Dirty Little Secrets
About Black History,
Its Heroes, and
Other Troublemakers

Claud Anderson, Ed.D.

PowerNomics Corporation of America

Publishers

A publication of
PowerNomics Corporation of America

Copyright © 1997 by Claud Anderson
Published by PowerNomics Corporation of America
P.O. Box 30536
Bethesda, MD 20814
(301) 564-6075
http://www.powernomics.com

Printed in the United States of America
ISBN 09661702-0-2
Library of Congress Catalog Card Number

All rights reserved. No part of this book may be reproduced or
transmitted in any form or by any means, electronic or mechanical,
including photocopying, recording, or by any information storage
and retrieval system, without the written consent of the publisher.

Cover design & layout: Robert Coleman Design

**To My Parents,
Family, Friends,
and Race.**

Acknowledgments

This book could not have been written and printed without the help of those people who unselfishly gave of their time and skills. I am indebted to my wife, Joann C. Anderson, Ph.D. for her constant support and encouragement; Flo S. Jenkins for her editing; Roger Lewis for providing me with materials from his black memorabilia collection; and the United States Congressional Library for their permission to reprint some of their rare photographs. A special thanks to *Emerge Magazine* for permission to reprint their covers.

Most of all, I am indebted to Anthony MacFarland for aggressively coordinating and pushing this book through the tedious publishing process in record time.

Contents

✪
Introduction

In my travels across the country as a public speaker on black issues in America, I am asked many questions by blacks and whites. The questions reveal how misinformed most people are regarding black history in America. They ask, "Why can't blacks emulate other ethnic groups?" "What have blacks contributed to the development of this nation?" Or, "Why can't blacks come together as a group and help themselves?"

It is not that my audiences are ignorant. Far from it. They are usually deeply concerned about black circumstances, politics and culture. They have come to hear me explain the thesis of my book, *Black Labor, White Wealth: A Search for Power and Economic Justice*, which attempts to guide African-Americans in their frustrating search for equality.

Ignorance of history makes the campaign for justice more difficult. Let us look at the label "Uncle Tom" as an illustration. This label is often used to describe a black person who sells out his race to profit himself. As a specific example, Supreme Court Justice Clarence Thomas appeared on the front covers of *Emerge Magazine* twice in the last three years---once with a bandanna wrapped around his head and once as a black lawn jockey. The magazine's covers and stories portrayed Clarence Thomas to be an Uncle Tom. But, based on Harriet Beecher Stowe's novel, *Uncle Tom's Cabin*, in which the name originated, blacks who intentionally place the welfare of the dominant white race above that of their own race more closely resemble Sambo, not Uncle Tom. Sambo was the character whose commitment to his white master was exercised even at the expense of his fellow slaves. In fact, it was Sambo who beat Uncle Tom to death for refusing to whip a black female. Whether Clarence Thomas is a Sambo is a question I will let you answer. But he is not an Uncle Tom.

You do not have to be a devotee of racial politics to find *Dirty Little Secrets* useful. American history in general and African-American history in particular are often

*Supreme Court Justice Clarence Thomas on the front cover of **Emerge Magazine** (November 1993).*

poorly taught in our nation's schools. Teachers and textbooks too often pass off myths and misconceptions as history. It is hard for students to see history as relevant to their own lives. For example, when history teachers teach about Shay's Rebellion that burned Jamestown, Virginia, the first colonial settlement, they do not teach that blacks fought to free white colonists from English rule even though the black race itself was being enslaved by the very same freedom-loving white colonists. During Black History Month, black children will see posted pictures of Sojourner Truth, but they are not taught that this fiery orator and activist was raised in a Dutch household and could speak only Dutch until she was an adult.

Despite improvements in recent years, black people are virtually non-existent in textbooks except for picking cotton, demonstrating or rioting during the Civil Rights Movement of the 1960s. School textbooks continue to gloss over or misrepresent the impact of slavery, Jim Crow segregation and civil rights in the building of this nation. No wonder students are bored by history, in general, and can see little relevance for it in their own daily lives.

This educational gap manifests itself in adulthood and produces adults without adequate background to solve the race-based problems of our time. Yet, as I have learned on the lecture circuit, Americans, young and old, are fascinated by black history. Humans have a natural curiosity about situations--whether tragedies or triumphs-in which unusual feats of strength and character overcome, or fail to overcome, seemingly impossible odds, the stuff of African-American history.

Discovering "dirty little secrets" about taboo subjects and peccadilloes of notable personalities adds excitement and educates in the process. This book tells intimate and little known details about the most misunderstood of all subjects: the history of the black race.

It is a compilation of bits of facts, or "factoids," tantalizing stories, strange coincidences, contradictions and forbidden sexual exploits. Many of the black characters presented herein are little-known personalities. They are the unsung slaves, pirates, cooks, nurses, janitors, and cotton pickers. As you will see, most of them, in their own humble way, are heroes--although some are scoundrels who turned on their own race.

Many of the whites depicted were slave-owners who fought against the freedom of the black race. A few, as in the exceptional case of John Brown, are white heroes who fought and died for the black race. It is not standard history. It presents a vast area of untold history that your history teachers did not dare disclose. In a modest way, it tries to correct the historical record, which racists and ideologues have too often distorted.

History remains nearly 100 percent white history. These factoids fill some of the gaping holes in Western history, particularly American history, and show how, for centuries, black labor has been used to enrich, feed, clothe, house, protect, and pleasure various ethnic, racial, and religious groups. While black labor was the engine that drove civilizations around the world, black people were never allowed to develop their material and human capital nor control their own destiny. We still grapple with this fundamental disparity today.

Much information about race has been lost or buried in old laws and regulations, bills of sale, newspaper reports, letters, economic reports, and personal diaries. What you will learn herein will be surprising, if not downright shocking. Some items will be interesting and amusing. All of it is worth knowing, providing a more accurate picture of the past and present. After all, that is the true value of history's dirty little secrets.

1
Notable Firsts and Lasts

The first truth is no greater than the last.

Mini-Facts

• *On January 1, 1804 Haiti's new black republic proclaimed itself a free country and abolished slavery. Haiti was the first, and to date, the only black country to successfully revolt and overthrow a European colonial power.*

• *In 1865, General William Sherman issued reparations in Special Field Order #15, providing some land for ex-slaves in South Carolina and Georgia. In 1996, the State of Florida compensated the black survivors of the Rosewood, Florida massacre.*

• *In 1900, Bert Williams and George Walker became the first black recording artists when they made several records for the Victor Talking Machine.*

• *The phrase "gospel music" was first widely used starting in 1875, when a book called Gospel Hymns and Sacred Tunes appeared in the North.*

❂

Darken the Mind and Charge a Black Tax

With its infamous "Asiento de Negroes" (Negroes enslavement contract) of 1517, Spain not only became a major slave-trading nation, it was the first nation to enact a public policy of enforced illiteracy for blacks. Prior to the Asiento policy, black Africans in Spain or any Spanish territories who sought an education were allowed access to it. Blacks were represented in various professions throughout Europe as well as Africa. When Spain slammed the door on black enlightenment, it became the global model for planned black illiteracy.

Juan Latino, a free black man, was probably the last person of his race to receive a college education in Spain before the Crown and the hierarchy of the Catholic Church officially condoned black enslavement in place of Indians. Latino was awarded a bachelor's degree from the University of Granada at the beginning of the 1500s. He went on to become a professor of grammar and Latin in Granada, Spain, and became a noted poet. He published his first book of poetry in the mid-1500s. Proceeds from the sale of his book must have surely come in handy since during this same time period Spain enacted a "black tax." This was not a general tax. It mandated that free, professional and educated blacks pay a "special" tribute or tax.

Three centuries later, free black males in Southern states across America were required to pay a similar annual tribute called a "capital tax." As with Juan Latino in the 1500s, free black males in America, regardless of educational achievement or profession, had to pay, simply for existing. (1)

❂

First Black Born in America Was Not a Slave

In 1619, an unknown Dutch frigate brought 20 blacks from Africa to Jamestown, Virginia, where sailors traded them into indentured servitude in exchange for food, water, and ship supplies. By early 1624, the first black child, William, was born to a black couple, Anthony and Isabella Tucker, in Elizabeth City, Virginia.

Shortly after William's birth, the Tuckers took him back to Jamestown to be baptized in the local Church of England. Thus William, the first African born in an American colony, had the double first "honor" of also being the first black to be baptized.

Equally noteworthy is the fact that he was born at a time when neither he nor his parents were considered slaves. After the Tucker's arrived on the Dutch warship, they were traded into indentured servitude for approximately three to four years. By the time of William's birth, they were out of servitude and intermingling with white immigrants just arriving in the colony. Formal slavery did not start in America for another 40 years after William's birth, but records were not kept on blacks, so it is unclear what happened to William or the parents of the first black born in America. (2)

The First Thanksgiving?

Thanksgiving is the holiday on which we thank God for His bounty and blessings. Thanksgiving, with its displays of pumpkins and pilgrims is one way Americans proclaim their love of country. Yet, the true origin of Thanksgiving and its celebration reveal an unsettling combination of myths and facts.

First, pilgrims did not introduce the tradition; American Indians had observed autumn harvest celebrations for centuries before the first Europeans arrived on the continent. Second, although George Washington set aside days for national Thanksgivings, it was President Abraham Lincoln who proclaimed the day a national holiday back in 1863. Ironically, this was the same year he issued his historic "Emancipation Proclamation" which, symbolically at least, freed more than five million black people from slavery. Although the first "official" November Thanksgiving was the first holiday that all black people in America were able to give thanks for being free from the chains of servitude, no public connection was made between the two events.

Lincoln did not make any religious connections to the Thanksgiving holiday. His motives were purely nationalistic. Having divided the nation over the slavery issue, and the ensuing Civil War, Lincoln felt the Union needed all the patriotic fervor that such a holiday observance could engender. While black people were the primary justification for proclaiming a national Thanksgiving holiday, no symbolic forms of blackness have ever been associated with the holiday. And, not until after the 1890s were American Indians included in the tradition. Moreover, no one used the term "Pilgrim" until the late 1870s. Probably the only truth about Thanksgiving, as it is commonly practiced, is that it started off as homage to patriotism and has remained as such until today.(3)

A Dubious Distinction

Anthony Johnson had the dubious honor of being the first American to hold a black person as a slave for life. And because Johnson was black himself, the distinction is even more notable.

Johnson arrived in Virginia from England as an indentured servant in 1621, just two years after the first blacks had arrived in Jamestown. After working off his two-year servitude, he earned enough money to purchase a small tract of land and several servants. Over the next few years, he acquired an additional 640 acres under the "head rights system," a law that rewarded him for increasing the number of slaves he owned. Thanks to the free labor, Johnson became one of the richest black men in the area, just three years before Virginia legally recognized slavery.

Johnson's loyalty was to wealth, not race. John Casor, one of Johnson's initial 13 slaves, complained to a visiting white planter that Johnson, his black master, had held him in servitude longer than the seven years that he was legally required to serve. Sympathizing, the white planter told Casor, "If I were you, I would just up and leave." Casor followed the advice. After Johnson found out that his servant had departed, he filed a lawsuit against the white planter for damaging his property by encouraging his servant to leave.

Dominated by white slave owners, a local court ruled in Johnson's favor, stipulating that Casor did in fact belong to Johnson for life. It ordered the white planter to pay damages for influencing the black slave to run away. The ruling was a harbinger. Although slavery existed unofficially in the North American colonies, just 20 years later, the colonies, with Virginia playing the lead, officially legalized slavery. By 1665, they went a step further; they emulated Anthony Johnson and enacted enslavement laws that authorized whites to own blacks for life or in perpetuity.

Nearly two centuries later, the black/white emulating cycle was nearly complete. Many conservative blacks had begun to purchase black slaves in hopes of moving to the same class level as white slaveholders. On the eve of the Civil War, more than 6,200 black slaveholders were sprinkled throughout the South. Still, not all whites liked the idea. Within a generation of the Civil War, the states of Delaware, Connecticut, and Kansas reversed the 1643 Anthony Johnson Virginia court decision. The court decision stated, "a black person could not hold another black as a slave because it elevated and equated black slaveholders to white slaveholders." To allow a black person to escape his blackness by becoming a black slaveholder not only confused the slavery issue, but, defeated the primary purpose of racism: group-based, not individual-based, subordination and exploitation. (4)

✪
The First African-American Poet

In 1746, a black woman named Lucy Terry witnessed a bloody Indian massacre in Deerfield, Massachusetts. She wrote a rhymed description of it. The lengthy poem was so powerful that she was publicly recognized for the language that she used in recording the event. A sample of the power and feelings of her words were reflected in such lines, as:

> "....The Indians did in ambush lay, Some very valiant men to
> slay, The names of whom I'll not leave out: Samuel Allen like
> a hero fought; And though he was so brave and bold, His face
> no more shall we behold; Eleaser Hawks was killed outright,
> Before he had time to fight, Before he did the Indians see, Was
> shot and killed immediately;..."

Lucy's written poetry was quite an accomplishment for an uneducated slave. Born in Africa, Terry was kidnapped and shipped to America as an infant. She grew up in Deerfield, Massachusetts, where more liberal racial attitudes provided her the opportunity to master English, despite the fact that the colonies in the early 18th century had penalties of a $100 fine and 39 lashes for anyone caught teaching a black to read or write.

Through determination and the aid of liberal white educators, Terry earned a special place in black history. She was the first known African-American to write a poem on American soil, and thus became this nation's first African-American poet. (5)

✪
Slaves Parroted Elected Officials

Until the early 18th century, free blacks in the South had little more freedom or opportunity than slaves in the North. Free blacks placed great emphasis on social imitation of whites, "putting on airs," dressing up and emulating white high society. Northern slaves, especially those in New England were more interested in putting on "political airs" or mimicking the pomp of government. This was true despite the fact that neither slaves, nor free blacks, could hold elected office until after the close of the 19th century.

That prohibition did not stop them from enjoying the trappings of power. Throughout the 18th and 19th centuries, slaves in a number of New England cities and towns initiated "Negro Election Day," an annual event at which slave communities elected their own governors, judges, sheriffs and magistrates. These "elected" positions gave those who held them more status within the black community. But the black leaders did not exercise official political power and could do little to help their people. Occasionally, they were able to unofficially represent the interests of blacks in periods of conflict or controversy.

Noting the importance that blacks placed on status and title, whites often ridiculed those who imitated white politics by giving them ridiculous titles such as "Governor," "Mayor," and "Your Honor." As mocking as these titles were, in most instances, they stuck and were accepted as their personal names. (6)

❂
First Ministers Were Licensed to Control

The American war for independence gave blacks, both free and enslaved, cause to express their interest in religious freedom. But fearing blacks would use the Bible to seek freedom, education, or black unity, whites applied strict limits to black religious services. While a few blacks, mostly "house" as opposed to "field" slaves, were allowed to attend services with whites, they were required to sit in separate all-black sections.

Once white slaveowners realized that religion could serve as an excellent mechanism to control slaves, they allowed field blacks to attend services as long as they were accompanied by a white "overseer." Because owners did not want black field hands in their own churches, they built modest chapels for them on their plantations.

By the latter part of the 18th century, whites in many slave states decided to allow blacks to build their own churches and conduct their own religious services. This change of heart may have been motivated in part by a sincere desire to encourage the Christianizing of blacks, but the relentless push for increased control was never far from the surface. In response to independent services conducted by and for blacks, a national policy evolved requiring whites to select and license all black preachers. Dominant white society controlled black religion, its ministers, and churches. Catechisms for religious instruction of slaves commonly bore such passages as:

> Q. Who gave you a master and a mistress?
>
> A. God gave them to me.
>
> Q. Who says that you must obey them?
>
> A. God says that I must.

A black congregation had the potential of being a source of unrest, so slaveowners allowed only the most pliable, compromising, and controllable blacks to become licensed as the ministerial head of black congregations. The licensed black ministers were expected to encourage their fellow blacks to be meek, obedient, and accepting of whites as masters. In this arrangement, blacks were to remain loyal to whites, and worldly gratification was postponed until after death.

The licensed black preachers were supposed to defer to secular authorities on political matters and avoid comments on the injustices blacks suffered. Since blacks could not develop businesses nor enter the professional ranks, the ministry became a business as well as a job. Black ministers began cropping up across the nation. Unlike in white communities, they became instant leaders. Popularity, respect and income security came with the position. There were no educational requirements, only a social obligation to support the status quo between the races.

It was not difficult to find blacks in every community and plantation willing to accept the prescribed leadership role for a preacher. In 1783, for instance, Jesse Peters became one the first blacks to receive a preaching license. He was appointed to lead America's first Negro Baptist Church, located in Silver Bluff, South Carolina.

Joseph Willis was the first to deliver a Protestant sermon west of the Mississippi River, where the budding minister also moderated the first statewide Baptist organization, the Louisiana Association. Black churches are now the oldest black business in America and one of the few to survive integration. (7)

William Leidesdorff: A First In Many Things

Occasionally a child is born who is destined to become many things for his people. William Alexander Leidesdorff was such a child. Born in 1810 to a white father from Denmark and a black mother from the Virgin Islands, Leidesdorff lived a life of firsts, including being the first black man with the Dutch last name of "Leidesdorff."

When William was a boy, the interracial family moved from the Virgin Islands to New Orleans. After his father died in 1839, Leidesdorff relocated to California. Like many Americans who went west, he became a naturalized Mexican citizen. The Mexican government gave Leidesdorff a land grant of 35,000 acres nestled on a bay on the California coast. The terrain was among the most spectacular on the entire coast line. Unbeknownst to the young man at the time, the tract would one day become the city of San Francisco. Eventually, Leidesdorff lost the title to the land, but the details are unknown.

At 29 years of age, Leidesdorff became the first black diplomat when he was named sub-consul to the Mexican territory of Yerba Buena, a name still borne by an island in the San Francisco Bay. After the United States annexed the California territory from Mexico, he became something of a financial adventurer and builder. In 1847, he launched the first steamboat on the San Francisco Bay. Leidesdorff went on to build the first and largest hotel in Yerba Buena, known as the City Hotel. The hotel was destroyed by one of the city's great fires.

Leidesdorff was one of the town's most prominent citizens. He served as the city's treasurer, established its first public school, and organized the first horse races in the state of California. He died in San Francisco at the age of 38 and left no known will or heirs to his estate. Joseph Libby Folsom, a captain in the United States Army living in the Bay Area, sought possession of Leidesdorff's estate. Folsom located Leidesdorff's uneducated mother and siblings in the West Indies, and offered them $8,000 for Leidesdorff's entire estate, valued at $500,000. Purchase of the land holdings from Leidesdorff's uneducated family at such a low value was a windfall for Folsom, and clearly unethical.

Even after his death in 1848, Leidesdorff achieved several other firsts. Laid to rest beneath the stone floor of downtown San Francisco, he became the first black man to have a street in downtown San Francisco named after him. Leidesdorff Street runs through the heart of the financial district, and pays tribute to a black pioneer. (8)

❂
The First Persecuted Witches

With rare exception, it seems, intolerance breeds intolerance, especially when the combination of blackness and the supernatural are involved.

In 1679, just a little over a decade after slavery was formally introduced, a black woman known only as "Wonn Negro" testified in a witchcraft case in New England. Against whom she testified is unclear from available records. But it was probably against another black woman, because shortly thereafter, a black woman named Mary Black was tried, convicted, and imprisoned for witchcraft. Mary Black petitioned the court the following year, won her appeal and was released.

Black women were prime targets for witchcraft charges. Such was the case in Salem, Massachusetts, in 1692. The legendary Salem Witch Hunt began when the daughters of a well-known minister and an influential citizen were challenged for frightening and unusual behavior. The girls apparently ignited the fire storm by pretending they had satanic powers. A local doctor diagnosed the girls as "bewitched" and under the influence of an "evil hand." When the town began to take them seriously, the girls confessed they had concocted the stories of satanism. Their admission, however, was too late to save the women accused of witchcraft.

The first person charged with practicing witchcraft was Tituba, a West Indian slave who had taught the girls sorcery and fortune-telling games based on Caribbean traditions. Accused of witchery, Tituba was jailed and tried. After being flogged mercilessly, she confessed and implicated two other women. Only by admitting she was a witch was she spared execution.

Others, some of them black, were also arrested and tried for witchery. Four confessed to being witches and were spared. Many were not so fortunate. Nineteen women were hanged, and a man was pressed to death under a pile of stones.(9)

❄

California's First and Last Black Governor

Don Pio Pico was born in 1801 and was one of a number of highly influential, politically involved African-Mexican families that founded the city of Los Angeles. Pico earned a niche in history when he was appointed by the Mexican government as governor of the California Territory. In that position, he represented the interests of the Mexican government during a critical time in its relationship with the United States.

Chief among the problematic issues was slavery. Southern planters and their slaves were pouring into Texas to establish cotton plantations, but Mexico, which still controlled Texas and California, prohibited slavery. In the end, American frontiersmen and planters intentionally triggered a war with Mexico to justify slavery and the annexation of southwestern lands--what would become the states of Texas, New Mexico, Colorado, Utah, Nevada, Arizona, and California.

Following the fall of the Alamo and a mercifully brief war between the United States and Mexico, the United States laid claims to the new lands. The two countries signed a peace treaty in 1847. Don Pico was quickly removed from office, becoming the first and only black--not to mention Mexican--governor of California.(10)

❄

The First Cowboys

Contrary to the images created by Hollywood, black slaves were America's first authentic cowboys. The word "cowboy," in fact, originally had nothing to do with roping cattle and hell-raising in the high plains. The word "cowboy" grew out of social customs that did not allow black males to be addressed as "mister" or "men," especially "gentlemen" or any other title that conveyed status.

Fifty years before there was an American Southwest, cowboy, with the diminutive term "boy," was often applied to black slaves in the Southeast who worked at cow pens. Their job was to herd livestock in Georgia, Alabama, and South Carolina. The label "boy" was a constant derogatory term for a black male, that included not only "cowboy," but "house boy," "field boy," "stable boy," and "under boy" (personal body servants during the Civil War).

Notable Firsts and Lasts

Black "Buffalo Soldiers of the West. (Library of Congress)

After the Civil War, new land rush laws sparked the westward movement. Fifteen million new European immigrants arrived in the latter part of the 1800s, but the ranching and cattle industry of the Southwest, especially along the Texas Gulf Coast, was wholly dependent on black labor. Many of the slaves served as cowboys before they were freed. Nearly one-third of the 35,000 cowboys who drove cattle north from Texas between 1866 and 1895 were black.

Many of these black cowboys distinguished themselves in the cattletowns of the old west. Some of their achievements were a credit to their race, others were not. In Dodge City, for instance, the first man shot was a black cowboy named Tex, an innocent bystander to a gun battle. The first man ever to be arrested by authorities in Abilene, Texas, was an unknown black man. His black friends were so outraged by his arrest for what they felt was a trivial matter, that they shot up the town and used the ensuing confusion as a cover to stage a jail break for their friend.

Nat Love was another black cowboy with questionable character. Widely known as "Deadwood Dick," Love was said to have ridden with Billy the Kid, Jesse and Frank James, and Buffalo Bill.

Cherokee Bill, another black cowboy, "was similar to Billy the Kid in everything but skin color," according to one historian.

Not all black cowboys lived the kind of dangerous, short lives in the old West that is the Hollywood stereotype. Thousands of black cowboys were lawmen, popular heroes, Buffalo soldiers, or just plain ranchers and farmers. Yet only a few black cowboys--good or bad--can be found in the history books. (11)

❂

First Horse Racing Jockeys Were Black

From the early days of horse racing until the early 20th century, most of the handlers, trainers, breeders, groomers, and jockeys were black slaves. Black jockeys dominated the racing industry throughout the 19th century.

Blacks were responsible for the daily care of livestock on farms and plantations. They performed similar duties in city carriage houses and race-track stables. It was a natural step for blacks to move from caring and grooming horses to riding and racing them. In the first Kentucky Derby, 14 of the 15 jockeys were black. In that race, a black jockey, Olive Luis, rode Aristides, the winning horse.

Isaac "Ike" Murphy, born a slave in Lexington, Kentucky, in 1861, was considered by some the greatest jockey of the 19th century. Murphy's mother did laundry for a racing stable, and in his early years he exercised horses for stables in the area. Because most jockeys of the time were black, it was not difficult for Murphy to enter the profession. He rode his first race at the age of 14. During his 20-year career, Murphy raced 1,412 times, winning 628. Racing in the Saratoga, New York, circuit in 1882, he won 49 of his 51 races. Murphy won his first Kentucky Derby in 1884, repeating his feat in 1890 and 1891. Five years later at the age of 35, he died of pneumonia. After his death, Murphy was inducted into the Halls of Fame of two race tracks--Pimlico, Maryland, and Saratoga, Florida. Isaac Murphy, Jimmy Lee, and Oliver Lewis established track records at the Kentucky and American Derbies that still stand today. (12)

❂

The Last Derby Jockeys

Jess "Long Shot" Conley, who earned his nickname by riding numerous underdogs to victory in the 1890s, was the last black jockey to ride in the Kentucky Derby. Riding Colston in 1911, Long Shot Conley finished third in the Kentucky Derby, the last major racing event to permit black jockeys.

When big business entered the sport, blacks saw their roles reduced to non-riding, menial jobs. During the first decade of the 20th century, whites and Latinos replaced blacks in the racing industry. One the few relics that remain as a testament to black involvement in professional racing are the rare lawn jockeys that guard suburban driveways.

Some students of black history believe these icons evolved not from the black jockey era but from the image of the loyal slave coach footman steadfastly holding his master's lantern. Lighting the lanterns was a way to signal other slaveholders that a slave had run away. Ironically, the lawn jockeys began to disappear from drive ways about the same time blacks were disappearing from the race track circuits. (13)

✪

The First to Bleed

Four days after the Civil War began, the blood of a black soldier was shed. On April 18, 1861, Nicholas Biddle, a former slave who had volunteered for the Union army, became the first black in uniform wounded in the Civil War. While traveling with an advance guard of Pennsylvania troops through Baltimore, Maryland, to guard the nation's capital, Biddle was felled by a rock thrown by a slavery supporter. Baltimore, Maryland was a slaveholding city within a slave state which was sympathetic to the Southern Confederacy.

While enroute to Washington, D.C., the black Union troops ran a gauntlet of hostile, anti-Union and possibly anti-black crowds all across Maryland. Upon reaching Washington, Biddle and fellow troop members were quartered in the Capitol building. A pool of blood, which ran from the wound in Biddle's face, marked the spot on the Capitol floor where he laid that night.

The Union was saved, but Nick Biddle was not. He was buried with little fanfare in an obscure "colored churchyard" in Pottsville, Pennsylvania. (14)

✪

The Last to Die

On May 13, 1865, a black sergeant with only the last name of Crocket, was the last soldier, black or white, Union or Confederate, to be killed in the Civil War.

At the time of Sergeant Crocket's death, the war, for all intents and purposes, was over. But his unit had yet to receive word. General Robert E. Lee, the leader of the Confederacy, had surrendered on April 9, 1865 to General Ulysses S. Grant, commander of the Union Army, at Appomattox Courthouse, Virginia. Following suit, Confederate General Joseph Johnston surrendered to Union General William Tecumseh Sherman on April 28, 1865. Several days later, May 2 or 3, Confederate President Jefferson Davis was captured and imprisoned. At that point, the war was over.

But the news was slow to arrive to military forces in the West. As late as May 13, the 62nd United States Colored Infantry from the North was still meeting resistance from Confederate soldiers at White's Ranch, Texas. It was in this final conflict that Sergeant Crocket was killed, becoming the last officially reported war death. Since the Confederacy had surrendered a month earlier, it appears that Sergeant Crocket truly died in vain.(15)

❂

President Arrested by Black Policeman

The old English adage that the king does no wrong does not apply in America. President Ulysses Grant was probably the first and only American President to be arrested, and it was a black, District of Columbia policeman who performed the deed. In the late 19th century, Officer William West was on duty at 12th and M Streets in Washington, D.C., when he noticed a horse and carriage approaching him at a frightening pace. Dashing into the oncoming traffic, Officer West grabbed the reins and brought the carriage to a halt.

Looking inside and recognizing President Grant, Officer West apologized profusely and waved the President on. But President Grant, aware of the public relations nightmare in appearing above the law, insisted that Officer West book him for violating the district speeding law. Officer West took the President to the nearest police precinct. For professionalism as an officer of the law, President Grant later promoted Officer West to a mounted policeman. (16)

❂

The First Black Newspaper Had Purpose

In 1827, just 34 years before the Civil War commenced, *Freedom's Journal*, the first newspaper edited by and for black Americans, was published. The paper grew out of the collective effort by the black community to protest the anti-black bigotry of the *New York Inquirer*, an influential white-run newspaper.

In support of slavery, Mordecai Manuel Noah, the *Inquirer's* eminent Jewish publisher, went out of his way to vilify and degrade blacks. To counter Noah's propaganda, John B. Russwurm, the Rev. Samuel E. Cornish, and other free blacks met in the New York home of Boston Crumwell, a respected leader in the city's small free-black population. After a series of discussions, the leaders selected Cornish and Russwurm, two of the youngest but best educated men among them, to accomplish the job.

Freedom's Journal was considered subversive literature in the South, and blacks were prosecuted for possessing copies of it. The *Journal* sold well among blacks until its editorials began to focus more on a fringe "Back to Africa Movement," rather than the daily issues confronting black communities across the country.(17)

✪

Black Face Symbolized Jim Crowism

Jim Crow, which today is synonymous with legalized segregation, was originally a character in a minstrel song and a dance popularized in 1828 by a white comedian named Thomas D. Rice, or "Daddy Rice," the father of America's black face minstrels. The idea for the Jim Crow character was derived from a song and dance Rice saw performed by a black stable boy who lived directly behind Rice's theater. Donning tattered clothing and blackface, and singing in "darky dialect" tempered by his thick New York accent, Rice was so good that his fellow thespians eventually dubbed him "the first and best knight of the burnt-cork." Jim Crow eventually became a stock character in all of Rice's minstrel shows.

Rice was later joined in the minstrel circuit by a crowd of newly arrived white immigrants eager to entertain whites by imitating blacks in a derogatory fashion. Once established, the black-face minstrel shows became popular fare throughout the country. At least 30 full-time companies performed the shows in the decade immediately preceding the Civil War.

Blackface was taken abroad in the 1900s. In preparation for the signing of a trade treaty with Japan, American sailors aboard the Commodore Matthew C. Perry even performed a shipboard minstrel show for a Japanese audience. The program stated that the sailors would appear as "colored Gemmen of the North" and "Neggas of the South." The Japanese audience ate the show up, laughing uproariously at the antics and dialect of white sailors in blackface. The blackface "Sambo" soon became a part of Japanese culture and language, so much so that 150 years later, the Japanese were still producing "Sambo" artifacts and advertisements for "Darkie" toothpaste. Blackface characters spread to other countries. As recently as 1996, Latin American companies advertised pizza with "Sambo" images. Darkie Toothpaste, advertised today as "Darlie," is sold in France and Japan. Official Jim Crow segregation laws were abolished during the apex of the Civil Rights Movement when Congress enacted the Civil Rights Act of 1964 and the Voting Rights Act of 1965. But the psychological and social damage of Jim Crowism had spread far and wide and did not die with legal segregation.(18)

❂
Black Schools Were Taboo

By the early 19th century, the idea of educating free black children was still highly unpopular with whites who saw it as subversive to the interests of whites. Dominant white society had enacted an endless number of laws, ordinances, and public policies designed to keep black children non-competitive with white children. Black children were to be an illiterate or semi-skilled, menial labor force for the personal comfort and wealth building of white society. Consequently, white society sought to shut schools for free blacks as soon as they opened. Many who profited from black suffering and planned illiteracy, followed the social policy that "no light was to enter the brain of a black child."

The destruction of the Richmond African School is a case in point. In 1811, Christopher McPherson, a wealthy free black, hired Herbert H. Hughes, a white school master, to teach at McPherson's newly created school for free blacks. With the consent of a few caring white masters, a smattering of enslaved children also attended. Total enrollment amounted to only 25 students.

McPherson was so pleased with his initial success that he boasted of the school in an advertisement in the *Argus*, a Richmond newspaper. In the ad, he recommended that every black community combine its resources and establish similar schools for black children. Richmond whites did not share McPherson's enthusiasm. Within days of the school's opening, a band of leading white citizens confronted Samuel Pleasance, the editor of the *Argus*, and demanded that future ads for the Richmond African School be rejected. Pleasance disagreed, but dutifully yielded to the public pressure.

Hughes, the white schoolteacher, was made of sterner stuff. He bought space in the *Argus* himself, defended the school, and pledged to continue teaching until authorities closed it. The powers-that-be took Hughes's challenge. Richmond officials summoned McPherson to court and asked him to demonstrate why his school should not be declared a public nuisance. The police harassed McPherson, forcibly drove Hughes out of town, and shut down the black school.

Months later, McPherson advertised his desire to establish "a seminary of learning of the arts and sciences" for blacks as soon as he could find a "proper tutor." This time, before he could reopen the school, the police arrested McPherson and shipped him to Virginia's Williamsburg Lunatic Asylum.

The lesson intended for blacks was obvious: Any black man who dared to educate black children had to be crazy.(19)

❂
The Last Returned Fugitive Slave

Until the eve of the Civil War, escaped slaves were still returned to their masters in the South under the Fugitive Slave Act of 1850. Lucy Bagby Johnson was the last fugitive slave captured and shipped back to her former owner under the Act.

Police officers abducted Johnson from the home of a white employer in Cleveland, Ohio, in 1861. A group of local white citizens organized to protest Johnson's arrest, acquiring the assistance of sympathetic lawyers who successfully defended her in court. But as soon as she was set free, United States Marshals, once again acting under the Fugitive Slave Act, arrested her. A federal commissioner who heard the case turned out to be sympathetic, offering money to buy Johnson her freedom. But he also ruled that "the law was the law" and Lucy Johnson had to be returned to her West Virginia master who was unwilling to accept compensation for her freedom.

When the Civil War began, Johnson's determined master tried to maintain his ownership by moving her further into the deep South, where pro-slavery sentiments were more rigid than the rest of the country. Johnson was eventually rescued from her owner's vicious grip by a Union officer who took a liking to her. After President Lincoln issued the Emancipation Proclamation, Johnson met and married another former Union officer who had settled in Cleveland, Ohio. The couple remained there until her death in 1906. (20)

❂
The Last Boat Load of Slaves

International slave trading was outlawed in the United States in 1807, but illegal international and domestic legal slave trading continued right up until the Civil War began. The *Clothilde* docked in Alabama in 1859 with a slave cargo making it possibly the last ship to bring illegal slaves into an American port. The ship carried approximately 130 men, women and children who had been kidnapped from Tarkar, a village in West Africa. The ship's captain, William Fowler, eluded federal authorities patrolling the Mississippi Sound, unloaded his ship in Mobile, Alabama, then said farewell to slave trading by burning it.

Unfortunately, for Fowler, the pending Civil War had drastically closed down most slave markets. He was unable to sell the slaves, so he set them free as soon as the war started. This last shipment of black slaves was able to stay together and formed a village, Africa Town, in an area known as the Plateau, near Mobile. They were probably the only blacks able to keep their African customs, names, and language. Descendants of these black slaves can still be found in East Mobile. Cudjoe Lewis, the last of the original Tarkar slaves, died in 1935. (21)

The Last Black Slave Dies

On October 2, 1979 the last former black slave died. Charlie Smith, who claimed to be America's only living former slave, passed at an unbelievable one hundred and thirty-seven years of age. Smith lived in North Florida, in the heart of the old Cotton Belt. In a public ceremony in the mid-1970s, Governor Reuben Askew of Florida recognized Smith with a special certificate of merit. Smith's mind remained lucid on his personal life, slavery, and black history up until his death.

2
Heroes and Heroines

There will arise a champion to fight my cause.

Mini-Facts

• *In the late 1890s, James Parker, a black man, knocked down and captured Leon F. Czolgosz, the assassin who had just shot President William McKinley at the Buffalo Exposition.*

• *In 1895, W.E.B. Dubois was the first black person awarded a Ph.D. from Harvard University. He was the first to introduce the concept of Pan-Africanism and became recognized as black America's most prominent scholar and activist.*

• *In 1908, Jack Johnson defeated Tommy Burns in a 14-round boxing match in Sidney, Australia to become the first black heavyweight champion of the world.*

✪

A National Hero: John Brown

On the morning of December 2, 1859, as John Brown's body hung from the gallows in Charleston, Virginia, free and enslaved blacks across America kneeled and wept in his honor. They prayed for his soul because they knew they had lost a friend and devoted protector. Ironically John Brown was a decendent of Peter Brown, a passenger on the Mayflower that brought the first freedom seekers to America.

Even the name John Brown sounded black enough to give black people comfort. But John Brown was not black; he was a white revolutionary who believed he had been ordained by God to free the black race from enslave-

ment, even if it meant his own death. He made himself a controversial figure in American history by launching a violent, no-holds-barred attack
against institutionalized slavery.

With his message from God and a party of 21, including his sons,
daughters and five blacks, Brown invaded the state of Virginia, captured the
town of Harpers Ferry, seized the U.S. armory, and freed some 50 slaves.
With this series of revolutionary acts, the white militant almost single-
handedly created the passionate emotional climate that led to the Civil War.

More than any other white before or since, Brown confronted the issue
of black liberation forthrightly and at a high personal cost. He sacrificed
not just his own life, but the lives of a number of his own children. In paying his last respects to Brown, Frederick Douglas said, "Brown's struggle in
the cause of freedom was superior to mine. Mine was a small light; his was
a burning sun. Mine was bound by time; his stretched away to the silent
shores of eternity. As a black man, I am willing to speak for the slave; John
Brown, a white man, was willing to die for the slave. How do you explain
this?"

John Brown's raid on Harpers Ferry appears to have failed primarily
because it was not supported by visible black leadership. In preparing for
the raid, John Brown wanted a black leader such as Harriet Tubman or
Frederick Douglas to join his crusade and call the slaves to arms. Brown
believed black slaves would not rally to an unknown white man. But both
Tubman and Douglas declined to join his party. After seizing and holding
Harpers Ferry for two days, Brown's judgment was proven correct. The
slaves did not rally to his side. Outgunned, Brown waited too long for the
slaves to rise up, allowing federal troops the time to travel from
Washington, D.C., and capture his raiding party.

Ironically, John Brown, a white man, was a national hero to blacks, just
as Hayward Shepherd, a black man, was a traitor to blacks. Hayward
Shepherd, a black railroad porter, recognized Brown's raiding party as it
rolled into town. Rather than assisting the liberators, he tried in vain to
warn the town and was promptly killed by the raiders. After hanging Brown
and his party for attempting to free slaves, the town erected a monument
honoring Hayward Shepherd, for his contribution to black enslavement. (1)

John Horse: A Black Hero

The runaway slave, John Horse, had the distinction of being one of the few, if not the only black in American history who stood up to and fought both slave holders and the United States Army. He did so for more than 50 years of his life and, amazingly, was never defeated in battle nor captured.

When John Horse escaped slavery, he chose Florida as his sanctuary around 1820. Like hundreds of other runaway slaves, he assisted in building the "maroon" settlements and allied with Seminole Indians against slave hunters and military incursions. Since Seminole Chief Osceola was married to a black woman named Morning Dew and had several mixed sons, the Seminoles were more receptive to black runaways than other Indian tribes. John Horse and Wild Cat, one of Osceola's sons, were top lieutenants and battle strategists for the Seminoles.

The Indians and blacks fought General Andrew Jackson and his military command to a standstill during the various Seminole Wars in Florida. White mercenaries and militia reported to the United States government that black runaways and leaders like John Horse were the "best soldiers that the Seminoles ever had." After three great Seminole Wars, the government defeated the Black-Seminole Indian alliance, in part, by capturing Chief Osceola under a flag of truce. When Chief Osceola died in prison, John Horse and Wild Cat became the Seminoles' new leaders. In 1844, John Horse, Wild Cat and other chiefs traveled to Washington and met with President Polk to develop a peace accord. As a compromise, in the 1850s, both Horse and Wild Cat were asked to assist the government in relocating the Seminoles to Arkansas. Horse took his black maroons with him to this new Indian territory.

Seminoles and black Indians did not find peace in the new territory. They were constantly harassed by their old enemies, Creeks, Chickasaws, Cherokees, Choctaw, and whites; all of whom were slave traders and slaveowners. Horse and Wild Cat labored to feed the black and Indian families. But, after white slave hunters murdered Wild Cat, John Horse concluded that 50 years of fighting was enough. He decided to relocate to Mexico. John Horse packed up his black and Indian families and rode off into the setting sun, towards Mexico. They were never seen nor heard from again. (2)

A Black Hero Brought Christmas Cheer

During the Christmas holidays in 1811 in Richmond, Virginia, a black slave showed compassion for his fellow man that is frequently spoken of but rarely demonstrated. On the day after Christmas, Richmond high society gathered in a local theater to see a visiting play. During the play, a prop boy dropped a lamp that immediately ignited the flimsy scenery and set the theater ablaze, trapping a large number of wealthy white slaveowners inside.

A slave and blacksmith named Gilbert Hunt, who happened to be outside the theater, rushed to the burning wood structure. Strong and agile at six feet two inches, Hunt fearlessly stood beneath the burning building and caught the screaming people as they were lowered out of the window one by one by a Dr. James McCaw. The last woman, Dr. McCaw's own sister, was so large that Hunt, unable to catch her, used his body to break her fall and save her life. Despite Hunt's heroics, more than 68 whites and five blacks perished in the fire. In the aftermath of the tragedy, petitions urging that Gilbert Hunt be emancipated in appreciation for his heroism were ignored by his owner.

Then history repeated itself, and Hunt was once again a great hero. This time, during a great fire at the city's penitentiary, prisoners were trapped on the second floor of the jail. The only escape route, windows, were covered with heavy iron grates. Hunt rushed to the scene. He held a fireman on his shoulders who used a crowbar to tear out the grating embedded in the bricks. Once again declared a local hero, Hunt was again denied meritorious manumission. By this time, however, he had earned enough as a blacksmith to buy his own freedom. He remained a hardworking tradesman until his death in 1863. Half a century later, a tablet to his memory was permanently affixed to the wall of Richmond's Monumental Episcopal Church.(3)

Harriet Tubman: Female Role Model

Without a doubt, Harriet Tubman was a bareknuckled freedom fighter and liberator of her people. As the progenitor of the Underground Railroad, a metaphor for helping fugitive slaves escape to Canada or free states, Tubman did a man's work and bore the lash. Although her spirit was as strong as her body, she carried a pistol and was prepared to use it to engender respect from whites and intestinal fortitude from cautious blacks. At great risk to her own life, Tubman made repeated trips into hostile southern areas to draw enslaved blacks out of captivity. Over a 30-year period, she led more than 300 escaping black slaves to freedom in the North.

According to legend, Tubman announced her departure times on the Underground Railroad at least twice a day by singing the hymn "Steal Away" and "Follow the Drinking Gourd" within ear shot of slave cabins. To guide the runaway slaves, the songs suggested that they follow the tail of the Big Dipper constellation to the North Star. After escorting hundreds of runaways to freedom, Tubman was finally able to entice her own parents into the Underground Railroad and to guide them North as well to "freedom's land."

She supported John Brown's Harpers Ferry raid and would have accompanied him had she not been ill. Later, during the Civil War, she served as a nurse and spied for the North. For over a generation after the Civil War, she cared for poverty-stricken freed slaves. After a 40-year fight with the United States government, she finally received a Civil War pension in the early 1900s, just before she died. (4)

The Gun-Toting Female Mail-Carrier

Throughout history, black women have been forced to act and perform like men just to survive. One such woman was Mary Fields, known as Black Mary. Reportedly born a slave in Tennessee in 1832, Black Mary lived first in Mississippi and then in Ohio. Later, she moved to Montana where she became one of the most memorable characters in the annals of Western history. Tall and weighing in at more than 200 pounds, she was a gun-toting stagecoach driver and the second woman ever to regularly drive a United States mail route. A crack shot, she wore a .38 pistol strapped under her apron. Black Mary's reputation earned her many dangerous routes inhabited by Indians and mail bandits. Her reputation for expertly employing her weapon to protect both the mail and herself dissuaded many would-be-robbers. At her death by natural causes in 1914, Black Mary was mourned by her townspeople as a black pioneer. (5)

⊙

The First Black Naval Hero

Robert Small was born a slave behind the Cotton Curtain but became a black hero. Just after the outbreak of war in 1861, Small, who had learned about ships and sailing from his father, was made pilot of the Planter, a steamboat the Confederacy used to transport guns and ammunition to the rebel army. On the night of May 12, 1862, the ship docked in the Charleston, South Carolina, harbor, and the Planter's white officer went ashore. After alerting the seven other African-American seaman aboard, Small donned a captain's dress uniform, took control of the ship, and steered it out of the Charleston harbor, past the guns of Fort Sumter and into a northern port behind Union lines.

Neither the North nor the South commanded much of a Navy, even though ships were vitally important to the moving of military troops, supplies, and weapons. So the Northern Union was delighted with Small's escape and military gifts. They needed the ship, its valuable cargo, and its skillful and courageous pilot. The Union Navy expressed its appreciation to Small by making him the chief pilot on the Planter. After the Union used the ship in its successful attack on Charleston, Small was promoted to Captain. Later he left the Union Navy, joined the Union Army and was awarded the rank of Brigadier General. Small's military career ended with the Civil War because national public policies returned to its pre-Civil War prohibition of blacks holding high military status, especially during peace time.

Reconstruction policies offered Small an alternative career. He left military service and entered politics. He was elected to the South Carolina state legislature, and in 1876 became a United States Congressman, serving four terms. President Benjamin Harrison later appointed him customs collector for the port of Beaufort, South Carolina, where he served until his death at the age of 76.

Robert Small was a high ranking military officer and politician, but first and foremost, he was black America's first naval hero. (6)

⊙

Black Political Heroes

Frederick Douglas was born a slave in 1817 to a white father and a black mother who gave him the name, Frederick Augustus Washington Bailey. In 1838, as a young adult, he escaped from slavery. As a fugitive, Douglas became a militant political leader who spoke at abolition rallies throughout the North.

When his best selling autobiography, *Narrative of the Life of Frederick Douglas, An American Slave*, was published, he earned a reputation as an outspoken and eloquent black hero. Although Douglas was a political radical, he frowned upon black nationalism. He based his views and tactics on the principles of compromise and non-violence. Those principles were adopted a century later by India's Mahatma Gandhi, who in turn served as a role model for Dr. Martin Luther King, Jr., the Nobel prize-winning black civil rights leader.

Prior to the Civil War, Frederick Douglas was the most prominent and respected black in America. But unlike John Brown, a white man who was willing to pay the ultimate price for black freedom--"to die for black people"-- Douglas did not match his rhetoric with action. Because Brown believed that black slaves would not join a group of freedom fighters led by a white man, he beseeched Douglas to join him on the raid on Harpers Ferry. Douglas refused to join Brown, arguing that the plan did not stand a chance of succeeding.

Prior to his death in 1896, Douglas revealed the real reason behind his decision not to join John Brown in the raid on the Harpers Ferry armory to secure weapons for a massive slave revolt. Douglas confessed that he refused to join the freedom riders, not so much because he thought Brown's raid would fail, or because he opposed violence, but because the most famous black man in America, was afraid for his life. History suggests that Frederick Douglas did not mind being a black hero, but he did not want to be a black martyr.(7)

⊙

More Unsung Black Heroes

Following the Civil War, the North neglected the plight of freed slaves in favor of welcoming new immigrants, mostly white Europeans, streaming into the country. The federal government abandoned blacks after enacting constitutional amendments to give the former slaves paper freedom--political and civil rights. At the same time, the government withheld the economic and social rights essential to black progress. As a result, many blacks lacked the tools and resources necessary to compete in the job and business markets. The "black codes," enacted by the old southern plantation owners and politicians in the winter of 1865, immediately following emancipation, made black people even more vulnerable. The black codes replaced the defunct slave codes of 1705. The black codes mandated that every Southern black had to have an annual labor contract--in writing--with a white landowner in his possession by the first of January or risk being charged with vagrancy, jailed and assigned to public work projects. Anti-black sentiments were so intense that many blacks fled the South for the relative safety of the North and Midwest.

In 1879, two black men, Henry Adams of Louisiana and Moses "Pap" Singleton of Tennessee, led an exodus of some 40,000 blacks from Louisiana, Mississippi, Alabama, and Georgia for the Midwest. Many traveled to states like Kansas that initially opened their borders. But as the number of destitute blacks in the state grew, the climate became increasingly hostile. Hotels, restaurants, and boat lines refused to accommodate the black newcomers. Singleton became so discouraged by the treatment of his compatriots that he mounted a campaign, ultimately unsuccessful, to encourage blacks to migrate to Liberia or Canada.

In the same year, Edwin P. McCabe, a lesser known black activist, unsuccessfully campaigned to create a "Negro state" in the Oklahoma Territory. The Cherokee Strip in the Oklahoma Territory was also briefly considered as a site for a black homeland. This movement failed as well. The proposal went down in flames not only because of the predictable lack of federal support and private assistance, but because of the hostility of Indians as well as whites. In any case, the Oklahoma Territory was no more prepared to accept blacks than Kansas, Iowa, or Nebraska.

The Civil War freed blacks from the physical chains of slavery, but not from its handicapping legacies. (8)

✪
Father of the Country Given Poison Peas

Phoebe Fraunces, the daughter of a black West Indian man, saved George Washington's life on the eve of the Revolutionary War. Fraunces was the daughter of

"Black Sam" Fraunces, the owner of a well-known tavern in New York City where George Washington and his officers customarily met to dine and discuss plans for a war with England.

In 1776, the British were well aware of Washington's entertainment and culinary habits. Hoping to head off a revolt for independence, the British planned to kill off the colonies' military leadership. They devised a simple, dastardly plan: poison George Washington. Their agent was the Irishman Thomas Hickey, who had won Washington's confidence and served as his bodyguard. Hickey courted Fraunces because she served Washington and his party when they ate and drank at her father's tavern.

After developing an intimate friendship with Fraunces, Hickey gave her a dish of poisoned peas to serve to Washington when he came for dinner. Despite her newly developed friendship with, and romantic feelings for Hickey, Fraunces became suspicious of the Irishman's actions and warned Washington, who threw the peas into the yard. Chickens who ate the discarded peas immediately fell dead. For his assassination attempt, Hickey was hanged before a crowd of 20,000 in New York City.

Both Miss Fraunces and her father, Black Sam, were officially recognized by the Continental Congress for their service to the fledgling country and given a sum of money. Later, when George Washington became America's first President, he appointed Fraunces White House steward. (9)

⚙

Richard Allen: The Father of the Negro

Philadelphia and the Mason-Dixie Line, the official boundary between the nation's free and slave states, were only a few miles apart. This geographic proximity allowed white slaveowners to travel North to "the city of brotherly love" in order to randomly abduct freed blacks and Northern slaves who they claimed were runaways.

Reverend Richard Allen, born a slave in Philadelphia in 1760, was one such victim. Allen was seized by slave traders who signed sworn affidavits that he was a fugitive. After many prominent Philadelphians, black and white, testified on Allen's behalf, the charges against him were dismissed and the white slave trader was imprisoned for perjury.

After the ordeal, Allen, who converted to Protestantism at 17, went on to convert his master, buy his freedom for $2,000, become a preacher, and founded Philadelphia's African Methodist Episcopal (AME) Church, of which he was the first bishop.

A pioneer among black abolitionists and president of the first national black AME Church convention in the Western world, Allen played a pivotal role in defining black politics. He personified the values of hard work, refusal to accept subordinate status and emphasized collective action. In a nutshell, Allen's thesis was black empowerment. In fact, he was so closely identified with the movement for black freedom and independence that some called him the "father of the Negro." (10)

⚙

David Walker: A Rare Black Militant

Born the son of a slave father and a free mother in Wilmington, North Carolina, David Walker grew up to become a Boston businessman and abolitionist. Walker's claim to fame came in 1829, when he circulated a pamphlet titled *Appeal*, a powerful plea for black liberation. The *Appeal* circulated widely in the North and South, and many credited it with provoking slave revolts and helping to shape the public debates that led to the Civil War.

In his fiery writings, Walker condemned the intentional enslavement, criminalization, and impoverishment of the black race. With the exception of black Africans, he pointed out, all races of the earth were born free. He railed against the commonly held perception that blacks wanted to be white, insisting that they preferred to be just as their Creator had made them.

Urging that his brothers show no fear because God was on their side, Walker contended that any man not willing to fight for this freedom deserved to remain in chains and even to be butchered by his captors. Insisting that death was preferable to slavery, he said that if an uprising occurred, slaves must be willing to kill or be killed. A man who refused to defend himself was worse than an "infidel" and "undeserving of sympathy." Apparently, Walker's veiled threat or challenge did not fall on deaf ears.

In response to Walker's statement, the state of Georgia offered a $10,000 reward for Walker if taken alive and $1,000 if dead. A year after the offer, in 1831, the abolitionist died under mysterious circumstances. Some claimed Walker died for his people's freedom. Others claimed he was murdered for the bounty. (11)

✪

A Master Felt the Golden Rule

On rare occasions during the Civil War, black slaves exercised a measure of revenge for their mistreatment while in captivity.

One slaveowner, who took perverse pleasure in beating naked female slaves, was captured by the Union army in 1864. The Union general, a devout abolitionist, ordered the slaveowner stripped and bound to a tree. The general ordered black male soldiers to whip the white slaveowner. When they finished, three female slaves who the slaveowner had regularly beaten for minor infractions, took their turn, settling some old, painful scores. The black female slaves had gotten their chance to "do unto others as they have done unto you." (12)

✪

A Slave Who Was a Double Spy

The Union won the Civil War in part because it had the advantage of more industry, soldiers, technology, and a centralized form of communication. Essentially, the North had both the military material and moral high ground. On the other side, the Confederacy was able to put up a valiant struggle because it owned the greater concentration of wealth, had trained military leaders, and millions of unpaid slave laborers who supplied food, military supplies, and care for unattended white families and farms.

The presence of five million black slaves, however, was a knife that cut both ways. A small number of slaves were heroes because they refused to assist the South. Instead, they chose to organize subversive forces within the Southern Confederacy. They refused to work. Others hurt the pro-slavery cause by feigning loyalty while serving as spies, saboteurs, and guerrilla forces for the North.

Thousands of runaway slaves enlisted in the northern war to serve as soldiers, construction workers, wood cutters, cooks, skilled craftsmen, and servants. A total of close to 200,000 black men formally helped the Union Army rout their Confederate counterparts. Some historians posit that without black support, the North would not have won the Civil War. (13)

✪
Heroes, But Not Citizens

The Revolutionary War, the first major conflict between this land and a foreign power, generated heroes from the ranks of blacks, both free and slave.
In 1780s, just before the Revolutionary War, the slave, Thomas Peters, became a black military legend. Peters and 20,000 other black slaves sided with the British during the war in hopes of gaining their freedom. Peters was an excellent soldier who received many accolades. But when his side went down to defeat, so did his hopes for freedom.

A few years later, in 1788, a black slave named Dick Pointer saved the lives of many white settlers one early morning at Fort Donnelly, Virginia, by single-handedly holding off a surprise Indian attack until the garrison awoke and came to his aid.

Louis Pacheo was another little-known black slave-turned-hero of the third Seminole war. Not only did he get revenge for his enslavement, but he exacted it against a famous military leader, Major Francis Dade of the United States Army. Pacheo was a runaway slave who had joined the Seminole Indians in Florida. He convinced the military that he could be trusted to guide them to various Indian and black rebel hideouts. Instead, Pacheo led Dade into a trap in Florida. Pacheo led Major Dade and his hundreds of troops and Creek Indians into the swamps where Chief Osceola and his men were waiting in ambush. Pacheo's plan was so well executed that only four of Dade's men survived what was later termed a massacre. Pacheo's allies, other black runaways and Seminole Indians, honored him as a hero.

Numerous other blacks also emerged from the three Seminole wars as heroes. John Caesar, a black slave in South Carolina, was a double hero for saving lives in South Carolina with his medical cures and for taking lives as a warrior in Florida. In the 19th century, Caesar developed antidotes for several poisons. For his medicinal achievements, his home state of South Carolina granted him meritorious manumission from enslavement as well as 100 pounds in cash.

Several years later, in the 1820s, Caesar joined the struggle of runaway slaves and Indians in Florida. Within a short time, he became a feared and valiant black warrior. He was a leader within the Seminole tribe and led raids on plantations in border states to free and recruit slaves into the cause. His raids focused national attention that eventually brought an end to the Seminole War. Like so many other runaway slaves, John Caesar was a hero and role model of black leadership.(14)

A Time for Slave Revolts

Many students of human behavior and historians have wondered why black slaves suffered such inhumane treatment for so many centuries and attempted so few revolts. People do not typically revolt when conditions are so oppressive that they have no hope of succeeding. The slavery system was comprehensive and effective. They were not only heavily outnumbered, but they had no weapons to speak of, or training to use them. Confined to plantations, they had little knowledge of the physical terrain of the South. Few could read or write. Their skin color made them highly visible targets for the white militia that patrolled the roads night and day to quell potential unrest. Most of the North was still allied with the southern slaveholders, and blacks did not have irate African nations crossing the Atlantic seeking revenge and to free their enslaved people.

Even though slaves often considered themselves little more than the working dead, they knew that a failed revolt meant certain death. In both direct and indirect ways, many slaves found ways to resist, even under the most treacherous of circumstances. Most slaves were so overwhelmed by the magnitude of their situation that they preferred to withdraw from reality or psychologically join their white oppressors. At a subtle level of resistance, slaves nonetheless responded to white oppression by feigning illness, crippling themselves, committing suicide, poisoning their masters, and setting fire to the properties on which they labored. More aggressive slaves escaped to "maroon" settlements and Indian communities in the wilderness, where they often plotted against their oppressors. Maroons were groups of escaped slaves who established their own communities. They routinely raided slave plantations for food, supplies and to liberate other slaves.

While most slave revolts in America were small and ineffective, at least three chilled the hearts of southerners. The three key revolts were led by Gabriel Prosser(1800), Denmark Vesey(1822), and Nat Turner(1831). These revolts set the stage for the ultimate revolt, the Civil War of the 1860s, that ended slavery as an institution.(15)

❂
Slave Couple Couldn't Wait

Many slaves took to heart a challenge from abolitionists that they should seize every opportunity, using any means necessary, to break free. Mark and Phillis were slaves, owned by John Codman of Charleston, South Carolina, who grew tired of their chains.

Learning that Codman had granted their freedom in his will upon his death, they decided not to wait. There was always the possibility, after all, that he might outlive them both. Taking matters into their own hands, they poisoned Codman. But their plot was uncovered by white neighbors. For killing a white man, Mark was hanged and Phillis was burned alive. They were said to have died believing, however, that they had done the right thing. Other slaves would continue to adhere to the belief that desperate times called for desperate measures. God, they believed, helps those who help themselves.(16)

❂
A Song of Slave Revolts

It was a capital offense not only for a slave to plan or participate in a revolt, but even to imagine it. Rigid measures were taken to block the access of slaves to any tool or resource that could conceivably be used as a weapon. What slaves lacked in means to revolt, they made up for in spirit and determination. They dreamed about slave heroes. The following song captures this spirit and desire for freedom:

Arise! arise! shake off your chains!
Your cause is just, so Heaven ordains;
To you shall freedom be proclaimed!
Raise your arms and bare your breast,
Almighty God will do the rest.
Blow the clarion's warlike blast;
Call every Negro from his task;
Wrest the scourge from Buckra's hand,
And drive each tyrant from the land!
(Chorus)
Firm, united let us be,
Resolved on death or liberty!
As a band of patriots joined,
Peace and plenty we shall find. (17)

1800: The Prosser Conspiracy

The Gabriel Prosser conspiracy was one of the nation's most carefully planned insurrections. Inspired by the successful Haitian revolt at the turn of the 19th century, Gabriel Prosser, a 24-year old rebel slave, sounded the dawning of the new age of rebellion in America.

After months of planning, Prosser proposed leading a slave revolt against the city of Richmond, Virginia, in August, 1800. The black insurrectionists were instructed on how to gather and use clubs, swords, and other objects as weapons. Prosser's intentions were to divide his rebel force into three columns; one to attack the penitentiary which was being used as an arsenal, a second to capture the power station and a third to attack the city itself. If the citizenry refused to surrender, the rebel leader planned to kill all the whites. He would grant an exception to those he felt had been somewhat kind to blacks, primarily Quakers, Methodists, and Frenchmen.

The rebels aimed to gather large supplies of guns and powder and capture the state treasury. They calculated that when this had been accomplished, they would control the resources to hold off counter-attacks for several weeks. They hoped word of the slave revolt would then spread across the country and that slaves from the surrounding territory would arrive to fortify their ranks. With a large enough revolt, they felt whites would have little choice but to come to terms with their demand for emancipation.

On the day of the revolt, however, a severe Virginia storm washed out bridges and roads, making it impossible for the 1,200-plus revolutionaries to get to the gathering point. When only 300 slaves showed up at the designated time, Prosser temporarily postponed the rebellion. On the morning of August 30, before Prosser could reschedule the undertaking, he was betrayed. Two Richmond slaves, Tom and Pharaoh, informed their masters about Prosser's plans. Once exposed, Prosser and 35 of his compatriots had little chance to escape. They were quickly surrounded, arrested, and tried. As was to be expected, Prosser and his fellow slaves were found guilty of revolting for freedom and executed.

Long after Prosser was hanged, rumors hinted that between 2,000 and 50,000 slaves were ready to join his uprising. Many slaveholders were puzzled about the size of Prosser's conspiracy and why so many slaves were willing to join. One theory suggested the Virginia state seal, which depicted the mythological Virtus standing over a conquered Tyranus, had also motivated Prosser's support. The image on the seal, when impressed on dark wax, could be interpreted as a freed slave standing triumphant over his master. Believing this state seal had motivated blacks to revolt, many plantation owners hired guards at the capital, and changed the official seal. (18)

❂
The Denmark Vesey Uprising

In 1822, a few years after the Prosser Conspiracy, Denmark Vesey, a militant free black, organized a revolt in Charleston, South Carolina. Vesey had purchased his own freedom for $600, which came from $1,500 in lottery winnings. He was refused permission, however, to purchase the freedom of his children.

Fueled by anger that his children, not to mention his race, were mere chattel, Vesey vowed not to accept the self-mocking, acquiescing behavior expected of slaves. He demanded that blacks display racial pride and courage. When he saw Charleston slaves bow, tip their hats, and step into the street gutters to make way for whites, he screamed, "You deserve to be slaves." To express his anger in a more productive forum, Vesey became a Methodist minister who preached racial solidarity and freedom to his fellow blacks. Drawing on the text of the Declaration of Independence and the Old Testament, in his sermons, he admonished against inequality and urged slaves to resist their masters. So vehement were Vesey's arguments that some of his followers feared Vesey more than their masters or even God.

Vesey planned his uprising for nearly four years, patiently working out the details. He was well aware that several past revolts had gone awry when blacks squealed to their masters. To decrease that possibility, he let it be known that he would personally deal with any slave who betrayed him. But even with all of Vesey's threats, house slaves informed their white masters of Vesey's planned revolt--not once, but twice. Vesey never had a chance to carry out his threat of "breaking the neck of any slave who informed on him."

Based upon the word of slave informers, white authorities arrested and executed Vesey and 37 of his followers. Another 30 lesser participants were deported to the Caribbean Islands for re-conditioning. For Vesey, death was probably preferable to living with the knowledge that two of his own people personally profited from selling him down the river. For their treachery, the informers received meritorious manumission and monetary rewards. (19)

✪
Nat Turner, Sword of God

Of all the slave revolts, Nat Turner's was without a doubt the best known. In August, 1831, Turner and about 70 other black slaves began their long-planned insurrection. The charismatic slave believed the voice of God had instructed him to commence a death march across Virginia and the South to free four million black slaves. If necessary, he felt his band was justified in killing every white person who crossed his path.

Nat Turner began the killing with his own master, then proceeded from farm to farm. Within a few days, he and his co-conspirators had raided several plantations and butchered no less than 55 whites. The word of Turner's revolt immediately spread across the nation, throwing the white population into a panic. Many whites packed their families into buggies and fled Virginia and neighboring states. Haiti's successful slave revolt, which by this time was well known, made Turner's uprising white America's worst nightmare. To slaveowners, Turner represented an out-of-control, avenging black bogeyman.

The federal government placed the United States Marines on alert. For two full months, thousands of state reserves and militia members scoured the state for Turner's small but mighty gang of revolutionary slaves. Furious that slaves had the nerve to actually take up arms against them, white vigilante mobs roamed the countryside assaulting and slaughtering free or bonded blacks. In some cases, entire black families, women and children included, were massacred. Business and property owners conducted economic reprisals by refusing to employ free blacks or rent them homes or farm lands. Since whites controlled private property, indeed, the entire economy, their actions had serious repercussions on the black population.

Turner's small army was eventually located, surrounded, and defeated. Turner and his men attempted counter-attacks, but were vastly outnumbered. After going into hiding and eluding capture, he was finally discovered in a cave,

Picture of Nat Turner's 1831 rebellion (Library of Congress).

arrested without resistance, tried, and hanged. Nat Turner had responded to the prolonged suffering of his people. At his trial, the black warrior looked at the sea of hostile white faces. "I do not feel any guilt for what I have done," he declared. "Let God judge my acts." His earthly judges found him guilty of seeking freedom. He was hanged and decapitated. (20)

❂

Whispers From a Caribbean Nation

Toussaint L' Ouverture, a former carriage driver and natural military genius, led the slaves of Haiti and the Dominican Republic in a rebellion against Napoleon of France at the end of the 1700s. Napoleon and his army suffered a stunning defeat. This was the only time in the development of the Western world that white Europeans blinked and blacks seized their freedom. More than 60,000 blacks and whites perished in L'Ouverture's rebellion, creating Haiti as a republic of freed slaves.

Following Napoleon's defeat, France sent troops to Haiti to negotiate a peace treaty. Although they had been militarily trounced, French treachery was still alive and well. French military officials, displaying the flag of truce, managed to lure L'Ouverture to their Haitian headquarters, where they arrested him in 1802. He died in jail in the Alps in 1803. To stave off a chain reaction of black revolts in the United States, slaveholders tried in vain to keep the news of the Haitian revolt from the ears of black slaves. L'Ouverture had made an impact. Reportedly, "Wherever slaves chafed under chains, this man's name was whispered." (21)

3
Freedmen and Free Labor
We make distinctions without making differences.

Mini Facts

• *From the 15th to 19th centuries, a "black Holocaust" was carried out. Two-thirds of the 35 million slaves shipped out of Africa died en route to the Americas. Neither an apology nor reparations have been offered to the victimized black race.*

• *In 1787, the First Constitutional Convention met in Philadelphia to draft a Constitution that codified slavery and equated blacks to three-fifths of a human being. Following suit, the new Congress enacted the first immigration bill that placed a zero quota on black immigrants.*

• *At a Berlin Conference in 1876, European governments arbitrarily divided up the entire African continent into colonies, then exploited them until they were the most economically impoverished nations on earth.*

• *In the 1860s, the 14th Amendment to the Constitution was enacted to give blacks due process rights. Yet, for nearly a century afterwards, the U.S. Supreme Court ruled against every due process rights case involving blacks.*

❂
What Is a Slave?

What is a slave? A slave is a person owned by another person, has no rights and works without pay. The word "slave" was originally applied to a European ethnic group. According to the encyclopedia, it came from "Slav," a Russian people captured by the Germans.

Other sources say the word "Slav" originally meant "the people of glory" and suggested some kind of a religious identification or purification. In any event, the last enslavement of European whites occurred in the 14th century, when Arabs held the Mamelukes in captivity. Ancient slavery was an individual matter, resulting from a war, religious differences, or personal indebtedness. But, in any of these instances, enslavement was based on a power relationship between the slave and the master that allowed the slave to earn his freedom eventually. In ancient slavery, intermediaries such as the Catholic Church protected the rights and property of the enslaved and required the master to pay "freedom dues" to the slave upon his release.

The modern enslavement of blacks was different. Black slavery was a new socioeconomic system. Unlike all previous forms of enslavement, black enslave-

Modern slavery was based on skin color. (Library of Congress)

ment was based upon the "accident of skin color." Further, for the first time in the history of mankind, all formal religions, nations, and ethnic groups collectively moved against and supported the enslavement of black people. These first time occurrences against blacks at the same time the rest of the world was espousing the concepts of freedom, liberty, and equality for all men, led to enslavement being called a "peculiar institution."

Perhaps another reason it was called a peculiar institution was because it marked the beginning of Europe's social engineering of the black race. Before the Diaspora, or scattering of African blacks, Europeans considered black Africans to be exotic, exciting, but not necessarily inferior. As more and more European nations became slave traders and began to enjoy the wealth that it produced, Europeans came to classify Africans as stupid, uncivilized and less than human. They used all reasoning at their disposal to justify why whites treated blacks like no other human beings on earth. (1)

✪
Blacks Were Here Before the Mayflower?

The first black slaves arrived in America much earlier than typically reported in history books, probably as early as 1526. In the summer of 1526, 500 Spaniards and 100 black slaves founded a town near the mouth of the Pee Dee River in what is now South Carolina. Most of the members of this group were killed off by diseases and fights with local Indians. Matters worsened for the Spaniards, when in November of the same year, the slaves rebelled, killed many of their white masters, and escaped into the wilderness to live with the Indians. The approximately 150 remaining Spaniards then abandoned their settlement and retreated to Haiti. The black slaves that they left behind undoubtedly joined and inter-bred with the local Indian tribes. Their mixed offspring awaited the arrival of the European settlers who came nearly a century later. (2)

✪
A Public Edict Laid Foundation for Racism

Before the Maryland Colony came into existence in 1634, newly arrived European whites and African blacks intermingled and socialized reasonably well. In 1638, however, the Maryland Colony issued a public edict encouraging a separation of the races. It became the basis of public policy for race relations in America.

The Council for the Maryland Colony edict stated that, "Neither the existing black population, their descendants nor any other blacks shall be permitted to enjoy the fruits of white society." This public edict later became more commonly known as "the Doctrine of Exclusion."

Around the mid-1660s, various colonies picked up the Maryland Edict or the Doctrine of Exclusion and expanded it into enslavement laws for people of African descent. Once established, the laws became the basis for a national public policy on the exploitation of blacks that was passed on from generation to generation through social customs and public laws. The Slave Codes of 1705 required all individuals, churches, businesses, organizations, schools, and all levels of government to teach, justify and enforce the status of blacks as "a subordinate, excluded, non-competitive, non-compensated, managed work force for the personal comfort and wealth building of white society." This public policy remained in effect until the late 1960s.

The wave of computerized technology that began in the 1960s rendered marginalized black labor obsolete. It established a new public policy that maintained the inequalities between the races, absolved members of the majority society from feeling any guilt or accepting responsibility for what had happened to black people, and categorically denied support to public policy or programs that would shift control and ownership of wealth and power resources from whites to blacks. (3)

❂
Why Were Blacks Preferred Slaves?

It was not by simple chance that the black race was selected for enslavement. It resulted from a process of elimination. Europeans were not interested in enslaving members of their own race. Asians were protected by geographical barriers. Indians refused to be enslaved, indicating a willingness to die first. What group was left? Blacks! The Catholic Church recommended blacks because they felt one black slave was worth three to four Indian slaves. More specifically, African blacks were selected and effectively enslaved for at least five reasons: 1) They had an agricultural history based upon an extended family work system; 2) They lacked a broad sense of community based on skin-color and were divided along the lines of tribalism; 3) They were simultaneously invaded and enslaved by every religious denomination, national government, ethnic and racial group; 4) They lacked guns and exploding powder; and 5) Their "internal disposition" allowed them to accept enslavement. This combination of factors set the stage for African blacks to become the "chosen people" for enslavement. (4)

❂

Prescriptive Conditioning of Slaves

Historical documents contain countless references by whites to what they construed as the "ideal slave" attitude and behavior. The question so often asked is, "Since most slavery was not a voluntary state, how or what did white society do to make all blacks act alike and accept slavery?"

In 1996, Charles M. Christian, in his book, **Black Saga: The African American Experience**, offers his readers a look at how slaves were conditioned. He describes the steps that "seasoning sites" in the West Indies used to break in newly-kidnapped slaves. Slave conditioning sites taught blacks their place, status, future, and acceptable behavior patterns.

Slave traders and slaveholders often consulted with experts who successfully conditioned blacks and were able to keep them helpless and dependent. A properly conditioned slave, it was argued, would never break the psychological chains placed in his mind. Christian listed the following steps in the conditioning process:

Step # 1-Establish and maintain strict discipline to engender unconditional submission.

Step # 2-Create a sense of personal inferiority.

Step # 3-Instill fear in the mind.

Step # 4-Teach the slave to see the world only through the eyes of the master.

Step # 5-Reconstruct the slave to be a helpless and perfectly dependent individual. (5)

❁
What Are We Slaving For?

The words of a black slave summarized their existence.
>We bake de bread,
>Dey gib us de crust,
>We sif de meal,
>Dey gib us de huss...
>We skim de pot,
>Dey gib us de liquor
>An say dat's good enough for Nigger. (6).

❁
The Infamous Willie Lynch Speech

Willie Lynch was an expert at seasoning black slaves and lived in Jamaica. When the Virginia colony enacted its meritorious manumission policy in 1710, Willie Lynch went to Virginia to share his expertise. Upon his arrival in Virginia in 1712, he supposedly delivered the speech below.

Gentlemen:

I greet you here on the bank of the James River in the year of our Lord, one thousand seven hundred and twelve. First, I shall thank you the Gentlemen of the Colony of Virginia for bringing me here. I am here to help you solve some of your problems with the slaves. Your invitation reached me on my modest plantation in the West Indies where I have experimented with some of the newest and still the oldest methods for control of slaves. Ancient Rome would envy us if my program is implemented. As our boat sailed south of the James River, I saw enough to know that your problem is not unique. While Rome used cords of wood as crosses for standing human bodies along its highways in great numbers, you are here using the tree and the rope on occasion.

I caught the whiff of a dead slave hanging from a tree a couple of miles back. You are not only losing valuable stock by hangings, you are having uprisings, slaves are running away, your crops are sometimes left in the field too long for maximum profit, you suffer occasional fires, your animals are killed. Gentlemen, you know what your problems are; I do not need to elaborate. I am not here to enumerate your problems. I am here to introduce you to a method of solving them.

In my bag here, I have a fool-proof method for controlling your black slaves. I guarantee everyone of you that if installed correctly it will control the slaves for at least 300 years. My method is simple and members of your family and any overseer can use it.

I have outlined a number of differences among the slaves; and I take these difference and make them bigger. I use fear, distrust, and envy for control purposes. These methods have worked on my modest plantation in the West Indies and it will work throughout the South. Take this simple little list of differences, think about them. On top of my list is "age," but it is there only because it starts with an "a," the second is "color" (or shade), there is intelligence, size, sex, size of plantation, status on plantation, attitude of owner, whether the slaves live in the valley, on the hill, east, west, north, south, have fine hair or coarse hair, or is tall or short. Now that you have a list of differences, I shall give you an outline of action, but before that, I shall assure you that distrust is stronger than trust, and envy is stronger than adulation, respect or admiration.

The black slaves after receiving this indoctrination shall carry on and will become self-refueling and self-generating for hundreds of years, maybe thousands Don't forget you must pitch the old black vs. the young black male and the young black male vs. the old black male. You must use the dark skin slaves vs. the light skin slaves and the light skin slaves vs. the dark skin slaves. You must also have your white servants and overseers distrust ALL blacks, but it is necessary they trust and depend on us. They must love, respect, and trust ONLY us.

Gentlemen, these kits are your control; use them. Have your wives and children use them, never miss an opportunity. My plan is guaranteed, and the good thing about this plan is that if used intensely for one year the slaves themselves will remain perpetually distrustful.

Thank you gentlemen,
Willie Lynch, 1712 (7)

✪
What Was An Indentured Servant?

Blacks in bondage were called slaves, while bonded whites were called indentured servants. Servants were termed indentured because their contract was indented, or folded, along an irregular line and torn in two, master and servant each kept one half as a receipt until the termination date. Typically, indentured servant contracts were for four to seven years. At the completion of the contract period, the indentured party received pay, clothing, livestock, land, farming tools, and a weapon. A slave's bonded status was for life--his and all future offspring. When black slaves were emancipated in the 1860s, they were set free poor, landless, ignorant, weaponless, homeless, and naked. The various levels of government expressed no appreciation for the contributions of black people in building the nation nor did they issue an apology for what they had done to blacks.(8)

✪
Slaves Marketed On Easy Terms

African slaves were typically purchased at auction houses in the slave markets of major urban ports such as the District of Columbia, Charleston, New Orleans, Hampton and Savannah. For those who rarely left the rural areas of the country, slave wagons traveled the back roads hawking their slave wares at bargain prices. But, unlike large auction houses, they did not guarantee their "goods."

For those who did not have access to an auction house or roving slave wagons, there was always the mail order route. An interested slave buyer could order by mail specifying the size, sex, and even the tribe of the African slave he wished to purchase. Many mail order houses allowed slaves to be bought for a small down payment and reasonable payment terms of three, six, nine or twelve months. Needless to say, slaves damaged after purchase could not be returned to the auction houses, slave wagons, or mail order centers, for monies back. (9)

❂
Arabs: The Chief Slave Traders

For the purpose of spreading the Islamic religion and taking the mineral wealth of black African nations, the Arabs began enslavement of sub-Saharan blacks in the mid-700s A.D. After nearly 13 centuries, selling on an average of 1 million blacks every 100 years, one can estimate that Arab slave traders enslaved and financially profited from the sale of more than 13 million African blacks.

In July, 1994, several Arab diplomats and other spokespersons disavowed a *Washington Post* article that Arabs were still trading in black slaves in Mauritania, Ethiopia, and Sudan. The national press was challenged to prove that slavery still existed in those countries.

The *Baltimore Sun* newspaper accepted the challenge and sent two reporters, one black columnist from the *Sun* and a foreign correspondent, who was white, to Sudan to see if they could buy black slaves and prove beyond a shadow of a doubt that chattel slavery does exist in Sudan.

According to *The Washington Post*, the two reporters found clear evidence of slave raids on blacks in the south of Sudan. They actually bought two black slaves from Islamic fundamentalists for the price of $500 each. Having completed their mission, the reporters immediately returned the slaves to their aggrieved families.

Few people are interested in or understand the continued enslavement of blacks because the issue is confused and smothered under religious conflicts between Christians, Jews and Islamic religions. They failed to understand that black slavery is not a horizontal moral issue. It is a racial and economic issue. Neither the national political leadership, religious leadership, or traditional civil rights organizations have acknowledged current day black slavery as an

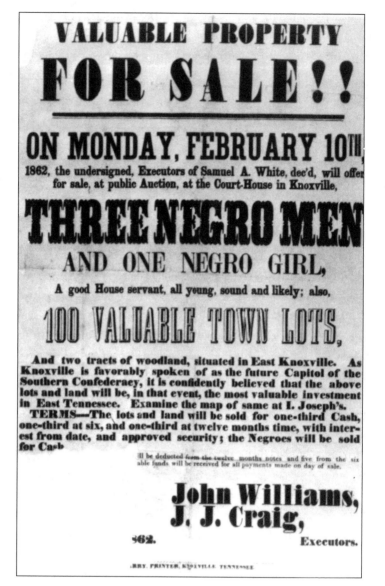

An 1862 notice of slave auction. (Library of Congress)

issue.

The Commander-in-Chief of the Garang Liberation Movement, a human rights group in Sudan, told a reporter of the ***Washington Post*** that, "the Islamic government army and its paramilitary auxiliary militias use slavery to destroy the African/non-Moslem dimension of Sudanese identity." Obviously, as long as blacks remain divided along the lines of religion, political party and class, they will forever be vulnerable to those who seek to enslave and exploit them. (10)

❂
Trickster Slave Uses Mother Wit

Being kept in a constant state of ignorance and deprivation because they were either slaves or second-class citizens left blacks little choice but to develop survival tactics that reflected the realities of their dilemma. They learned to use what was called "Mother Wit" to outsmart a more powerful and presumably more knowledgeable adversary. This tactic led to the image of a black trickster.

Some of the clearest images of a trickster at work occurred during slavery. For example, Cato, a slave living in Philadelphia, Pennsylvania, during the nation's revolutionary war, knew that he was in for a beating. His master had given him a letter to be delivered to the local jailer, who also worked as a paid slave beater. Suspecting his master's intentions, Cato asked an illiterate fellow slave to deliver the letter to the jailer for him. Sure enough, the letter stated, "Mr. Jailer, please administer a dozen lashes to the back of the bearer of this letter for me."

Although it was illegal to educate a slave, some became expert schemers. In this specific instance, Cato arranged to have done to another what his master had planned to have done to him. Cato was no hero, just a survivalist. (11)

❂
Rent-A-Slave Ad

Good neighbors routinely shared slave labor with non-slaveowners, as indicated in this ad from a Richmond newspaper:
Attention! Negro Owners
When your field work is completed for this season, I will feed
and shelter fifteen, one half an three quarter hands while they

are idle in exchange for their labor, to clear land for a period of four months or from the time you can spare any Negroes to me and you need them back. I will pay the owners a reasonable price for any accidental death or mutilation that may occur to one of these slaves, while in my possession. I will be totally responsible for any runaways. They must be stout and obedient, without the use of chains. A mutual indenture in writing will be honored. To those willing to participate in the above venture inquiries to the above notice are invited.

August 20, 1836

Subscriber Col. John C. Ballard

Residence Richmond, Virginia   (12)

4
Sex and Sensibility

For some, the blacker the berry, the sweeter the juice.

Mini Facts

• *Just a half of a century after the Mayflower Pilgrims landed on Massachusetts shores, the colony had lots of prostitutes, brothels and venereal diseases. As a matter of fact, Colonial Williamsburg, the capital of Virginia, had three of the biggest houses of ill-repute of all the thirteen colonies.*

• *In 1662, a Virginia law defined the status of a child from a black and white union as being the same as the mother. The status of the child of a white mother and white father was determined by the status of the father.*

• *In the mid-1700s, it was not unusual to see white women in the slave markets buying black slaves after carefully examining their genitals. Black females were routinely purchased by white men as sexual playthings and breeders.*

• *During President Lincoln's re-election campaign in 1864, the Democratic Party circulated a pamphlet that introduced a new word, "miscegenation," claiming Lincoln wanted to mix the races.*

The Criminalization of Black Sexuality

Within four years after the first 20 Negroes arrived in Jamestown, Virginia, in 1619, and were traded into servitude, a black female was charged with having sex

Black female slave abducted. (Library of Congress)

with a white male. By 1623, she was a freed woman who could do anything except engage in sex with white men. Yet, it was white males who were driving the practice of interracial sex. In some ways, it made sense for white men to look for sexual partners outside their race. Of the 1209 white persons in the Virginia colony in 1623, white men outnumbered white women by more than four to one.

The few white women who did come to the colony to work as maids were quickly paired off with white men. The remaining white men often found black women a convenient and, in some cases, preferable substitute for white women. Despite the popularity of interracial pairing, many colonialists decreed it a violation of both God's and man's law.

Thanks to his penchant for seducing black women, Hugh Davis, a white colonist, caused the word "Negro" to be entered into the criminal codes of the colonies. Caught in the act, Davis was officially charged with "abusing himself and defiling his body by laying with a Negro woman." For committing a sexual act with a Negro woman, Davis was physically beaten before a group of black spectators and made to acknowledge his lustful and unlawful sin. However, public whipping and humiliation were to no avail, interracial sex continued unabated. The sexual linkage between black women and white men had become a part of American culture. (1)

❂
Romance and the Ruling Class

For centuries, white male and black female sexual liaisons have been an expected and even accepted custom, a natural result of the power inequalities between the races and the sexes. White males had unlimited prerogative to use, and often abuse, black females for their own gratification, with or without permission from her or any other member of her race. This was especially true during slavery when black women had no way of resisting the advances of their owners. This inequitable and exploitative tradition continued long after slavery had been abolished.

For white men, the miscegenation ritual became a symbol of white manhood and racial dominance, regardless of whether it resulted from force, consent, persuasion, rights of ownership, or even romance. Because of the taboo nature of the subject, the meaning of the sexual relationships between black females and white males in the ruling class is still shrouded in mystery. Were the females generally taken against their will? Or, did black women indulge with white men for power and material benefits? (2)

❂
Thomas Jefferson's Mistress, Black Sal

The best known romance in the colonial period was between Thomas Jefferson and Sally Hemings, one of his black slaves. The romance began when Jefferson was in his 40's and ended when he was nearly 64 years of age. It is thought that Hemings bore five slave children for the President and author of the Declaration of Independence.

Rumors of the affair did not go unnoticed by Jefferson's political enemies.

His 1804 presidential campaign was bombarded with mudslinging gossip about his love life with various black mistresses, and their mulatto offspring, his "Congo Harem," as one detractor put it. Jefferson's opponents focused on his affair with Hemings, whom he allegedly impregnated while he served as American envoy to Paris. At the time, the black slave was just 16. In addition to the whispering campaigns about Jefferson and Hemings, one of President's contemporaries put the tale of his love life to verse:

> Of all the damsels on the green;
> On mountain, or in valley,
> A lasso luscious ne'er was seen;
> As Monticelian Sally.
> Chorus: Yankee Doodle, ho's the noodle?
> What wife was half so handy?
> To breed a flow of slaves for stock;
> A black amour's the dandy.
> When pres'd by load of state affairs;
> I seek to sport and dally,
> The sweetest solace of my cares;
> Is the lap of Sally.

Neither the allegations nor the verse stopped the immensely popular Jefferson from winning the election. Neither did they affect his behavior toward Hemings in particular and his slaves in general. The difficulty Jefferson's political opponents had in exploiting the issue were the result of Jefferson's distinct public images. He was perceived as a brilliant businessman, a statesman consumed with a passion for public service, and a devoted, protective lover of his black concubine and mixed-race children. Yet he was also viewed as a ruthless slaveholder who was alleged to have sold two of his own daughters to a New Orleans slave auctioneer for pocket change. The public often did not know which likeness to believe.

The mystery of Jefferson's moral nature as well as his feelings toward Hemings and his mixed-race children extended beyond his life. At his death in 1826, Hemings was 53. In his will, Jefferson freed everyone in the Hemings family--except the long-suffering Sally. She was willed, along with the rest of his slaves, to his white daughter Martha. Some felt he kept Sally enslaved to protect her; to keep her out of the public eye after his death. Either way, Sally remained in bondage at the Jefferson estate at Monticello for several years until Martha Jefferson quietly set her free. Sally then joined her family, which was living in a small house across the Potomac River from Washington, D.C. At the age of 62 in 1835, she died there in obscurity. (3)

Washington Fathered the Country and....?

The popular perception of George Washington is that of the honest world leader and devoted husband to Martha. But if we are to believe one story about Washington's actual conduct toward one of his black female slaves, reality was far different from perception.

Like most American presidents, George Washington was born into wealth, prominence, and power. And like many prominent men of his day, there were rumors that he fathered mixed-race children. Reigning as a veritable king over a massive plantation with hundreds of black slaves, many of whom he had inherited from his father, Washington had unbridled access to anything he desired.

Like Thomas Jefferson, the record suggests that Washington was more than just the father of revolution and country. It was also rumored that he had fathered several black children by one of his favorite slaves. But unlike those involving Thomas Jefferson, this allegation has not been fully substantiated.

Washington's alleged black mistress and their offspring were discussed in historian Richard Shenkman's *Legends, Lies and Cherished Myths of American History*. In the book, Shenkman writes that the only evidence for the charge was a letter written by Washington in which he admitted to having an "assignation with pretty little Kate, the washer-woman's daughter." The letter, which has never been authenticated, was circulated by British authorities in an effort to discredit Washington during the battle for independence.

Others have claimed that Washington died from a bout of pneumonia after a secret winter rendezvous with his black concubine. Seeking to protect his image and reputation, Washington's supporters insisted that it was his plantation manager, Lund Washington, who fathered a child by a black mistress. When the dust from the accusation settled, at least a few things were clear: a white male named Washington, living on the Washington plantation, had an affair with a black mistress and produced a mixed-race child. Which Washington was actually responsible remains a mystery that is unlikely to be resolved. (4)

✿

Vice Presidents' Black Mistresses

Jefferson, and possibly Washington, were not the only leaders to consort with black women. Romance between whites and blacks occurred at all social levels and classes. Richard Johnson, the Vice-President during Martin Van Buren's administration, had long and scandalous affairs with a procession of black women.

In his assignations, Johnson displayed honesty rarely seen among other national leaders engaged in such conduct. Rather than veil his private life in a shroud of secrecy and shame, the Vice-President freely acknowledged that he was the father of two daughters by a black slave named Julia Chinn. Having inherited Chinn from his father, Johnson took her as his mistress-housekeeper. But he had the courage to introduce her to white society as his wife. Not only did he acknowledge the children he had by Chinn, but he paid for their support and saw to it that they received an excellent education.

In seeking acceptance for his relationship with a black woman, Johnson was ahead of his time. When he attempted to introduce his daughters into white society, they were snubbed. Johnson's daughters eventually married white men to whom he bequeathed his property. The scandal of his affairs with a black mistress shocked the country, but Johnson ignored the attacks and negative public opinion. He refused to give up his political career, his daughters, or his black mistress. The relationship did not end until Julia Chinn died of cholera in 1833.

Despite his honesty, Johnson's behavior was not entirely enlightened. Chinn's death failed to quench his passion for black females. It may, in fact, have inflamed it. He immediately began another affair with a young slave woman of mixed blood that lasted for years. After being elected Vice-President by the United States Senate, Johnson took his third slave mistress, who proved unfaithful, running away with an Indian lover. Furious at being jilted, Johnson pursued, captured, and sold the young woman back into slavery.

Johnson then took as his lover the next best thing to his enslaved paramour--her younger sister. Even though she was only 16, he lived openly with the young woman for years. Johnson's political connections and reputation as a wealthy slaveholder sheltered him from reproach for his insatiable appetite for black mistresses, allowing him to become Vice- President of the United States. (5)

❂
Not With My Pig You Don't

The confusion of colonial race mores was not unlike the views on justice and bestiality. While tolerating the sexual peccadilloes of white male slaveowners toward their black female slaves, who were classified by law as less than human and equal to a "beast of the field," colonial society imposed the death penalty on anyone caught, or in some cases, simply accused of, indulging in sex with farm animals, beasts of the field. Since white males equated all blacks to beasts of the field and used black females as sex objects, apparently some forms of bestiality or indulging in sex with "beasts of the field" were acceptable. Even though the lines between blacks and animals were blurred, dominant authority occasionally drew a line in the sand.

A white male, George Spencer of New Haven, Connecticut, was caught in such a predicament. When a one-eyed pig was born in the town, the magistrates, casting around for an explanation, lighted on the hapless Spencer, who had the misfortune of also having but one eye. Interrogated about the possibility of bestiality, the frightened Spencer confessed, but then recanted. Under Connecticut law, convicting Spencer of bestiality required only the testimony of two witnesses. In their eagerness to execute Spencer, the magistrates admitted the pig as one witness and the retracted confession as the other. Spencer was hanged. (6)

❂
Famous Abolitionist Had a Black Mistress

Thaddus Stevens was a powerful abolitionist and member of the House of Representatives who often squared off against southern slaveowners, but shared their taste for black mistresses. On the question of black liberation, the representative was no hypocrite. Unlike the southern white males who were willing to degrade blacks while sexually exploiting them, Stevens forthrightly cared for them, both politically and personally. Befriending them, he fought for their rights as human beings.

An originator of the 14th Amendment of the Constitution, intended to protect suffrage by reducing the representation of states that deny blacks the vote, Stevens had reasons to be so inclined. During the last two decades of his life, he found comfort and happiness living with his housekeeper, Lydia Smith, a beautiful light-skinned mixed-race women.

✪
Sex and the Civil War

To many Americans, mention of the Civil War brings to mind images of Abraham Lincoln, Confederate flags, and half-naked black slaves walking on back roads. Little has been written of the flood of professional prostitutes, free sex chasers, sexually-transmitted diseases, and breakdown in Puritan morals brought on by the war.

Civil War soldiers, including many of the highest military leaders in the land, took time out from fighting to engage in sex with whites prostitutes. Their more frequent assignations, however, were with the even more vulnerable--and thus accessible--black female slaves.

Whether they were discovered on plantations or back roads, black slaves were routinely used as sexual outlets by both Union and Confederate soldiers. When General Joseph Hooker took command of the Union Army, for instance, his "realistic" recreation and socializing policies gave the troops great latitude to engage in nearly any form of sexual activity, supposedly to gain a measure of relief from the pressures of war. Red light districts and bordellos, with whiskey never far away, sprung up around Washington, D.C., and other large northern cities to accommodate the soldier's every taste. In fact, the very term, "hooker," which means prostitute, apparently sprang from General Hooker's own sexual habits. He loved visiting the row of bawdy houses on Lafayette Square in the nation's capital so much that it became known as "Hooker's Row."

Praising the sexual attractiveness of light-skinned, mixed-race women in song became central to American folklore. The state song, "Yellow Rose of Texas," celebrated the "high yellow" complexion of a beautiful light-skinned prostitute who ran a boarding house in Galveston. During the Union Army's occupation of Columbia, South Carolina, one citizen reported that "it was not unusual to see a Yankee soldier with his arm around the neck of a Negro wench, even in the common thoroughfare, or hugging and kissing a mulatto girl, when he could find one."

For the white troops, sex with light-skinned women was often preferable to dark-skinned ones. White soldiers often sang "Shall Brown," which commended a black servant's intention to leave his dark woman for the favors of a "new bright mulatto girl." Following their white counterparts, black men also considered mixed-race women desirable. Regardless of skin color, women were almost always available to the servicemen. Both the Union and the Confederate armies were shadowed by large parties of women. Some women went so far as to disguise themselves as male soldiers to more easily dispense sex, undetected.

While Puritan values maintained the facade of a Victorian society, illicit sexual relations were a reality. The soldier's sexual escapades were revealed in military records, newspaper reports, and personal letters to friends and family back home. But those knowledgeable about the activity acted as censors who weeded out many of the bawdy aspects of the Civil War years.

Medical records, however, were not necessarily subject to such suppression. According to the records, few soldiers bothered to practice the "safe sex" technique of the Victorian period, abstinence. During the war years, venereal diseases were commonly known by the euphemistic "ailments of Venus."

At one point during the war, records of the Union Medical Corps showed 212,000 cases of venereal disease out of 531,000 white and black soldiers. Clearly, 40 percent of all Union soldiers had not contracted the diseases from outhouse "toilet seats," as many claimed. The official medical records of Confederate soldiers were equally alarming, especially since penicillin had yet to be invented. In 1861, one Confederate artillery battery reported that 13 of its 45 men, nearly one-third, were hospitalized for venereal diseases--not exactly fighting shape. (7)

Slave Breeding...For Profit and Myths

International slave trading was officially ended in 1807, but the legal decree did not end the demand for black slaves, especially in the newly-formed Southern and Western slaveholding states. To satisfy the market, and undoubtedly to combine pleasure and profit, the old slaveholding states like Maryland, Virginia, North Carolina, and South Carolina turned to slave breeding. In this practice, fertile black women were prized as "breeders," and black men were valued according to their "studding abilities."

In both instances, myths often projected larger-than-life qualities onto black men and women. One of thousands of such tall tales involved "old breeding Joe." According to one old slave's recollection, the seven-foot tall Joe was the most virile black male slave in Virginia. Legend had it that his white master rented Joe out to a white man who lived in Suffolk County, Virginia. The man supposedly picked Joe up on Friday and locked him in a barn with 20 black female slaves. Joe was picked up on Monday and returned to his master. The next year, 17 black babies were born on the Suffolk County plantation, all on the very same day.

These tales may have put money in the white master's pockets, but they played havoc with his psyche. White men, often intimidated by the proported sexual powers of the black male, feared his gaining access to white women. By creating sexual fictions about black males, white slaveowners made them more attractive to white women and undermined their own sense of masculine sexual identity. White men tried to extract themselves from this paradox of their own making by making it a capital offense for black men to be in the presence of a white female. (8)

Nigger in the Wood Pile

The expression "there is a nigger in the wood pile" grew out of the Reconstruction period and spoke to sexual liaisons across racial lines. Although white men, rich or poor, had nearly total control over their sexual lives and those of black people, white women exercised at least nominal control over their homes, lives and sexual activities. They understood that white males' sexual escapades, whether with a prostitute, black mistress or extra-marital, were an acceptable, though seldom discussed, part of life. But once in a while, white women would play tit-for-tat and turn the tables on white males by sexually consorting with black men.

Following the Civil War, non-economic emancipation did not provide black people with the resources to establish stable lives. They were forced to migrate and forge for food and shelter. It was a practice of black men to stop at different white homes and offer to chop wood for a meal. Often after watching black men strip and chop the wood, white women would entice or order them into the bedroom for a sexual liaison. A black man had little choice. Obey and risk being caught. Refuse and risk being charged with rape. Apparently, most obeyed and moved on.

The "nigger in the wood pile" expression arose from associations made by the white men returning home and finding freshly cut wood. White housewives would tell how a wandering black man chopped the wood for a meal. Nine months later, when a dark skin or black baby arrived in the family, the white male would associate the chopped wood with the darker baby and proclaim, "There must have been a nigger in the wood pile."

Miscegenation produced darker babies in the white race centuries before the Civil War. Some historians estimate that tens of million of whites have some blackness in their veins. Thomas Sowell gave some indication of the frequency of white female-black male sexual relations in his book, *The Economics and Politics of Race*. Sowell stated that in the 1840s, more than 43 percent of the white, out-of-wedlock babies were fathered by black men. The "nigger in the wood pile" expression died with the invention of gas stoves and furnaces. (9)

5
Adventurers and Artists

Those who are afraid of their own shadow must live in the shade.

Mini Facts

• *In 1795, a black actor, for the first time, was allowed to play a role that was not a comic part. In James Murdock's, **The Triumph of Love**, the black actor played a romantic character.*

• *In the 1850s, approximately 2,000 free and non-free blacks were involved in the great California gold rush. A few found sizable amounts of gold that most used to buy their own freedom or the freedom of loved ones.*

• *In 1854, a London company published the first black novel, **Clotel**, written by William Wells Browns about Thomas Jefferson and his black mistress. In the American edition, a senator was substituted for President Jefferson, due to the sensitive nature of the subject matter.*

• *In 1877, when federal troops were pulled out of black communities in the South and West, many blacks straightened their backs, took up arms, and organized self-defense militia.*

✪
Who Was Here Before the Indians?

The Folsom people, who were of African origin, lived in the Southwestern part of the United States at least 10,000 to 15,000 years ago, according to archeological findings. If the findings are historically accurate, then modern American

Indians are neither "Native Americans" nor the "First Americans." It is logical to conclude than that the oldest Indian ancestors were African blacks. Clearly, all those white Americans who proclaim varying amounts of "Indian blood" are also confessing to having varying degrees of "black blood" in their veins.

The ancestors of modern day American Indians crossed the Bering Straits onto the North American continent approximately 5,000 - 6,000 years ago. In June, 1997 some archeologists claimed that European whites were in North America approximately 9,000 years ago, more than 3,000 years before Asians. Both groups came to North America after African blacks who passed across the North American continent and established communities in the Southwest. The oldest traceable population group on the North American continent were of African origin. The city of Folsom, Arizona, and Folsom Prison are name after the archeological findings in that area.

It is generally accepted that the ancestors of present day American Indians were Asians who migrated across the Bering Straits approximately 5,000 - 6,000 years ago. The presence of black Africans in the Southwest may offer an explanation as to why centuries ago, American Indians did not have Asian features nor yellow skin coloring. According to photographs, drawings, and written records, American Indians were dark complexioned. Similarly, Asian interbreeding with blacks could have produced Indians with oval eyes. Archeological studies strongly concluded that the Folsom people were the oldest population group on the North American continent and they were definitely of African descent.

There is a great deal of evidence that people of African descent had an early presence in North, Central, and South America long before Columbus arrived. In Central America, numerous monuments depict gods with Negroid features. Columbus reported from his visit to South America that the "Indians" there spoke of having seen black people. Later, the Spaniards also claimed to have seen black-skinned people in Colombia and Peru. Pyramids, statues, and other stone figures throughout Central and Latin America have Negroid physical features. Then, there is an equaling puzzling question, "Whatever happened to the 5 million black slaves that Spain shipped into Central America between 1501 and 1650 to dig in the gold and silver mines? Did they perish? Or were they assimilated into various populations throughout North, Central, and Latin America? (1)

⊛

Black Dramatist in the Old Roman Empire

In ancient Rome, African blacks were involved in all aspects of society. Some held high status and some were slaves. One of the most popular was Terence the Actor, an African slave who was such a brilliant dramatist that his owner, Terentius Lucanus, gave him his freedom and bestowed upon him a name similar to his own in recognition of Terence's genius in the dramatic arts.

The Roman Empire was famous for its theaters as well as its politics, sexual orgies, and its more violent forms of public entertainment such as gladiator fights and feeding Christians to the Lions. Latin writers referred to Terence as the "Afer" ("African") and as "Fusco" ("very dark").

For nearly 2,000 years, Terence's comedy acts and poetry verses have been studied, admired and imitated by scholars and dramatists. Terence himself, the slave who became a free man, has aroused the curiosity of scholars interested in the achievements of blacks in the age of antiquity. (2)

⊛

Antar, the Black Lion

Ask Americans, black and white, what they know about the literature of Africa and the Middle East, and someone is sure to mention familiar stories of *Ali Baba and the Forty Thieves*, *Aladdin and His Lamp*, and *Sinbad the Sailor*, known collectively as *The Arabian Nights*. Few are aware that these stories are based on the real-life exploits and romances of Antar, a black African warrior. This romantic hero was brave, virtuous and stronger than other men. But, unlike the main character in most legends and folk stories, Antar was not an imaginary hero. He was real life, flesh and blood. He walked the earth and was known sometimes in Arab history as "Abul Fouaris" (the father of heroes).

Throughout his lifetime, Antar was a chieftain, warrior, lover, hero, poet, the son of a slave and a champion of his people. Although his name is rarely heard in English-speaking countries, he is the hero of North Africa and the Middle East. Antar, the Black Lion, was born in slavery sometime around the middle of the 6th century.

Ignored by the wealthy chieftain who was his father and scorned by his slave mother, the young Antar was assigned to watch the field cattle.

When a fight broke out among rival tribesman over the possession of a famous mare, the 15-year old Antar threw himself into the battle, and came out a hero. As a reward, he was liberated from slavery by his own father and slavemaster.

In later years, Antar rose to become the leader of the Abs Tribe. Other tribes laughed at the Abs for having a young man who was not only black but an ex-slave son of their chief. Whenever Antar heard such put-downs, he immediately issued a physical challenge to anyone who wished to test his ancestry and blood. Many took up Antar's challenge. All failed to defeat him.

Antar died about 615 AD when a poisoned arrow pierced his back in the heat of a battle. Even though he was then nearly 90 years of age, his enemies dared not go near him until they were quite sure he was dead.

The story of Antar's life is as full of adventure, romance, and chivalry as any tale of knighthood. His deeds were spread by word of mouth throughout the Middle East, then set to writing in a book, *The Romance of Antar*. The book is considered among the literary classics of the world. One of Antar's poems is among the seven which hang at the entrance of the Temple of Mecca, the highest honor a Moslem writer can receive. (3)

❂
A Heritage of Tall Tales

Black African folk tales, like African-based popular music and dances, survived slavery. Whether blacks were shipped into the Americas or the Caribbean, the African legends, myths, proverbs, and folk tales, that were passed down through the ages retained remnants of African culture.

Animal stories seem to have been particularly popular in Africa as well as early African-American communities. Some of today's well-known animal stories have roots in the African continent, like the Uncle Remus tales and the Br'er Rabbit stories. The earlier Aesop stories about Br'er Rabbit (who was "Shulo the Hare" in Africa), apparently evolved into today's Bugs Bunny. "Br'er Rabbit," "Br'er Wolf," and "Sis Nanny Goat," are names which reflect the speech syntax of African blacks.

Joel Chandler Harris (1848-1908), a white journalist with the *Atlanta Constitution* newspaper, wrote stories in the African-American dialect based on legends and folk tales that had been passed down by slaves through their oral traditions. Harris, an advocate for fair treatment of African Americans after the Civil War, based his stories on tales he heard told by George Terrell, an elderly black man from Georgia, where Harris grew up.

In the late 1940s, one of Harris' stories was made into a movie, *The Song of the South*. Harris had his fictional creation, Uncle Remus, remark, "Put a spelling-book in a nigger's han's an dar' you loozes a plow hand. I kin take a bar'l stave an fling mo' sense inter a nigger in one minnit dan all de schools houses betwixt dis en de state er Midgigin." Black civil rights organizations protested the film produced by Walt Disney Studios because they believed the film perpetuated black stereotypes in Uncle Remus and the animals. Even when blacks are due credit for their contributions, their powerlessness and lack of control over resources allows others to distort their cultural heritage into negative stereotypes. (4)

❂
Did Columbus Discover America?

Africans discovered America and the Caribbean Islands before Columbus according to evidence offered by some scholars. Professor Leo Wiener, of Harvard University, in his writings, *The Presence of Negroes*, claims blacks were in the Americas long before Columbus. His argument is based on the proliferation of statues that posses typical Negro features, and African-like monuments located through Central America and the number of maroon colonies in Mexico. V. Riva Palacio was quoted in A. J. Rogers' *Book of Amazing Facts* saying, " It is indisputable that in very ancient times...the Negro race occupied our territory (Mexico) when the two continents were joined. This race brought its own religious cults and idols. The Mexicans had a black god, Ixlilton, which means black-faced."

The pre-existence of blacks in America before Columbus was supported by other historical accounts. According to author, James W. Loewen, "When Columbus reached Haiti, he found the Arawaks in possession of some spear points made of guanine. The

Indians told members of Columbus' party that they got the guanine from black traders who had come from the South and East. Guanine proved to be an alloy of gold, silver and copper, identical to the gold alloy preferred by West Africans, who called it "guanine." Islamic historians have recorded stories of black sailors going into the West. Genetic studies found that traces of diseases common in Africa were also found in pre-Columbian corpses in Brazil. Columbus' son, Ferdinand, who accompanied the admiral on his third voyage, reported that people he met or heard about in eastern Honduras, were "....almost black in color..." and probably African. The first Europeans to reach Panama, Balboa and company, reported seeing black slaves in an Indian town. The Indians reported they had captured them from a nearby black community."

Even if there had never been any reports of blacks in the Americas, their presence seems only logical. A look at the world globe suggests that Africans probably arrived in America before Europeans. If European explorers set out due west, they would land in Iceland or the extreme northern parts of the North American continent. If European explorers did not know where they were going, why would they sail southwest, against the currents, to get to the Far East. Contrarily, it was easier for African explorers to "discover" America because it is closer and directly west of the African continent.(5)

✪
Was Columbus a Racist?

For decades, Christopher Columbus has been regarded by Americans as a hero with a special place in history and a day of honor on the calendars. But, contrary to popular myths taught in schools, Columbus was not a good guy and there is serious doubt about his being the first mariner to "discover America." His behavior towards native inhabitants qualifies him as the first European to bring racism into the western world.

Records show that Columbus crossed the Atlantic Ocean three times, not in search of a new route to Asia for silks and spices, but seeking gold and other precious metals for the Spanish Crown. As a commissioned adventurer, he was promised "10 percent of the profits, a governorship over new-found lands, and all the fame that went with the new title of Admiral of the Ocean Sea," said historian Howard Zinn.

Accepting their financial assistance and reward offers, Columbus promised the crown as much gold as they needed and as many slaves as they asked. When Columbus and his crew arrived in the Caribbean Islands, they used the local Arawak Indians in their maddening searched for gold. When the search became futile, Columbus and his angry crew took out their frustrations on the defenseless Arawaks.

Many Indians were killed and mutilated. Others were driven to suicide. Within two years, nearly half of the 250,000 Indians on the island of Haiti were dead. By the year 1515, there were 50,000 Arawaks; by 1550, only 500 remained. A report in 1650 showed that none of the original Arawaks or their descedents were left. Although he failed to find gold, Columbus kept his promise to deliver slaves to the Spanish Crown. He took 500 of the strongest island Indians back to Europe with him as slaves. Nearly all of them died en route or shortly thereafter. The Crown kept its promise and rewarded Columbus with the title "Admiral of the Ocean Sea."

But life has its little just rewards, too. Just like the elusive Caribbean gold and the way the entire race of Arawak Indians faded from the earth, so did Columbus. Within eight years, he was relieved from his post as Admiral of the Ocean Sea, returned to Spain in chains, and allowed to sink into such profound obscurity that today nobody knows for sure where he is buried. Columbus Day celebrations cover up his navigational incompetence, arrogance, and racial inhumanity. (6)

An Explorer Became a God

One of the most well-known African-American guides, Estevanico, left Spain on June 17, 1527 and became the first foreigner to discover New Mexico. Serving as an interpreter, he joined the ill-fated Spanish expedition led by Panfilo de Narvaez, the Spanish governor of Florida and his army of 200 soldiers who sought to explore the territory in the Gulf of Mexico. Their ship wrecked off the shore of Texas and only Estevanico and three others survived. Due to Estevanico's facility with languages, he was able to negotiate with the Indians for food, shelter, and directions to Mexico City, thereby, saving the lives of his party. In reaching safety, they were recognized as the first explorers to cross the continent north of the Isthmus of Panama.

For his leadership role, Estevanico was rewarded and appointed to the position of lead scout on another expedition back into wilderness of Central America in search of the Legendary "Seven Cities of Gold." Estevanico disobeyed the Crown's instructions to remain with his search party. Pushing way ahead, he became separated from his party but allegedly found the City of Gold. He became the first fully African-American that the Zuni Indians had ever seen. He was viewed as a god, and gifts of precious metals and female companionship were bestowed upon him. When he expressed an interest in leaving, they forbade him to go. When he attempted to escape, they killed him out of fear that he would bring others into their community. He died a god and the "first" discoverer of the Southwestern United States and Mexico. (7)

❂

York Saved Lewis & Clark Expedition

In 1803, Thomas Jefferson commissioned Meriweather Lewis, Jefferson's ex-private secretary, and William Clark, a somewhat frontiersman, to explore and chart lands of the "Louisiana Purchase" that extended west from the Mississippi to the Rocky Mountains. Neither Lewis nor Clark had much formal education or training in botany, cartography, or Indian languages. To assist them in accomplishing their goal, they included in their party a black man, known simply as York, whose skin color saved the expedition from hostile forces.

In the early spring of 1804, Lewis and Clark with 48 experienced men set out from St. Louis to explore the uncharted northwestern portion of present day United States. York was very useful during their trek through Indian territory. Indians were aware of white-skinned traders and trappers even in the remotest areas of the West, but they had never seen a human with black skin. Various Indians, including the chiefs, approached York and attempted to wipe the blackness off. Failing, they accepted that the color was real and placed such a great importance on the skin color that it gave York a special acceptance among the Indians. He was given a choice of Indian women.

According to Lewis and Clark's records, at least one Indian took York into his village home for his wife's extra-marital sexual pleasures. Later, York was given a Shoshone woman, Sacajawea, who played an important role in the success of the Lewis and Clark Expedition. It was reported that York sired a number of mixed-blood offspring throughout the three-year trip. But, in addition to his skin color "magic" and sexual proclivities, York had linguistic skills and a natural diplomacy that were of great value in facilitating his master's odyssey through western badlands and wilderness. When the exploration was over, York gained his freedom and returned to Louisiana. After settling down there, he was made a chief of one of the local Indian tribes.

Lewis and Clark went their separate ways, with different degrees of success. Lewis who had always suffered outbreaks of uncontrollable paranoia, was found dead on the floor of a tavern in Natchez, Tennessee, apparently of a self-inflicted gunshot wound to the head. Clark, his friend, fared better. He became governor of the Missouri Territory and governed well, although he never learned to spell. (8)

Poet Lived in a Color-Blind World

Phillis Wheatley, a talented black female poet, became a popular national and international talent at a time when the nation was writing a constitutional law codifying that blacks were only three-fifths of a human being. Twenty years earlier, a white slave trader had kidnapped Phillis Wheatley out of Africa while she was but a child.

In America, she was bought and educated by her white masters, the Wheatley's of Boston, who granted freedom and, to a large extent, became her patrons. At the age of 17, she wrote the first book ever published by an American black person. When her poetry became very popular, she had an audience with General George Washington. Later, she was sent to London to be received by prominent Englishmen and promptly charmed the court circles.

She was seduced into believing the world was color-blind when it came to talent and skills. She concentrated on her writing skills and tried to find a world for herself beyond her race in high white society and its literary environment. She was apolitical. In none of her poems or publications did she speak out on the issues of race and slavery. She infused her writings with Christian sentiments

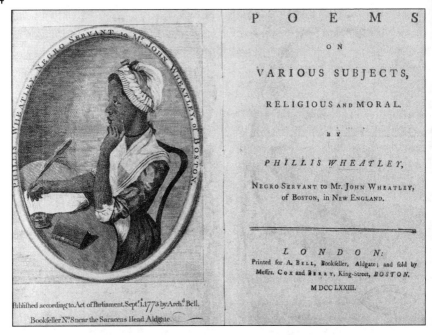

Phyllis Wheatly and cover of her book of poetry. (Library of Congress)

rather than social commentaries. She believed her acceptance came because she was a talented individual who just happened to be black-skinned.

In 1773, racial realities began to come home to roost. When her book appeared in London, someone bound a copy of it in the skin of a black person. The Wheatly family went bankrupt five years later. She was free but forced to fend for herself. She married John Peters, a free black man. Hardships worsened, causing her health to fail, and her husband was arrested and sent to debtor's prison. She died like most members of her race, black-skinned and poverty-stricken. (9)

❊

Black Humor of the Times

Classic literature in the library of every school carries venomous negative racism that passes uncontested as humor. Mark Twain's ***Huckleberry Finn***

(1884) contains a racist conversation between Huck and Aunt Sally after a steamboat blew out a cylinder head:

"Good gracious! Anybody hurt?"
"No'm. Killed a nigger."
"Well, it's lucky because sometimes people do get hurt."

Source: Mark Twain, *Huckleberry Finn* (10)

6
Colonizing and Colorizing

What is the value of my color?

Mini Facts

• *In 1660, Maryland and Virginia colonies passed laws concerning black and white servants. White servants could buy their freedom or collect freedom dues at the end of their contract period, but black servants' contracts were converted to enslavement papers.*

• *During the latter part of the 1700s, all five of the "civilized tribes" were slave holders, slave traders and slave chasers. Indians earned $20 for every captured and returned runaway slave.*

• *By the 1900s, every state in the United States had laws that defined who was black based upon parentage, varying quantities of black blood or the "one drop" of black blood rule.*

• *The "Black is Beautiful" concept emerged in the 1960s promoting a positive black image, unity, and the need for black people to control their own lives and communities.*

❁
Waiting for His Ship to Come In

The popular expression, "waiting for my ship to come in," was first used in the late 1600s as a formal explanation by Virginia Governor Alexander Spotswood to justify having been granted free title to more than 40,000 acres of choice "headrights" land along the James River on the strength that he was going

Slave ship from Key West Florida. (Library of Congress)

to bring in a boat load of black slaves.

Headrights land claims were used by white immigrants to get free or cheap land. The amount of free land that a person could obtain for importing slaves varied from 20 to 200 acres per slave. Governor Spotswood, like so many other prominent colonists, got as much free land as he could get under the government-sponsored policies.

Today, the expression, "waiting for my ship to come in," is little different from what it was 300 years ago. In part, it reflects hope and optimism, a belief that things will inevitably improve. No records are available to show just how many slaves Governor Spotswood eventually purchased or landed when his ship finally came in. Nor have any records been found to indicate that the government took back any of the headright land that Spotswood had been given.

Either way, Governor Spotswood, like millions of immigrant whites who came to America, acquired free land and got a windfall of wealth when black slaves were placed on the land. According to President Andrew Jackson, "a black slave brought 75 percent of the value to land." It is too bad that the mystical "ship" never came in for black slaves, since they never even got their 40 acres and a mule. Perhaps black people's ship did come in, but unlike Governor Spotswood, they were just not at the port to welcome it. (1)

❂

Blacks Had Their Ellis Island

Just as European immigrants had their Ellis Island to welcome them to America's shores, black people, America's only non-immigrants, had Sullivan Island as a major port of entry. Sullivan Island was located across the channel from the City of Charleston, South Carolina. It has been estimated that two-fifths of all black Africans who arrived in America during the early 1800s passed through Sullivan Island. Sullivan Island was a clearinghouse for slaves bound for plantations throughout the South. Before entering the Charleston slave markets to be sold, they were 'washed up,' sorted based upon sex, tribe, size and attitude. Some were withheld from market to undergo a "seasoning process." A few escaped to become maroons on neighboring Johns and Hilton Head Islands. Unlike Ellis Island immigrants who were processed into a new world of hope and opportunity, Sullivan Island represented a world of perpetual hopelessness, struggle and exclusion. (2)

❂

Black Race Produced All Kinds of Gold

Besides being considered Black Gold themselves, black labor triggered other gold rushes in the tobacco, cotton, and sugar cane fields of America and the Caribbean Islands. The first gold rush came from tobacco which was known as "yellow gold." As the world became hooked on smoking, dipping and chewing tobacco, major vertical industries developed. Tobacco was a primary generator of wealth, power, and businesses for whites. From the early 1600s until after the Revolutionary War of the 1780s, American blacks made up nearly 100 percent of the workers who grew, harvested and processed the tobacco in the factories of

Virginia, South and North Carolina. However, public policies, social customs, and state laws prohibited blacks from prospering from tobacco.

The billions of pounds of cotton produced by millions of black slaves became known as "white gold." Within one generation of the American revolution, the rush to raise cotton made cotton, "king." There was a push across the Southeast, into the Midwest to open up more land, bring in more slaves so more cotton could be produced. Cotton allowed human beings to wear something other than fabrics made from animals. Cotton became the "fabric of life." Cotton materials stimulated the economic infrastructure of nations and caused industrial revolutions on two continents. Black labor was again the driving economic engine, but black people were denied the fruits of their labor in raising, processing and marketing "white gold."

In 1849, a great gold rush occurred, with the discovery of gold in California. More than 6 million immigrants from every nation, except Africa, migrated to America in search of the precious metal. California, Texas, Arizona, and New Mexico were annexed into the United States as a direct result of America's fight with Mexico over slaves being brought onto the land for raising cotton. Many found new fortunes in the hills panning for yellow gold. Ironically, black people, the group whose presence produced so many gold rushes in America and around the world, were shut out of all of them. (3)

✪
Remember the Alamo?

Annexing Mexican land to extend slavery and grow cotton were the key factors that led to the Texas War and the fall of the Alamo. Beyond the textbooks, movies, and Saturday morning television myths, the freedom for which Davy Crockett, Jim Bowie, and the other hundreds of Alamo defenders were fighting, was the freedom to own black slaves. Mexico had outlawed human slavery, but white planters had moved onto and set up squatter rights on Mexican lands. Having been warned by Mexican authorities not to hold slaves on Mexican lands, white planters sought to circumvent the law by pretending their slaves had voluntarily signed life-time service contracts. The Mexican government rejected the white settlers' argument that their black workers were not slaves, but contracted, lifetime servants. General Santa Ana attacked and killed all the white settlers inside the Alamo. The battle triggered a Mexican-American War that lasted only a matter of weeks. After America won its war with Mexico, it annexed Texas and the southwestern territory. Surprisingly, when the Alamo is remembered, black slavery, the cause of the war, is never mentioned.(4)

"Too Many Slaves" Starts Revolutionary War

Too much of anything can be bad. During the early exploration of North America, slave trading companies across Europe encouraged immigration to America promising free land and slave labor. Millions of white Europeans departed their native land in search of the promised riches in a new land. But black slaves shipped into North America, outnumbered European whites six to one. By 1750, in the colonial America, the black slave population peaked at nearly 35 percent. Fearing that blacks and Indians might ally and subdue the colonists, the Continental Congress pushed England to desist in shipping any more slaves into the colonies. On October 20, 1774, the Continental Congress drafted the following resolution to end the slave trade.

"We will neither import nor purchase, any slave imported after the first day of December next, after which time, we will wholly discontinue the slave trade, and we will neither be concerned in it ourselves, nor will we hire our vessels, nor sell our commodities or manufacture to those who are concerned in it."

The Continental Congress resolution was a powerful statement, but it meant very little and fell on deaf ears in England as well as with many plantation owners because of the massive amount of money involved. The colonies desperately needed slave-produced products and wealth if they were going to attract additional immigrants and build a nation. The colonies had a dilemma. They needed blacks' labor to survive and prosper. They feared the possibility of an Indian and black slave alliance that could seize control of the nation. The colonists wanted a manageable black slave "minority."

As white fears continued to intensify, Thomas Jefferson proposed an immediate ban on slavery, but no later than the year 1800. This proposal, *The*

Declaration of Independence, in its original form, contained a scathing denunciation of slavery. But, the delegates representing South Carolina, Georgia, some slave-trading New England states, and other slave interests, deleted the language barring slavery and again defeated the resolution. Later, when the *U.S. Constitution* was written, it codified black enslavement and postponed outlawing international slave trading until the year 1807. (5)

⊕

Liberty Bell Rang First for Blacks

When "the bell" was first rung for liberty, it was for the liberty of blacks, not whites. Throughout this nation's history, in the praise of liberty, hoaxes and frauds have abounded and have been told to millions of children and adults alike.

According to Richard Shenkman, the ringing of the "Liberty Bell," to declare this nation's independence on July 4, 1776, began with George Lippard, a Philadelphia journalist. Lippard fabricated the ringing of the Liberty Bell on the Fourth of July in a book, *The Legends of the American Revolution* that he published in 1847.

The only thing true about his story was that the bell did hang in the Philadelphia, Pennsylvania, statehouse in 1776 when the founding fathers drafted the *Declaration of Independence*. But no one rang it for the signing, nor did Americans care much about the bell later. In 1828, the city of Philadelphia tried to sell the bell for scrap, but no one made an offer. The bell simply was not worth the expense of removing it from the building.

The bell contains the inscription, "Proclaim Liberty throughout all the Land unto the Inhabitants Thereof." But, the inscription, cast when the bell was produced in 1753, had nothing to do with the American Revolution. It was not called the Liberty Bell until long after the Revolution, and not in honor of the Revolution.

The first time anyone referred to the bell as the "Liberty Bell" was in a pamphlet entitled *The Liberty Bell*, by Friends of Freedom, distributed at the Massachusetts Anti-Slavery Fair in 1839. In the pamphlet, the bell symbolized the freedom of black slaves, not the independence of white Americans from Britain. The name Liberty Bell was coined in 1839 by anti-slavery activists. (6)

Colonial Graveyard for Slaves Discovered

On the southern tip of Manhattan, workers discovered Negro Burial Grounds, a cemetery dating to colonial times, while excavating a site for a new office tower. The cemetery contained the remains of at least 400 slaves and white paupers. Archaeologists suggested that it was the most significant U.S. archaeological discovery of the century. It was the only pre-Revolutionary black cemetery known in the United States. Analyses of the remains of children indicated that possibly 50 percent of New York's slave population died at birth or within the first years of life. Bone analysis indicated that many of the rest were worked to death at a very early age. (7)

Slavery Gave Birth to Capitalism

The international commercialization of black slavery changed the world and its economic concepts. The old European mercantilism was replaced by capitalism. Mercantilism meant profiting from the sale of a product, capitalism means profiting from another's labor. The word, "factory" was first introduced in the 15th century to describe Portuguese buildings that were used as holding places for slave at points along the West African coast.

The "franchising concept," as popularly known, was introduced by the English Royal African Company in 1668 to establish a monopoly on the slave trading industry. Like modern day franchising chains, for a 15 percent fee, the Royal African Company provided its franchised slave plantation owners with land, supplies, slaves, military protection, and a ready market for their raw, slave-produced cash products.

By the early 1800s, with a renewed interest in cotton production, plantations that had at least 100 slaves introduced a gang system of work. In the gang system, slaves were assigned work using an assembly line-type process that revolutionized the use of slave labor, introduced mass production and significantly increased productivity. Raw materials produced by slaves fueled both Europe's and America's industrial and banking revolutions. (8)

✪
Taxed Without Rights

Although free blacks were denied voting rights, civil liberties, business licenses and an education, they still were required to pay local, state taxes, and a capital tax. Failing to pay meant they could be imprisoned or re-enslaved. It meant that any local government or white person could lay claim to a free black person's property or material goods. They paid taxes for public services that they were prohibited from using. Besides general service taxes, blacks paid education taxes to support schools for white children. A gender based tax in many southern states in the 1840's required black men to pay an annual per capita tax, simply for being a black male. (9)

✪
Nation's First Anti-Smoking Campaign

Public policies stipulating "no smoking in public places" are not new. The nation's first no-smoking campaign was targeted at black tobacco growers and smokers.

Even though blacks planted and harvested nearly all of this nation's tobacco and made up almost 100 percent of the workers in the major tobacco factories of Virginia, Maryland, North Carolina and South Carolina, some local municipalities enacted ordinances that prohibited what blacks could do with tobacco after "picking it." In Charlottesville and Norfolk, Virginia, common councils passed laws that made it illegal for blacks to smoke in public places.

At the same time, nearly every southern state, and some northern ones, enacted laws to specifically prohibit free black farmers from competing with white planters in growing and selling tobacco. One law stipulated that blacks caught smoking 'yellow gold' in public were subject to a $1 fine and 10 lashes.

One Richmond, Virginia, newspaper told black smokers that "Cuffee" (blacks) will have to puff his villainous weed in private or suffer the consequences. Just to make sure, many laws prohibited blacks from even buying tobacco products.

The no-smoking policies were not designed to protect a black smoker's health but to subordinate the black race. Since public smoking was identified with freedom, whites perceived any black person smoking in public as an insult, or perhaps a threat. A black person smoking in public projected the appearance of being mature, free, and equal to whites. No smoking in public policies aimed to keep blacks, both physically and symbolically, in their place, in a subordinated child-like status.

The Founding Fathers Founded What?

The founding fathers wrote the principles of white rule into the U.S. Constitution. "We the people of the United States," meant we the free white people, and the free white people only. The Constitution guaranteed rights and freedoms for everyone but blacks. The black man could not assimilate. He was permanently nailed to the lowest rung of the social ladder. Neither freedom nor good work could force whites to recognize him as an equal human being. During the Revolutionary War, at least 17 delegates to the Constitutional Convention, or 31 percent of all of this nation's founding fathers, were slaveholders.

Collectively, they owned more than 1,400 slaves. George Mason, James Rutledge and George Washington were three of the largest slaveholders in the country at the time of the Constitutional Convention. In descending order, the slaveholders and the number of slaves they each owned were:

G. Mason, Virginia	300+	A. Martin, North Carolina	47
J. Rutledge	243	W. Dave, North Carolina	36
G. Washington, Virginia	216	W. Blunt, North Carolina	30
P. Butler, South Carolina	143	D. Jennifer, Maryland	20
C Pinkey, South Carolina	111	E. Randolph, Virginia	16
R. Spate, North Carolina	71	J. Blare, Virginia	15
C.C. Pinckney, South Carolina	70	J. Madison, Virginia	10
D. Carroll, Maryland	53	L. Martin, Maryland	10
G. Read, Delaware	9		

There was only limited discussion of the slavery issue among the attendees of the Convention. They were vested in the institution of slavery and there is little doubt that they fully intended to exclude black people from the rights that they would guarantee for themselves and other whites in the Constitution and Declaration of Independence.

All of the framers of the Constitution were wealthy members of the upper class of American society, but they wanted to please poor whites and assure them that they would always be above blacks, regardless of their income and wealth. By assuring them that they would never have to compete with blacks, the white wealthy class bought themselves an insurance policy forever against the formation of a poor white and black coalition. (10)

✪
High Office Holders Held Slaves

Many of America's historical public figures were "color-blind" to blackness and became slaveholders. Although slaveholding was greatest among employees at the lowest levels of government, the highest levels of leadership did their share of setting the tone by codifying enslavement. On the eve of the Civil War, analysis of the slaveholders in federal offices signal why there would be a national conflict. As examples; 11 of 16 U.S. Presidents, 17 of the members of the U.S. Supreme Court, 14 of 19 U.S. Attorney Generals, 21 of 33 Speakers of the U.S. House of Representatives, and 80 of 134 high-level representatives in the U.S. Foreign Service had been or were slaveholders. In a representative government, all of the Presidents from Washington through Jackson, except for John Adams, were slaveowners.

Popular leadership was willing to use the language of freedom and liberty or even willing to fight the wars against tyranny, but they were unwilling to abolish slavery or racial inequality in America. William Penn, like many other noted abolitionists invested heavily in the international slave trade through the middle of the 18th century. Obviously, profits overwhelmed humanitarian concerns and racial justice. But, at least one, a spouse disagreed with her slaveholding husband who was an extremely visible and popular slaveholder.

Abigail Adams wrote to her husband, John, in 1774 and expressed, "I wish that there was not a black slave in the Providence. It always appeared a most iniquitous scheme to me to fight ourselves for what we are daily robbing and plundering from those who have as good a right to freedom as we have."

Her husband, John Adams, answered her letter stating that, "There was no rational explanation for the inconsistency, except that most white slaveowners needed their free labor and the profits that it produced." (11)

Thomas Jefferson, a Hypocrite

Thomas Jefferson's harsh view of black Americans, whom he considered inherently inferior to whites, did not extend to American Indians. Jefferson was willing to contemplate white-Indian amalgamation.

In speaking of the Indians, he said in 1803, "We shall probably find that they are formed in mind as well as in body, on the same model with the 'Homo Sapiens Europeans'.... In truth, the ultimate point of rest and happiness for them is to let our settlements and theirs meet and blend together, to intermix, and become one people." At the same time, he left his own children to die as slaves. The following advertisement was run in a Richmond newspaper:

Notice

Thirty-two Negroes will be offered for sale on Monday, November 10th, at 12 o'clock, being the entire stock of the late John Graves, Esq. The Negroes are in good condition, some of them very prime; among them are several mechanics, able-bodied field hands, plough boys, and women with children at the breast, and some of them very prolific in their generating qualities, affording a rare opportunity to any one who wishes to raise a strong and healthy lot of servants for their own use. Also, several mulatto girls of rare personal qualities: two of them are superior. Any gentleman or lady wishing to purchase can take any of the above slaves on trial for a week, for which no charge will be made

Among the slaves being sold above, two were President Thomas Jefferson's mulatto daughters, Clotel and Althesa. He approved of the two girls being advertised as very superior for breeding. Worse still, Jefferson allowed them to be sold off into prostitution as mistresses.(12)

❂

Few Founders Voted for Bill of Rights

Although most of the delegates to the Constitutional Convention wrote and approved the Constitution, most were not involved in writing the Bill of Rights and overwhelmingly rejected it. A decade earlier, the Declaration of Independence stipulated that the role of government was to "secure" the inalienable rights of the people to "life, liberty, and the pursuit of property [which was later changed to happiness]."

But, the motion to have the Bill of Rights preface the Constitution was voted down ten to zero. Why was there such opposition to the Bill of Rights? Delegates, from Madison to Hamilton, offered sundry reasons, from simply being too tired to consider it, to harboring great concern that it might clutter up the Constitution. A delegate from South Carolina, C.C. Pinckney, gave the boldest and probably the most honest justification. Mr. Pinckney said a Bill of Rights in the Constitution would have made a hypocrite of slaveowners like himself, since bills of rights "generally begin with declaring that all men are by nature born free." "Now," said Pinckney, "we would make a declaration with a very bad grace, when a large part of our property consists in men who are actually born slaves."

In spite of delegate resistence, the Bill of Rights was enacted, but nearly all judicial interpretations have occurred in support of the dominant white society. Black America must routinely seek their rights through the enactment of civil rights laws, just as one would renew a driver's license. (13)

❂

Gerrymandering of the Black Vote

Elbridge Gerry, of Massachusetts, one of the drafters of the United States Constitution, is held responsible for the political technique of gerrymandering, which is the practice of dividing voting districts in an unfair way. It is ironic that as far back as the 1780s, Gerry's scheme began to deny blacks their voting rights, and centuries later, gerrymandering continues to deny blacks the benefit of their votes.

Since only white males attended the Constitutional Convention, Gerry's name is associated with other things that apparently no one felt were inappropriate or unseemly. During the discussion about the military and state militia, Gerry made an often ignored but famous remark in which he compared a standing army to an erect penis saying, it was "an excellent assurance of domestic tranquility, but a dangerous temptation to foreign adventure." Little discussion followed. Apparently Gerry had made his point.(14)

✪

Playing Population Monopoly

The *Federalist Papers* promoted the ratification of the U.S. Constitution. The papers caution that in a social democracy, based on the majority rule premise, the nation had to be ever on guard against tyranny by the majority. The authors discussed the relationship between the majority, a minority and tyranny. They knew that to avoid tyranny in a "majority wins" society, the majority had responsibility to ensure the rights of the minority. Moreover, the majority should do nothing to impede the minority from becoming the majority, just as the existing majority became the majority. Further, the *Federalist Papers* said that failing to protect the rights of a minority or permanently excluding them from input, constituted tyranny and relieved the shut-out minority from obligation to respect the rules and laws enacted by the majority. These were cardinal understandings of how a social democracy must work.

One of the first acts of the new 1790 Congress violated these founding principles. It passed a naturalization law that established a zero quota on black immigrants. While European, Asian and Hispanic immigrants continued to enter the country, this zero quota on blacks guaranteed they would be a planned, permanent minority and "loser." This zero quota remained in effect until 1965 when it was raised to one half of one percent for people of African descent. With a zero immigration quota, blacks depended strictly upon their natural birth rate to keep them even remotely competitive in a majority-wins society. Immigration policies and laws make blacks America's only permanently-planned losers.

There have never been any American refugee programs for blacks, regardless of the nature of their suffering or circumstances. There are daily opportunities for the U.S. government to bring fairness into immigration policies, but it has yet to happen. Europeans, Hispanics and Asians can immigrate for economic reasons, but Haitians cannot. Cambodian, Chinese, Koreans, Vietnamese and Latin American political refugees are accepted, but black African political refugees are not. While Cambodian and Cuban boat people are picked up and brought into the country, Haitian boat people are picked up and returned to their homeland. In 1996, approximately 3,000 sick and starving African blacks were allowed to drift aimlessly on a boat for two months off the coast of West Africa and not one Western nation or superpower nation would take them in. The inactivity of the United States spoke volumes about a nation that has sponsored immigration programs and public policies for nearly every ethnic group and nation on earth except black ones. (15)

7
Conservatism and Samboism

If terrorism comes to America, it will arrive on the wings of conservatism.

Mini Facts

• *In 1840, the U.S. Census Bureau reported 6,000 free blacks as slaveholders. The states of Delaware and Kansas enacted laws to stop blacks from being slaveholders since it gave them status equal to white slaveholders.*

• *Of approximately 850 free blacks living in New Orleans, Louisiana, during the Civil War, more than 642 were free black slaveholders. They formed two full regiments of black soldiers to fight with the Southern Confederacy to preserve slavery.*

• *December 24, 1865, the day before Christmas, the Ku Klux Klan (KKK) was organized in Pulaski, Tennessee, to resist Reconstruction and bestowing of civil rights on black ex-slaves.*

• *It was not until the 1940s that the term "Uncle Tom" acquired its current derogatory meaning of a fawning, submissive, compromising black man.*

❂
The Young and Naive

From the earliest beginnings in Africa until present day, black people have responded to various forms of racism and human exploitation in a manner that is totally inconsistent with normal human behavior and their own best interest. For whatever reasons, they have placed compassion and love for others above that of their own people. They have sought individual acceptance and advancement at the expense of their racial group. Contrary to conventional wisdom, it is difficult to blame such behavior entirely on the "slavery conditioning process."

Blacks were displaying such inappropriate behavior patterns before and during the early years of black enslavement. As early as 1704, when "The Eagle," a galley slave ship had taken aboard 400 captured black slaves off the coast of Africa, a young black boy displayed the sort of inappropriate behavior that has been a bane of black people's protracted dilemma.

After just a few days in captivity, the slaves decided to revolt while they had a measure of temporary freedom at supper time. One of the older slaves who had broken free attempted to strike the captain of the slave ship in the head, seize his weapons and take control of the ship. But, a black youth around 17 years of age to whom the captain had granted several favors, took the older slave's blow on his own arm, breaking the bone.

The young slave's interference allowed the captain of the slave ship to recover and rally his crew. Under the captain's leadership the revolt was put down, the black revolters were slain, and the ship continued to the slave colonies in America. When the ship landed, the captain granted the boy his freedom with some money. The youth was placed in the service of Robert "King" Carter so that he could learn how to provide for himself in a nation where blacks were slaves.

Until present time, many blacks choose being liked and getting along above getting out of their socioeconomic dilemma, regardless of how they are treated. (1)

❂
Free Black Slaveholders

Up until the end of the Civil War, many free blacks sought to maintain their privileged status over bonded blacks supporting the Southern Confederacy in its Civil War with the Northern Union. The exact number of free Negroes in the United States who fought with the Confederate military forces to perpetuate slavery is not known, but there were thousands.

Of the total number of free blacks in America on the eve of the Civil War, it is reported that about 6,230 were black slaveholders. Racial realities of the time encouraged most of them to live in and farm around large southern cities like Atlanta, Charleston, and New Orleans. Some blacks purchased other slaves to set them free, especially if they were family members. But, according to some reports, other black slaveholders often treated their black slaves as badly as any white owner on a rural plantation.

Like their white counterparts, black slaveholders and other conservative blacks' primary interest was to maintain their social status and profit from their slave investments. It was apparently just good business judgment for them to side with and fight on the side of the South. In a review of 28,000 Confederate troops held at New Orleans on November 23, 1861, seven months after the outbreak of the Civil War, there were two full regiments of black Confederate soldiers.

At a personal level, Preston Roberts, a Negro, was one of those soldiers. He was an unofficial quartermaster of General Nathaniel Forest. He was given the Cross of Honor, the highest Confederate medal, and until his death in 1910 was treated in all respects like a white man in the South. (2)

✪
In the Mind of Sambos

Many free conservative blacks held other blacks, including slaves, in contempt and disparaged them publicly. Anxious to ingratiate themselves with white society, conservative blacks vigorously defended slavery as the proper status for the majority of blacks. John Chavis, a free black preacher and schoolmaster, opposed emancipation and urged his white friends to resist the abolitionists' onslaught. He denied that Congress had the authority to legislate against slavery because, the laws of the country have had slaves the property of the holder equal to his cow and his horse and he has a perfect right to dispose of them as he pleases." Other conservative blacks were equally as vocal, urging blacks to accept enslavement for themselves and their offspring forever.

Harrison Berry was a 40-year old slave shoemaker and the owner of the business of S.W. Price of Covington, of Atlanta, Georgia. Berry knew how to read and write. He wrote a pamphlet entitled, *Slavery and Abolitionism, As Viewed by a Georgia Slave*.

Berry's pamphlet urged slaves to be submissive to their white owners, to accept their fate. He argued that blacks could never achieve anything without the approval and support of whites. He had little if anything positive to say about white Northern liberals and abolitionists, and accused both of promising to help slaves escape but ignoring them afterwards. He warned potential runaways that "subordination of the poor colored man in the North is greater than that of the South."

Berry carried his arguments further by saying that he would rather have his family bound by law as slaves with a master to protect them than be a free person without any means of support.

As a result of his pamphlet, Berry became perhaps the sole Southern slave whose message was circulated nationally. Unfortunately, he used that opportunity to declare his complete support for slavery in a published tract that sold for 25 cents a copy. (3)

❂

Conservative Blacks Conserved What?

Robert Carlos DeLarge, a conservative and naive black politician, who was elected to office during Reconstruction turned the clock backwards on blacks living in South Carolina. Apparently, as soon as DeLarge was elected to the South Carolina legislature in 1868, he immediately introduced a bill to remove or repeal all political impediments and punitive measures against white ex-Confederates and former slaveholders.

DeLarge filed this bill even though black ex-slaves had yet to receive any compensation or reparations for 260 years of enslavement. Worse, President Andrew Johnson had just vetoed a bill to provide ex-slaves with 40 acres and a mule. DeLarge believed that since blacks were the majority population in South Carolina, they should not appear to be too harsh or vindictive towards their "precious" white masters. He felt it was a time for healing and blacks should be humble and forgiving and allow whites to set the social and economic agenda for the black masses.

DeLarge soon got his wish. White minority politicians took over the state legislature, enacted Black Codes, which in effect re-enslaved blacks by forcing them into another 100 years of peonage or semi-slavery. DeLarge's political naiveté and bill laid the foundation in South Carolina for what was more commonly called "Jim Crowism." Similar naiveté was demonstrated by black leadership during the great Civil Rights Movement that occurred a century later. They accepted public claims of a "color-blind," equal opportunity society without having resolved the historical inequalities between the races. (4)

✪
Wealth Encouraged Black Conservatism

Oppressed black people turned against their own people for various reasons, but most often to acquire advantages over other members of their race. Once those who are set free have been recognized, rewarded and elevated by the dominant society, they are threatened when other members of their race break free or urge them to re-identify with the group. They become conservatives, and like any good conservative, they accept that there must be some losers in life. They will do whatever is necessary to maintain the status quo between the races so long as they personally remain elevated. Black conservatives and Sambos want more than anything else to live in the class society where they can escape the stigma of being members of the black race that they themselves are degrading.

William Johnson, a wealthy, free and conservative black in the early 1800s, is a fine example of a freed black who placed his personal interests above the needs of his people. Shortly after receiving his freedom, Johnson started a small business with money acquired from whites. He used it to make more money. As his life style changed, he began to despise the social behavior and economic conditions of blacks. Eventually he disassociated himself from blacks and carefully cultivated the habits of whites. He bred horses, hunted, gave his daughter music lessons, and lined his study with books. He treasured his friendship with the wealthy white elite who embodied the values he most admired.

Towards the end of his life, he made the final leap away from blacks. He purchased a sprawling farm outside of Natchez, Mississippi, hired a white overseer, and bought some black slaves. The man who had made his way up as a barber and money lender concluded that the ownership of land and black slaves were the "keys to happiness." (5)

❂

A Domestic Slave Trader

Andrew Durnford, who owned a Louisiana plantation which he worked with some 75 slaves, was finely tuned to the planter ideology and considered himself a patriarchal master in the best tradition of the Southern master.

Although Durnford railed endlessly against the seeming incompetence, laziness, and ignorance of his "Negroes," he took pride in playing the role of their master and protector.

When Norbert Rillieux, a French-trained free black engineer who had invented a new method of refining sugar, offered Durnford $50,000 for use of his plantation to test the process, the planter turned him down, noting that he could not give up control of his black people. Durnford's "people" of course were slaves, and he treated them as such, even though he had their same skin color. With the rare exception of his personal black bodyguard, he never showed any interest in releasing any of "his people" from bondage.

As early as 1680, laws had been passed prohibiting blacks from having white "indentured servants," but until the late 1840s there were no prohibitions of blacks owning other blacks as slaves.

Consequently, in 1835, Durnford traveled north to Virginia to purchase additional hands for himself and his white friend and mentor, John McDonogh. During his trip, he confronted, perhaps for the first time, the southern distaste for black slave traders, as opposed to blacks who bought slaves for their own use, and he consciously manipulated that distaste to obtain slaves at lower prices.

Yet, throughout a lengthy discussion with McDonogh on what Durnford called "Negro traders," he showed not the slightest understanding that the term applied to him and that what he was doing to his own people was treasonable. These possibilities were lost on him because he fully identified with the white slave-owning elite.

Many wealthy free blacks, like Durnford, considered themselves more white than black, no matter their actual racial heritage. They showed little sympathy for the slave and had few qualms about the morality of slavery. Durnford's northern educated son, had no greater sense of identification with blacks than his father. He supported some amelioration of slave conditions, but not their emancipation. Like father, like son. As slaveholders, they believed in slavery, but were willing to accept a plan to return blacks to Africa, "the land of their fathers," if the government was willing to re-pay them the monies that they had invested in their black slaves. (6)

✪

Uncle Tom's Cabin

In 1852, Harriet Beecher Stowe wrote and published *Uncle Tom's Cabin*, which was reputed to have been based on the real life of an escaped black slave named Josiah Henson. The book became a national and international best seller, selling 300,000 copies within the first year. In spite of the book's popularity, many of the book's white critics challenged the book's authenticity. In the state of Maryland, where Josiah Henson was born in 1789, the book was banned and one free black was sentenced to 10 years in prison just for owning a copy. Witnessing this kind of abusive treatment heaped on black people, especially his parents, was the driving force in Henson's life. He wanted out of slavery and

Promotion for a production of Uncle Tom's Cabin. (Library of Congress)

decided to escape to Canada on October 28, 1830. He devoted much of his life helping other blacks escape. Years later, while passing through Andover, Massachusetts, he met with and told his story to Harriet Beecher Stowe. Rather than writing a book entitled, **Uncle Henson's Cabin**, Stowe chose to call it **Uncle Tom's Cabin.** (7)

❂

Myths of Happy Slaves

Contrary to myths promoted by pro-slavery forces, historical records indicate that blacks were anything but happy-go-lucky slaves. The happy slave myth was fabricated to suggest that slavery was a natural state for blacks, who had no interest in overthrowing their white masters. There were claims that blacks had a genetic "internal disposition" that made them ideally suited to be slaves. To ensure that the reality was always consistent with myth, the dominant society maintained laws, public policies and social customs that labeled blacks apathetic, but punished them for being aggressive and assertive; that equated them to animals then mocked them for imitating white society; that called them poor and ignorant, then denied them the fruits of their labor and educational opportunities; and that argued that blacks should remain with their own kind, while enacting fugitive slave laws, that prevented blacks from running away from white enslavement to join their own people.

If nothing else refuted the happy-slave myth, the hundreds of attempted slave revolts, poisonings and other acts of rebellion against white masters surely did. (8)

A Notable Quote

" If a land owner cheated or beat his black tenants,
that is his business! If a black is the victim of white
violence, he must have done something to deserve it!
Above all, the black must be kept in his place." (9)

❂
A Black International Slave Trader

There are always exceptions, and there were a few blacks in the international slave trading business. Unfortunately, in too many instances, they were the worst of the lot, for they officially sanctioned the trading of black flesh for personal and racial profits.

There were African chiefs who from the 12th through 19th centuries supported the enslavement and sale of Africans to traders from around the globe. Few however, were able to become international slave traders in the conventional sense. In the late 1800's Tippoo Tibia, a black slave trader and ivory hunters from Zanzibar, East Africa, was the first man to penetrate the center of Africa. In pursuit of black slaves, he explored territory nearly as large as the United States. The rumors of the ferocious fighting skills of African warriors and the denseness of the jungle kept most whites out of Sub-Sahara Africa. But, Tibia's maps inspired white explorers and traders like Stanley, Weismann, Cameron, and others who sought the riches of Africa. Tibia himself, died in Europe in 1905, as a very rich man from the exploitation of Africa's human and mineral wealth. (10)

❂
Professional Slave Beaters

Prior to the Civil War, there were hundreds of professional slave beaters throughout the South who physically and psychologically disciplined the nearly six million slaves. Slaveowners hired professional slave beaters to deal with slaves for various reasons ranging from being too fearful to too caring. Most simply wanted someone who would whip a slave quickly and well.

Even though the master's whip was the sign of authority, some slaveowners wanted to be seen as fair, kind, and generous. So, at Christmas time or on any special occasion, the master wanted to be seen passing out the goodies to the slaves. They diligently avoided being identified with inflicting pain on their slaves. Overseers and straw bosses were normally authorized to punish slaves, but in special cases they brought in the professional beater, who not only knew how to best beat a slave, but also enjoyed their work.

To market their services, professional slave beaters advertised. In urban areas, they advertised in taverns and churches. In rural areas, they advertised in cotton plants and supply stores. Many beaters advertised their special kind of whipping expertise.

In accordance with their special arrangements with the slaveowners, professional beaters performed their duties with discretion on the plantation and in storage sheds in rural areas, in basements or enclosed back yards in the cities.

Seasoning a black slave. (Library of Congress)

Typically a slaveowner would have a contract with the beater. The owner would simply write a note to the beater indicating the number of lashes or other forms of punishment desired, and the slave to be punished would be sent with the note to the beater. (11)

✪
Free Blacks Opposed Slave Revolt

By the late 1700s, so-called slave revolts were becoming rather common throughout the colonies. But one of the most unusual slave revolts took place in Louisiana. Charles Deslandes, a free mulatto, led a revolt of 300 to 500 slaves that took place approximately 35 miles from New Orleans.

Whites fled as blacks armed themselves with cane knives, picks, axes, clubs and a few firearms. They moved from one plantation to another wreaking destruction and killing at least one white. What makes this revolt even more unusual was not the fact that it was led by a free person, nor a mulatto black, nor the fact that it was halted by white state militia and federal troops. What makes this revolt so unusual was the fact that free blacks joined with the federal troops and militia against their own enslaved people who were merely struggling to get what everyone else had: freedom.

How could free blacks go against their own people fighting to be as free as they were? Where was justice? The freedom-seeking slaves only killed one white person, but the local whites took revenge against the revolting slaves by killing nearly 100 and displaying their heads on poles along the road to New Orleans as a lesson to all other slaves. Maybe the answer to why free blacks went against their own people was in the social statistics of the community.

Prior to the Civil War, of more than 850 free blacks living in New Orleans, more than 600 of them were slaveholders of their own people. Equally as amazing was the fact that during the Civil War, free blacks from New Orleans mounted two full regiments of blacks who fought with the Confederate South to preserve black slavery. Free blacks who fought to preserve the Old South called themselves, "Mulatto Conservatives." They believed a little bit of whiteness made them better than their darker skinned, enslaved brothers and sisters.(12)

✪
Andrew Jackson Misled Blacks

Blacks, both free and bonded, were vulnerable to challenges of fighting for their freedom and a better quality of life. Just as General George Washington promised blacks their freedom if they helped the colonies in the Revolutionary War, then betrayed them, General Andrew Jackson did the same thing in the War of 1812.

Realizing that Britain had him outnumbered with troops, Andrew Jackson went back to the old trick and issued a proclamation at Mobile, Alabama, urging free and enslaved blacks to become involved in the war. Jackson invited them "to share in the peril and divide the glory." He promised blacks that if they participated, they would be "recognized and rewarded" for defending the land. His words suggested freedom for slaves. Blacks volunteered in large numbers. Two battalions of 500 free blacks each fought with General Jackson to liberate New Orleans from the British in the last battle of the War of 1812.

These "free men of color" were the largest single force of black men ever assembled on American soil. They joined with whites and other social outcasts, such as Indians, and pirates, to hold the battle lines against a well-equipped British army. When the battle ended, the British had lost more than 2,600 soldiers while the American ragtag force had lost only 21 men.

Jackson thanked his forces and forgot his promise of freedom to blacks. The best that he did for blacks was to indicate in a letter to a government official that he believed the British commander, Sir Edward Pakenham, had been killed by a shot fired by one of his black volunteers. Saying publicly that the "President and the nation will applaud [your] valor" was his way of sharing the glory with blacks. None of the black fighters were allowed to march in the New Orleans victory parade.

The slaves who fought to keep America free were even more disappointed when they learned they were keeping it free only for whites. White slavemasters were grateful to Jackson for preserving their way of life and returning to them their black slaves. (13)

✪
Harpers Ferry's Sambo Monument

Hayward Shepherd, a black porter for the Baltimore and Ohio Railroad at the train station in Harpers Ferry, Virginia, was the first person who was killed by John Brown and his party in their raid on the night of October 16, 1859.

Brown and his party had gone to Harpers Ferry to free and arm black slaves, but Shepherd, sitting on the station's porch, recognized the raiders and suspected their intentions. In turn, the raiders realized his intentions: to warn the town of the raid. To stop him, Brown's raiders shot and killed him on the spot.

Photograph of the Hayward Shepherd monument.

For his action, the United Daughters of the Confederacy and the Sons of Confederate Veterans erected a 900-pound granite monument to Hayward Shepherd. It contains the following inscription:

On the night of October 16, Hayward Shepherd, an
industrious respected colored freeman, was mortally

wounded by John Brown's raiders, in pursuance of
his duties as an employee of the Baltimore and Ohio
Railroad Company. He became the first victim of this
attempted insurrection. This boulder is erected by the
United Daughters of the Confederacy and the Sons of
Confederate Veterans as a memorial to Hayward
Shepherd, exemplifying the character and faithfulness
of thousands of Negroes who, under many temptations
throughout subsequent years of wars, so conducted
themselves that no stain was left upon a record which
is the peculiar heritage of the American people, and
an everlasting tribute to the best in both races.

What the inscription neglected to say, of course, was that Hayward Shepherd
died because he chose to place the way of life of the white citizens of Harpers
Ferry above the welfare of his own people. (14)

✪
White Female Exposed Revolters

Within two years of Cato's 1739 revolt, a plot of similar magnitude took place in
New York City. When a fort on what is now the Battery, went up in flames on March
18, 1741, and was followed by a succession of other fires, rumors were afloat of a
slave conspiracy to destroy the city of New York and massacre all the white citizens.

Free blacks were arrested and imprisoned whether under suspicion or not. A
month or so after the destruction of the fort, Mary Burton, a white indentured servant to John Hughson, an innkeeper, was called before a grand jury to testify
about an alleged burglary planned in her master's home. Pressured by the jury,
Mary Burton sang like a canary, and when she was through, had implicated three
blacks, Caesar, Prince, and Cuffe, in a plot to rob, burn down the town, kill all
the whites, and make themselves the city's rulers.

She also implicated her master, his wife, and another white woman, Peggy Kerry,
in the conspiracy. Kerry was involved in a sexual affair with Caesar, the black man.

Hell has no fury like a woman scorned. There are accounts that suggest Burton had an affair with Caesar, which may have prompted her accusations. (15)

Booker T. Washington: The Great Compromiser

Booker T. Washington was invited by conservative whites to speak at the Cotton States and International Exposition in Atlanta on September 18, 1895. Washington's speech was one of the most memorable, and most devastating, in the history of this nation.

Washington's remarks, popularly known as the Atlanta Compromise speech, were delivered to a racially segregated, southern audience. At a time when black people were being lynched at a rate of one a day and denied all of their basic Constitutional rights, Booker T. Washington encouraged blacks to accommodate whites by renouncing their interest in racial equality, to accept a subordinate status and structural economic inequalities in exchange for some "separate but equal educational assistance" throughout the South, but especially for his school in Tuskegee, Alabama.

Washington counseled blacks to, "Cast down your bucket where you are....to stay farmers, mechanics, and domestics." He further comforted whites by stating, "That in all things purely social, we can be as separate as the fingers on the hand" and urged whites to hire negroes rather than immigrants "because negroes were the most patient, faithful, law-abiding and unresentful people that the world has ever seen."

"The wisest among my race understand that the agitation of questions of social equality is the extremist of folly." The white audience was elated. The men gave Washington a standing ovation and the women threw flowers. With the exception of black conservatives, blacks in the convention center and across America were shocked and hurt. While still suffering the pains of 260 years of slavery and a failed Reconstruction, black people sat and cried in the aisles of the convention hall. They knew at that moment Booker T. Washington had traded away their future and there would be dark days ahead.

They were right. In the year after Washington's speech, the United States Supreme Court handed down its famous Plessy v. Ferguson decision, and the legal doctrine of Separate-but-Equal, the basis for Jim Crow Segregation. (16)

❂
Washington Took Licking, Kept Ticking

As the 20th century ushered in depressive times for black Americans, most of them held Booker T. Washington responsible and were not unhappy about what happened to Washington at the hands of a white man in New York in 1911.

Even though Washington had long been the darling of white social conservatism, they turned on him when he was charged with violating one of their most sacred taboos. Washington was severely beaten in New York City for allegedly approaching a white woman. This incident caused conservative black leaders to rush to the defense of Washington, while many black leaders found irony and some satisfaction in the beating saying, "See, we told you so!" In their minds, Washington was acceptable to white conservatives so long as he stayed in his place: the one that he proscribed for all blacks.

Numerous black leaders, especially W.E.B. Dubois and other black leaders continued to denounce Washington and his conservative philosophies. In the summer of 1903, Washington spoke to a large audience at a Boston church. William Monroe Trotter, a black activist, and his supporters challenged Washington with provocative questions which caused a commotion and fist fight.

Prior to his death a couple of years later, Washington publicly expressed regrets over his Atlanta Compromise speech and the fact that it was used by the conservative social forces within white society to discriminate against and subordinate black people. Long after his death, many of Washington's beliefs have served as beacons for business-oriented black minds.

❂
Sambo, Not Uncle Tom

Knowing that Uncle Tom was a fictional character is very important, but what is even more important is understanding that the Uncle Tom character in the book, *Uncle Tom's Cabin*, was not the bad guy.

Admittedly, Harriet Beecher Stowe's Uncle Tom character was humble, nonviolent and very religious. But such personal characteristics could just as easily have applied to 98 percent of nearly every enslaved as well as free black person. It is important that the character's traits be considered with attention to his strengths.

In the novel, Uncle Tom refused to beat other slaves for falling short on their daily cotton picking. When necessary he would take cotton from his own sack and place it in the sacks of other slaves who were short to prevent them from being beaten. He defied Simon Legree, the white slavemaster, by refusing to whip female slaves to make them more obedient. Nor would he tell where escaping black slaves were hiding across the river.

The label "Uncle Tom" is not an appropriate label for a white person in black skin, according to the character developed in Stowe's novel. Sambo would be a more apt name and description of a black person who sells out his people to advantage himself. Sambo was the character totally committed to the white master and who used every opportunity to undermine the other slaves. Sambo enjoyed following the Master Simon Legree, and offered to show him how to "tree the coons." Sambo in *Uncle Tom's Cabin*, like many black conservatives, operated under misleading colors. Or, as an old farmer said, "They run with the hounds while pretending friendship and brotherhood with the rabbits." It was Sambo who beat Uncle Tom to death for refusing to whip a black female. It is the real life "Sambo personality" and not "Uncle Tom," who is black people's worst nightmare. (17)

❂
Was It a High Tech Lynching?

Since for most of his life, Clarence Thomas had been educated, socially mentored, politically and financially supported by and married into the dominant white race, it is not too difficult for him to conclude that the world is truly color-blind.

He openly opposes public assistance, affirmative action, quotas, economic justice, set-asides or any public policies to correct the structural inequalities between the black and white race. Even though he had been on the public payroll most of the working days of his adult life, he was a constitutional conservative hypocritically opposed to public sector jobs.

On July 2, 1991, when President George Bush nominated Clarence Thomas to fill Thurgood Marshall's seat on the United States Supreme Court, Bush said, "Thomas was the most qualified person for the job." Shortly thereafter, Clarence Thomas' Supreme Court confirmation hearing became one of the most politically contentious, hypocritical, disturbing and yet comical political spectacles in the history of Senate confirmations.

With the exception of the Urban League, Southern Christian Leadership Conference and black conservatives, Thomas was overwhelmingly opposed by black America because of his insensitivity to race matters. His nomination split the nation racially, with white America overwhelmingly supportive of him. If his nomination was not designed to insult and divide the nation, why wasn't a person more acceptable to blacks nominated to fill a "so-called" black seat?

Most politicians knew Thomas was nominated, not because of his legal experiences nor scholarship, but because he was a conservative black who could be counted on to carry "political water" for conservative white groups. In spite of black America's disapproval, the general feeling was that a rising tide of conservatism would easily confirm Thomas and use him to impede blacks from using the judicial system to redress their grievances.

The insult to black America began to backfire in an unprecedented series of events from October 11 to 14 after professor Anita Hill, a black woman, testified at the hearing. As the entire nation sat glued to their television sets, Anita Hill in calm, measured tones, charged Thomas with sexual harassment and told her version of Clarence Thomas' sexual habits, his appetite for X-rated adult movies, favorite porno stars, unwanted sexual advances he made on female employees, and ribald language about "pubic hairs on coke cans."

As the nation vacillated between disgust and belly laughter, Clarence Thomas defended the remainder of his honor by accusing the senators on the confirmation committee of conducting a "high tech lynching." Clarence Thomas, the conservative, who has made a career proclaiming that white racism could never stop a black person from achieving, screamed racism and wrapped himself in "blackness" when he was charged with sexual harassment.

Millions of Americans watched the hearings and debated over who was telling the truth. Eventually, the conservative Senate committee confirmed Thomas and black Americans anguished in anticipation of the pain that his future judicial decisions would surely bear. (18)

From Justice Thomas to Uncle Tom

Emerge Magazine, a black publication caricatured Justice Clarence Thomas on the front cover of two editions as an "Uncle Tom." In a 1993 edition of the magazine, a full head-shot of Clarence Thomas, with a colorful Aunt Jemima-style hankie on his head, adorned the cover page. The ultra-conservative and only black member of the U.S. Supreme Court subsequently commented on the front-page of the *Washington Post* newspaper saying, "I am not an Uncle Tom." *Emerge Magazine* again made Thomas a caricature on the front cover of the November, 1996 issue, dressed in boots, breeches, a jacket and cap and holding a lantern. The African-American publication proclaimed, "Uncle Thomas: Lawn Jockey for the Far Right".

To explain the symbolized relationship of jurist Thomas as a "lawn jockey," *Emerge Magazine's* editor cited the history of black jockeys and black faced lawn ornaments. He told how a grateful George Washington was said to have put a statue of Jocko Graves at Mount Vernon. Graves, one of the first African American volunteers in the Continental Army, froze to death tending the horse for his commander, who was crossing the Delaware River. (19)

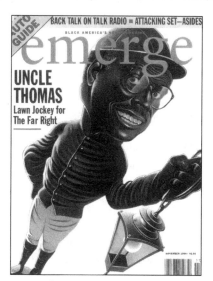

*Supreme Court Justice Clarence Thomas on the front cover of **Emerge Magazine** (November 1996).*

⚙

Economic Darwinism

Major corporations were attracted to and supported Ronald Reagan's bid for governor of California and President of the United States because he promised to use the powers and resources of government to help them make money. Conservative support for Ronald Reagan was pure socioeconomic Darwinism-- a survival of the strongest, not the fittest.

Justin Dart, multimillionaire owner of the Dart Drugstore chain explained his support for Reagan saying, "All I gave a damn about was that he [Reagan] was philosophically oriented in the right direction....Look, for instance, at such issues as abortion, NAACP, equal rights, and all those. Those are all, forgive me, trivial issues as far as I'm concerned. There are two basic issues that are overriding as far as I'm concerned: That is our [dominant society's] economic health, economic leadership, or economic dominance, and our military defense ability...The minor issues, like the Watts riots, they come and go.

This is socioeconomic Darwinism, unchanged, as it has existed in this country since slavery was first introduced. (20).

8
Businesses and Inventors

In every respect, blackness was a business.

Mini Facts

• *In 1704, most business advertisements for buying and selling slaves occupied a major place in the first newspaper printed in the colonies, the **Boston Newsletter**.*

• *Later, in 1741, Benjamin Franklin, a philosopher and inventor, had the dubious honor of running the first magazine ad seeking the whereabouts of a black runaway slave.*

• *For the first time in this nation's history, land became more valuable than a slave after the Civil War, when slavery ended.*

• *In the 1870s, one of the largest and most successful black businesses in America was the Chesapeake Marine Rail Way and Dry Dock Company of Baltimore, Maryland.*

✪
Slaves Introduce Rice to America

Uncle Ben's Rice, with the smiling face of a black man on the box, remains a popular consumer item, but social pressures from the Civil Rights Movement of the early 1960s caused many such labels to disappear.

The smiling black face on the label of Uncle Ben's Rice may have been degrading to blacks, but it was an historically accurate representation of the people who raised and harvested rice. African slaves introduced and taught southern white plantation owners how to plant and harvest rice in the coastal wet lands of nearly all of the southern states. Slaves showed their masters how to build rice-water trenches and dams, how to build canals, and how to construct containers to hold the rice.

The English slavemasters were unfamiliar with growing rice because rice crops were indigenous to Africa and the Far East. Rice production required highly regimented, experienced task workers who were physically capable of doing long hours of back-breaking work. Plantation owners watched slave advertisements looking for those special slaves "skilled and accustomed to rice planting." (1) Slaves assigned to the rice fields of the southeastern states suffered a high mortality rate from stagnant water-related illnesses, infections, and diseases. Their work hours were much longer than blacks working in cotton or tobacco fields. Considering the physical demands of raising rice, bending over and walking barefooted in cold water all day, and not receiving one penny for the labor, it is difficult to imagine why Uncle Ben was smiling on those rice boxes.

✪

Foundations Laid in Public Transportation

Black Americans were more involved in mass public transportation a century ago than they are today. In the late 1800s, blacks invented and filed for patents on a number of transportation related devices. As examples, in 1897, A. J. Beard invented a train car-coupler; in 1888, A.B. Blackburn invented a railway signal; in 1874 Brown and Latimer invented a water closet for railway cars; in 1897, R.A. Butler invented a train alarm; and in 1891, George Toliver invented a propeller for vessels. Although they were fresh out of slavery and the literacy rate among slaves was 50 percent, black inventors filed hundreds of patents for transportation devices.

What was even more impressive was their ability, with limited capital and training, to develop businesses in nearly all forms of public transportation. Blacks built and operated their own railroad lines in Pine Bluff, Arkansas, and Jacksonville, Florida. How these railroad lines compared to whites is unknown. But the black-owned railway in Pine Bluff, Arkansas was eventually taken over by whites. Blacks were much more competitive in the public bus business. From the 1930s until the early 1960s, blacks in Winston-Salem, North Carolina, had the distinction of owning and operating the only city-chartered black bus line in America, the Safe Bus Company. The company had over 500 buses, maintenance buildings and other properties. It was a major employer of black drivers, mechanics, maintenance crews and administrative staff. Although for years, the company serviced only black communities, in the 1950s it won the bid against the Duke Power Bus Company, the city's white-owned line, and began servicing both black and white communities.

The integration process and black efforts to ride on the front of white buses, hurt the black bus line. The Safe Bus Company went under and the white bus line reclaimed the chartered bus service.

During the same period, Winston-Salem also hosted two black-owned cab companies. Integration helped put both of them out of business. Today, these pioneering businesses are gone, and blacks can no longer boast of black-owned cabs, bus, and railway lines. (2)

❂
A Machine to Clean

In 1812, Thomas L. Jennings was the first black American ever issued a patent for an invention. Jennings' patent was for a dry-cleaning process known as "dry scouring." Jennings understood the importance of racial accountability. As result of his invention, he established and operated a dry cleaning and tailoring business in New York City. He used most of his profits to support the abolitionist cause. Jennings became an early activist for the rights of his people and later served as assistant secretary of the First Annual Convention of the People of Color in June 1831 in Philadelphia. (3)

❂
Thomas Fortune and His Powerful Pen

Thomas Fortune was born a slave in Marianna, Jackson County, Florida. Even though he had little formal education and the little that he received was poor in quality, Fortune made major contributions in education, economics, politics and poetry that improved life for all black people. He was hailed as "the ablest and most forceful editorial writer ever." Fortune breathed life into the saying, "The pen can be mightier than the sword," and used his writing skill to protect and advance himself, his family and his race. Fortune was well known for attacking and hurting his opponents with his pen, wit and paper. It was rumored that President Theodore Roosevelt once said, "Tom Fortune, keep that pen of yours off me!"

In 1880s, Fortune founded the first civil rights organization in the United States, the National Afro-American League, in the United States, the forerunner of today's NAACP. He also single-handedly integrated the New York City Public Schools, the nation's largest public school system. In 1996, the United States Postal Service considered issuing a commemorative stamp for Thomas Fortune, an overlooked but powerful black bridge builder in American history. (4)

⚙

Consumers Wanted the Real McCoy

When customers ask for the "real McCoy," they are asking for the original product, not an imitation. This comes from the experience of a black inventor, Elijah McCoy. Elijah was the son of fugitive slaves, George and Mildred McCoy, who fled a Kentucky plantation via the underground railroad and arrived in Detroit, Michigan, in 1841. Later, the family moved to Ontario, Canada, where Elijah was born. George McCoy opened a cigar manufacturing plant in Ypsilanti, Michigan, in 1864 and used the profits from his business to send Elijah to study mechanical engineering in Edinburgh, Scotland.

Elijah returned to Ypsilanti in 1870 and opened a mechanics shop. He was a prolific inventor and also served as a fireman for the Michigan Central Railroad, where he was in charge of lubricating all moving parts of the engine. His most famous invention was the lubricating cup. He received a patent for this invention in 1872. Some national and international industries discovered McCoy was black and refused to allow him to lecture to their staffs and students. Moreover, they refused to use his invention and used an inferior imitation instead. Loyal customers who used McCoy's lubricating cup claimed an advantage over their competitors. In their advertising they made sure that everyone knew they had the "real McCoy" and any other brand was a cheap imitation. In all, the "real" McCoy had 87 inventions and 57 patents including the lawn sprinkler. McCoy's other inventions, patents, and credit are lost in the pages of history. (5)

✪
Co-Inventor of the Reaper Didn't Reap

In the 1830s, a slave named Jo Anderson worked with Cyrus McCormick and co-invented the famous McCormick Reaper, which practically revolutionized farm harvesting. But Anderson received neither profits nor credit for his contribution to the invention of the first mechanical reaper. Like other slaves, Anderson dreamed of ways to make farming chores easier and, thereby, lengthen his life. As a slave, Anderson could not own property, nor could he file for a patent until after the Civil War in the late 1860s. In some instances, a slave's invention or assistance with an invention qualified him for "meritorious manumission," an earned achievement release from slavery. But in the instance of Jo Anderson and the reaper, Cyrus McCormick went into this nation's history books and to the bank with the money. Jo Anderson, his black co-inventor, just went away. (6)

✪
A Black Furniture Maker

Today it is difficult, if not impossible, to find a black furniture manufacturer. Yet, in 1836, Henry Boyd, a black man, built and operated a bed manufacturing factory in Cincinnati, Ohio. Considering the social-racial times and circumstances, it was no small achievement for Boyd to start and operate a factory. Boyd established his competitive furniture business during the white backlash to Nat Turner's slave rebellion in Virginia, and as whites were reeling from the prominent role played by runaway slaves in the Third Seminole War in Florida. Most freed blacks sought to reduce their visibility and vulnerability.

Not so with Boyd. At its peak, his furniture manufacturing firm required four buildings and had 20 to 50 employees. He strengthened his business by inventing a machine to produce rails for beds. But since blacks were prohibited by political and social customs from obtaining patents until after the Civil War, Boyd had to register his patent in the name of a white man. The bottom line is that the national policy prohibited blacks from being competitive with whites. Boyd's buildings were constantly damaged or destroyed by "mysterious fires." The old saying that lightening never strikes twice in the same place did not apply to his furniture factory. According to the local fire marshal, Boyd's building just happened to be located on the one spot where lightening strikes occurred repeatedly, defying normal probabilities. Boyd eventually had to quit his business because he lacked insurance coverage and did not have supplemental funds to continue paying for fire damages. (7)

○

Jasper and His Many Inventions

Since slaves performed nearly all the heavy, life-shortening labor, it was in their self-interest to invent labor and life-saving devices, or make suggestions on how to reduce labor demands.

Jasper, a black slave, was a skilled tanner and rope-maker. Working closely with his white master, he emerged as a creative inventor in the 1840s. He was credited with inventing a machine that automatically wove fish nets. The Haitian government contacted Jasper's master and expressed a willingness to purchase a special gun powder-making machine Jasper had invented, if the master was willing to allow him to travel to Haiti to install the machine and train the operators. Jasper's owner sent him to Haiti, but the boat on which he was traveling blew up and seriously injured him. After he recuperated from his injuries, when he returned to America, Jasper refused to return to his white master. A few years later, he enlisted in the Union Army during the Civil War and fought to end slavery.

After the Civil War, as a freed man, it was rumored that he returned to Norfolk, Virginia, and perfected his gun-powder maker and other inventions, including a reaper and mowing machine. (8)

✪
The Invention of the First Incubator

Although it is often said that "an idle mind is the devil's workshop," this was not the case with Jim, a black slave who used his mind and time to create what was probably the first chicken incubator. According to the account of Charles A. Bullock, a white male from Petersburg, Virginia, his father often told him how a black slave invented the first chicken incubator.

Bullock recalled his father's story saying, one day Jim's master discovered him burying eggs in various parts of the manure pile. When reprimanded, Jim explained to his white master, "This manure is gonna hatch eggs for you and the missus. Manure got the same heat as the hens because I have tried both of them." Jim continued working with the eggs and they did hatch.

The experiments proved to the master that Jim was right. Heat indeed caused the eggs to hatch. Jim's master decided to put the information to work. He built a box to comfortably hold the eggs, while a container for a small fire underneath kept them warm. That was the first egg incubator and Jim, the black slave, had "thought it up." Unfortunately Jim never got credit nor wealth for his idea. (9)

✪
Black Business Cycles Repeat Themselves

Blacks enjoyed limited success as businessmen, usually in "safe," non-competitive businesses that served the black community. Besides a few professional services such as teaching, banking and insurance, most black entrepreneurs made their living providing hair care services and products, domestic service, food preparation, catering, crafts and publishing weekly newspapers. These were primarily personal service businesses, and were considered "appropriate" opportunities for blacks. Such services produced some of the most affluent blacks in the country and represent the beginnings of a black upper class.

White and black customers alike sought black barbers and beauticians for their skills in hair care. These services were often provided in the customer's office or home.

Black businesses frequently grew out of culinary expertise. Consequently, some of the better black cooks and caterers in the North successfully operated restaurants and taverns.   For example, in 1762, Samuel Fraunces, known as "Black Sam," went to New York in the pre-Revolutionary period and became a leading caterer and restaurant owner. He paid 2,000 pounds for the De Lancey Mansion on the corner of Broad and Pearl streets and opened a tavern.

Before long, Fraunces' Tavern was the social center of the city and many historic events were born there. For instance, in 1768, the New York Chamber of Commerce was organized in a meeting at Sam's tavern. About 20 years later, at the end of the Revolutionary War, George Washington also bade farewell to his officers in Sam's tavern.

A few blacks competed with whites in mainstream businesses. In cities like Baltimore, Maryland, and Jacksonville, Florida, blacks owned railroad lines. They owned a bus company in North Carolina, movie studios in Jacksonville, Chicago, and Los Angeles, and an oil drilling company in Oklahoma. Other blacks even ventured into building and operating broom and mattress factories. By 1914, blacks had established some 50 banks and nearly as many insurance companies.

During slavery, blacks were the artisans, carpenters, craftsmen and builders. It was only natural that, in the few instances where they were allowed, they formed businesses around those skills. But, after the Civil War, in nearly every skilled trade, or artisan's craft, newly-arriving immigrants from southern Europe bumped blacks out of those businesses and organized whites-only unions that prohibited blacks and kept them out for another century. (10)

✪

Black Inventors

With a national public policy that excluded blacks from any educational process, and most areas of business, it is amazing that blacks produced as much as they did. Approximately 96 percent of all the blacks in America were slaves; so they could not own physical or intellectual properties. Greedy slaveholders had little difficulty "borrowing" or expropriating the inventions of slaves or free black people. Even when blacks were allowed to file patents, they had to overcome endless legal and illegal barriers.

Until 1858, the inventions of slaves were by law the property of the slaveholder. The number of inventions produced by blacks will never be known because they were credited to whites. For example, a black slave named Ned invented a cotton harvester. Ned's machine was so efficient and labor-saving that his master, O.J. Stuart, of Pike County, Mississippi, attempted to patent the invention in his own name in 1857. Stuart argued that since he owned Ned, he owned anything created by Ned. Had Ned been able to drag his case out for a couple of years, he could have gotten both a patent and credit for his invention. Despite that kind of negative racial climate, little known black inventors continued to offer their scientific and industrial gifts to America and the world.

Shirley J. Davidson, a graduate of Howard University in 1893, is credited with inventing the first mechanical calculator that may have been the forerunner of modern day adding machines and calculators.

Henry A. Bowman, of Worcester, Massachusetts, was awarded a patent for a flag making process in February, 1892. When his business began to succeed, his white competitors came after him. He was unable to hire an attorney to help him legally protect his business and his invention, so a powerful white firm took his patent and put him out of business. Stripped of everything, including his pride, he simply vanished from the city.

The year 1892 was a good year for a few other black inventors. Every housewife ought to feel indebted to Sarah Boone, who came up with the idea of putting collapsible leg supports on a narrow wood board, covering it with soft padding, and calling it an ironing board. Prior to her ironing board, people typically ironed clothing on a wood plank placed between two chairs, tables or boxes. Thanks to Sarah Boone, the ironing board is a standard feature in every home. (11)

A Few More Unknown Inventions

The greatest flood of patents came after the Reconstruction period, between 1870 and 1900. During this time, more than 300 patents were awarded to blacks. Most of the inventions were small household, farming or work-related devices, but they symbolized the drive and creative ability of a people. Among the inventions patented after the Civil War and before the turn of the century was Louis Temple's toggle-blade harpoon, designed to lock itself into a whale's flesh. Other inventions included folding beds, street sprinklers and sweepers, cooking ranges, rug and egg beaters, riding saddles, motors, golfing tees, portable weighing scales, gas burners, envelope seals, pencil sharpener, nailing machine, cotton chopper, horseshoes, mop, potato digger and corn husker, dust pan, potato chip, fountain pen, curtain rod and lemon squeezer. Although patents were issued on every one of the 300 devices, in all too many instances the black inventors lacked financial resources to mass produce, market or profit from their inventions.

Only a few were as lucky as Beard, a former slave, who invented the automatic railroad coupler, also known as the Jenny Coupler. His invention allowed trains to be joined together without human assistance. Beard's coupler was patented on November 23, 1897. He later sold the invention to a New York firm for $50,000.

Individual blacks made major contributions in spite of racism, slavery, planned ignorance, and the denial of the opportunity to enjoy the fruits of their labor and creativity. Historical facts suggest that America owes a debt of gratitude to all the unknown and unrewarded black inventors. (12)

✪

Black Images in Advertisements

First Aunt Jemima ads. (Roger Lewis Black Memoribilia Collection)

While most blacks were denied credit for their inventions, negative black images on products was a popular form of advertising. In a few rare instances, black images were those of the original black inventor. Most were just caricatures of blacks on products identified with or primarily produced by blacks.

Two of the most recognizable black images on products were Aunt Jemima and Uncle Ben. According to the black version, a black woman named Jenkins created the recipe for Aunt Jemima pancake flour and her picture became the logo on the box. Having neither business skills nor money, she lost her recipe to a large, white firm. A similar story is told about blacks and rice. There are no records available on what kind of monetary compensation these two blacks received, if any. (13)

Buying Black Movement

In the 1920s and 1930s, blacks began to leave the South for better jobs and what they hoped would be improved racial conditions in the North. They most often moved to large metropolitan areas with heavy industrial development. As northern ghettos began to form, blacks began to feel their economic and political strength amass. Group cohesiveness and group capital spells power.

During the early 1930s, in the urban areas where blacks now lived, they began to advocate group economics and group politics, especially where they spent their hard-to-come-by dollars. They had clear goals for their group activities. Blacks began a "Consumer Buying Power" movement in Chicago. They used pickets and boycotts to force white business owners, especially those that had large black clientele and customer bases to employ blacks in their businesses. In New York, Adam Clayton Powell, a young black community activist, minister and future Congressman, led a four-year employment effort that added ten thousand black workers to the telephone company, the electric company, the bus line, and department stores. In black communities throughout America, organizations began to use the same tactics to get blacks jobs.

In Washington, D.C., the strategy of using your consumer dollars to create employment opportunities was captured in the slogan, "Don't buy where you can't work." Once blacks galvanized around the economic boycott, over 90 percent of the neighborhood stores changed their hiring policies. Other white businesses feared they would become boycott targets and began to employ blacks.

Boycotts worked because white businesses were situated in black communities and depended upon black customers for survival and profit. A generation later, whites insulated themselves from the possibility of black economic sanctions and relocated their businesses to all white suburbs and their primary customer base. Anti-boycotting laws were even enacted to stop blacks from withholding their money from white merchants. (14)

9
Blood Lines and Blood Phobias

The power is in the blood.

Mini Facts

• *Until their expulsion in 1492, centuries of occupation of Spain and Portugal by Arabs and Moors resulted in a large number of mulattos who were absorbed into the European blood line.*

• *In 1924, the State of Virginia enacted miscegenation laws defining a white person as one with no trace of any blood other than Caucasian, or with 1/16 or less of Indian blood.*

• *In 1966, Representative Adam Clayton Powell, who used his white appearance and congressional powers to aid blacks, convened the nation's first Black Power Conference*

• *By 1985, as a result of four centuries of miscegenation, at least 75 to 90 percent of all people defined as American blacks have some white ancestry.*

❂
Africa: The Birth Place of All Mankind

In the beginning, "The Lord God formed man of the dust of the ground, and breathed into his nostrils the breath of life; and man became a living soul. God then planted a garden eastward in Eden; and there he put man who he had formed." (Genesis 2:7-8) These quotes, of course, are from the Bible, and indicate that all men had a single point of origin. More contemporary sources seem to back up the biblical account. Roland Oliver, a foremost scholar on African history, noted that the first creature generally recognized as the ancestor of man, was found between Ethiopia and what is now the

Republic of South Africa, sometime between 1.5 million and 4 million years ago.

However, up until 1950, many historians and archeologists would not acknowledge mankind's African origin. Then came two findings of great importance. In the Olduvai Gorge, a canyon leading into the Serengeti Plains in what is now northern Tanzania, the remains were found of "homo erectus," a man who lived about 1.5 million years ago. He or she was an ancestor of black Africans.

Recently, the *Washington Post* reported another significant scientific finding based on DNA genetic studies. According to the article in the *Washington Post*, (in August 1997) analysis of patterns of variations in DNA suggested that all Caucasian and other non-blacks derived from a common black ancestral population in Northeast Africa.

So whether one accepts the origin of the creation of man in the Holy Scriptures, archaeologists' findings in Africa, or the scientists' DNA findings, it seems that all human life began in Africa, then migrated to Europe, Asia, the Americas and every other nook and cranny of the planet. (1)

❂
Who Built the Great Pyramids?

Egypt's pyramids hide many a secret, dirty and otherwise. Within the pyramids are traces of a society that long since passed into antiquity along with mathematical and racial riddles that have never been solved. One secret of Khufu's Great Pyramids has been the racial identity of its builder. Khufu, the King of Egypt who was called Cheop by the Greeks, was the architect and builder of the Great Pyramid. He lived during the late 2600s B.C. Obscured by time and historical omissions, few viewers of the Great Pyramid, ever knew that its builder was a black man.

Scholars believe that he must have been a powerful ruler to have made his subjects build such a large pyramid in his honor. According to the *Afro-American Almanac*, the Great Pyramid, contains 2,500,000 blocks of time-tested granite. With each block weighing two and a half tons, this Great Pyramid covers more than a dozen acres of land. Scientists, engineers, and scholars are still struggling to determine how this feat was achieved without the benefit of advanced technology and machinery. They most often assume this feat of architecture was achieved by a non-black, but there is the possibility that modern DNA genetic testing could confirm the race of

Cheop, the great king and pyramid builder. (2)

✪
Woman Shaped Religious Kingdoms

"I am black, but comely, O ye daughters of Jerusalem, as the tents of Kedar, as the curtains of Solomon...I am the rose of Sharon, and the lily of the valley." These lines from the Song of Solomon (1:5), in the Holy Bible, describe the Queen of Sheba, and hint at her role in determining the course of great nations and major religions. Three thousand years, and conflicting fragments of history told in the Bible, the Talmud, the Koran and the legends of various Middle Eastern nations, have minimized her name and obscured her race. But, this is the story that is told of her.

She was a beautiful black woman. As Queen, she ruled the rich and powerful Arabian nation of Sheba during the time that Solomon, the son of David and the King of the Hebrews, was building his Temple of Jerusalem to house the Ark of the Covenant. Fearing King Solomon and his powers, the Queen of Sheba went to Jerusalem to establish a relationship with him. She was impressed with Solomon's wisdom and wealth.

They fell in love and their love affair produced a son called Bayna-Lehkem, "the son of the wise man." The legend goes that after the son became a man, he stole the Ark of the Covenant, transported it back to Ethiopia and buried it within the ancient Church of Axum. The imperial house of Ethiopia traced its line from the Queen of Sheba and King Solomon through their son Menelik, down through Haile Selassie, who ruled until he passed decades ago. (3)

✪
Aesop, A Black Slave

Millions of children and their parents are familiar with the fables like the tortoise and the hare, and the ant and the grasshopper. They know these are Aesop's fables, but few know his racial origin. Even fewer of Aesop's fans know that his impact goes beyond his "stories." Aesop was a gifted black man who lived, suffered, and died as a slave in ancient times. His great mind and wit were a powerful influence on the thought and the moral views of many of the world's great thinkers. The philosophies embedded in his fables had a major influence on the development of ancient and modern societies. Plato, Socrates, Aristophanes, Shakespeare and other great minds of the Western world, thought about and found inspiration in his simple stories.

Aesop is believed to have lived during the 6th century, before the birth of Christ, in ancient Greece. His name meant "Ethiop of Africa."

Hundreds of years after Aesop's death, in the 14th century, his fables were first presented to the public by Planudes the Great, a scholarly monk who researched and wrote Aesop's biography. In the 17th century, French poet and author Jean de La Fontaine wrote a biography of Aesop. Both Planudes and de La Fontaine proclaimed Aesop's African origin and described his broad flat nose, thick lips, black skin and kinky hair.

This description of Aesop as an old black slave, the teller of tales and fables, gives him a special place in black history. He is the classic-era counterpart of more modern day Uncle Remus and his tales. Socrates spent his last days putting Aesop's fables into verse. The mass entertainment markets, print and electronic media, have kept alive and perpetuated the wit and fables of this black slave. (4)

☢

What Five Black Presidents?

People in bars, board rooms and living rooms across the country have at one time or another entertained the question of whether America would ever elect a black to be President of tthe United States, and if so who would be the first. According to Joel Augustus Rogers, in his book, *The Five Negro Presidents*, the questions are moot. Rogers believes that America has had at least three black Presidents--Thomas Jefferson, Abraham Lincoln and Andrew Jackson--and two black Vice-Presidents, Hannibal Hamlin and Warren G. Harding. Joel Augustus Rogers was a well-known and highly-respected researcher who authored numerous books and articles in the 1930s and 1940s.

Rogers' assertions, while not supported by conclusive evidence, tend to reflect the circumstances of their times. Every state had laws that defined who was black. Some states classified a person as black when they had 1/8th, 1/16th, 1/32nd or even "one drop" of black blood. Considering the cultural and ritualistic pattern of white men sleeping with black women, there is a high probability that many whites elected to the highest offices across this nation were "legally black."

✪
Jefferson

According to Rogers, Thomas Jefferson, the third American President, was black. Rogers cites the denunciation of Jefferson in the ***Johnny-Cake Papers***. Rogers quoted the political paper as saying, "Thomas Jefferson, son of a half-breed Indian squaw, sired by a Virginia mulatto father..." The paper also called him "a half-nigger." Town gossipers and members of the opposition party picked up the rumors of Jefferson's heritage and gave them wider circulation. But, again, no proof of the allegations has ever surfaced.

Rogers alleged that Andrew Jackson, "Old Hickory," the son of an Irish white woman who intermarried with a mulatto Negro, was legally black. In support of his assertion, Rogers further stated, "What gave an air of truth to this allegation was that the elder (brother) died before Andrew was born. His widow went to live on the Crawford farm where there were Negro slaves, and one of these was proported to be Andrew Jackson's father. In his book, Rogers stresses that Jackson was conceived after the death of his real father, whose name he bore." Most historical documents indicate that Jackson's acknowledged parents were poor white immigrants from Ireland. Some newspapers even printed stories alleging that Jackson's mother was a prostitute brought to America by British soldiers. None except Rogers assert that Jackson was the offspring of mixed parents. On the other hand, history leaves no doubt that Andrew Jackson had very little love and affection for either blacks or Indians. (5)

✪
Lincoln

The second black President of the United States, according to Rogers, was Abraham Lincoln. He was depicted as a Negro by his opponents and called "Abraham

Africanus the First." Why did Lincoln's political opponents call him an African? According to Rogers, the texture of his hair and skin color appeared to be more Negroid than Caucasian. His skin color was like that of a mulatto, his black hair was coarse, and he had brown eyes. These physical characteristics caused many to think it was possible that Lincoln had some black blood in his veins.

Lincoln's political enemies may have called him a Negro because they perceived him as sympathetic to the plight of Negroes and felt they could hurt him with the accusation. Ironically, Lincoln's interest was not in saving a black enslaved race, but saving the Union, which prospered through its exploitation of blacks. (6)

Rogers also says that Lincoln's vice-presidential running mate, Hannibal Hamlin, was a Negro. He stated that after Vice-President Hamlin was elected to office, he was attacked on the Senate floor because of his dark skin coloring. Hamlin allegedly responded to his attackers saying, "I take my color from nature. You get yours from the brandy bottle. Which is more honorable?" Rogers quoted a newspaper editorial in *The Chicago Democrat* (June 4, 1861) that blasted Lincoln with, "...the possible dire effects on the country if a free Negro is elected to the vice-presidency." R.B. Rhett, the succession leader of the political faction from Charleston, South Carolina, said, "Hamlin is what we call a mulatto. He has black blood in him." Rhett quoted the same article in *The Chicago Democrat* of June 4, 1861, which said, "The constant theme in the South for the last two months has been the election of the abolitionist Lincoln and the free Negro Hamlin." Whether or not Hamlin was black or white remains unanswered. Either way, General Butler of the Union army told the Secretary of War in the 1860s that in recruiting Negro troops, he would like to have a "regiment of mulattos, about the complexion of Vice-President Hamlin." (7)

✪

Harding

While President Woodrow Wilson was busy betraying black people in preparation for World War I, black Americans felt a sense of justice when they heard the rumor that Wilson had unknowingly chosen a black vice-presidential running mate. Shortly before election day, newspapers heralded the story Warren G. Harding, Woodrow Wilson's Vice-President, was a Negro.

Fuel was added to the fire when millions of flyers were circulated proclaiming that, "Harding's father is George Tryon Harding, obviously a mulatto; he has thick lips, rolling eyes, chocolate skin, and his mother, Phoebe Dickerson, a midwife of whose ancestry little is known, was white." Wilson betrayed and barred blacks from government jobs. Was it possible that President Woodrow Wilson had unknowingly locked himself into the White House with a black Vice-President?

According to J.A Rogers, Harry Daugherty, the Attorney General, in San Francisco discovered over 250,000 copies of the flyers announcing that Harding was a black, but President Wilson ordered all of the flyers destroyed. Allegedly, the true stories about Presidents Wilson and Harding are contained in a rare book, **Warren G. Harding, President of the United States**. Supposedly there are only three known copies and they are said to be worth approximately $200,000 a copy. When a representative of the Republican Party publicly asked Harding whether or not there was any black blood in his family, according to Rogers, Harding responded, "How should I know? One of my ancestors might have jumped the fence!" (8)

❂
Roman Catholic Church Hid Black Popes?

The Pope is the spiritual leader of the Roman Catholic Church and from his seat of authority in the Vatican Palace in Rome, Italy, the power of the Pope extends to all aspects of church affairs around the world.

The Catholic Church is proud to state that unlike other positions of authority and leadership, the office of the Pope has continued unbroken since Saint Peter, venerated as the first Pope. It is commonly accepted that the Catholic Church has only elected white males to the Papacy since St. Linus, in 67 A.D., but according to author Ross D. Brown, the Catholic Church has had at least three black Popes and a number of black saints. The three African Popes were St. Victor I (189-199 A.D.), Melchiades (311-312 A.D.), and St. Gelasius I (492 A.D.).

How does the Catholic Church square the conflicting facts? They were one of the first religious denominations to recommend and sanction black enslavement, contending that blacks were inferior human beings. Yet, they had already elevated blacks to the "infallibility" of popehood, and the high calling of sainthood. Was it because racism against blacks did not begin until the 15th century, while black Popes were elected to their position centuries earlier? The spirit of God works in mysterious ways. Perhaps with these reasons in mind, while in Jamaica in 1992, Pope John issued an apology to the black race for the historical role that the Catholic Church played in the international enslavement and subordination of the black race. (9)

✪

They Were Less Than Pure

The State of Virginia, all set to enact racial integrity laws in the 1940s, received an emotional jolt when George S. Schuyler, in his book *Racial Intermarriages in the U.S.* made public the results of his thorough investigations into the genealogies of high level Virginia government office holders. His book announced sad news to many whites. Virginia was a very racially-mixed state, even among the American Indians. This posed a "little problem" for a large number of whites who publicly claimed to be "pure" white or mixed with "pure" Indian blood.

Schuyler's research was more specific and indicated that about 45 percent of the nation's white population had some quantity of black blood in their veins. The black blood came in through black Indian ancestors. This black blood exposé included most of the big money first families or "blue bloods" of Virginia, who after learning about the black blood in their veins, undoubtedly skipped many social teas.

The Richmond News Leder in Richmond, Virginia, further stirred the pot by saying that among those living and dead, those who would be classed as blacks, if a racial integrity bill or the one "drop of black blood" law was enforced, would be:

> 2 United States Senators
>
> 1 United States Ambassador to France
>
> 5 Army Generals
>
> 2 Presidents of the United States
>
> 2 Secretaries of War
>
> 3 Distinguished Southern Novelists

3 Governors of Virginia

1 Speaker of the House of Representatives

2 Bishops

3 United States Congressmen

1 Rear Admiral

2 Judges of the Virginia Supreme Court and
many of the foremost officers of the
Confederate Army.

The *Richmond News Leder* concluded by warning its readers that, "Virginia, of course, is not the only state that could offer similar blood mixing, if a careful survey were conducted." Needless to say, policy makers quickly lost interest in enacting a racial integrity law. (10)

10
Scoundrels and Other Outcasts
They were scoundrels, but they were our scoundrels.

Mini Facts

• *Between 1699 and 1845 as many as 50 slave mutinies at sea took place. One of the most noteworthy was the Amistad revolt when 54 slaves seized the ship, sailed into New York and won their freedom in a celebrated Supreme Court case.*

• *In 1711, a number of frightened white citizens petitioned the Governor of South Carolina to post a reward of 50 pounds for the capture of Sebastian, the feared leader of a band of raiders and runaway black slaves.*

• *In 1735, black slaves revolted aboard the Dolphin, overtaking the crew and the captain. But both the captives and the captors were killed in an explosion on board the ship.*

• *On April 18, 1818, Andrew Jackson fought the battle of Swanne, Florida, against a force of Native Americans and blacks. Jackson won, but characterized it as a "savage and Negro War."*

❂

When Piracy Was Better Than Slavery

When confronted with a choice, many blacks preferred piracy over slavery. They sometimes became pirates to escape slavery or they were taken into piracy as contraband from captured ships. Blacks made the transition easily because pirates, like black people, were marginalized social outcasts. Both survived the best way they could, with few friends and many enemies.

Runaway slaves and pirates were "wanted people" who did whatever was necessary to survive. They had bounties on their heads. There was little difference from being a black slave and being a black pirate. In piracy, blacks were often leaders or captains-in-charge. Blacks typically made up a major part of the crew of social misfits and outcasts.

Literary research suggests that 25 to 30 percent of an estimated 5,000-plus pirates who were active between the years of 1715 to 1725 were of African descent. Any black tough enough to survive and escape from slavery was well qualified to join the ranks of the pirates.

During the 15th and 16th centuries, piracy was rampant on the seas. Pirates attacked vessels carrying slaves and slave-produced products. They routinely attacked ships going to and from Europe, Africa, the West Indies and the Americas. During the heyday of piracy, black pirates wreaked revenge on various colonial governments and private business shipments. Ships leaving large ports such as Charleston and Port Royal were regularly looted until colonial officials demanded protection from the English Royal Navy.

Pirates spread the risk and were equal-opportunity raiders. Joining up was a simple thing for runaway slaves. All they had to do was to follow the rules which were few and easy to learn. "Honor among thieves" was the prevailing rule. "Share and share alike" was a close second. For example, one British captain looted his own ship, then turned the ship, its loot, and captives over to Edward Teach, more commonly known as Blackbeard, just so he could be accepted into Blackbeard's crew.

Blackbeard was such a popular and feared pirate that many runaway slaves joined his crew as a safe haven. At one time, nearly 60 of Blackbeard's 100-man crew were black ex-slaves. Of Blackbeard's crew, the next most feared pirate was Caesar, a trusted black man who was second-in-charge of the ship. In 1718, Lt. Henry Maynard and a crew of Virginia sailors killed Blackbeard, but while they were celebrating their victory, they discovered Caesar with a lighted torch, preparing to carry out Blackbeard's last order to blow up the ship's power magazine if the ship were seized by government officials. After subduing Caesar, Maynard's crew took him and nine other prisoners back to Hampton Creek, Virginia, and without the benefit of a trial, hanged all of them.

The rare instance when blacks were totally in charge of a pirate vessel occurred when a white pirate crew elected them to command the ship. Diego Griello, a runaway slave from Havana whose nickname was "Lucifer," was such a pirate commander who on three separate occasions defeated government warships deployed to capture him. Griello plagued Spanish shipping lines for nearly three decades.

Among black pirates, the baddest of all, at least in reputation, was Lauren de Geoff. He led more than a thousand men during his 1683 raid on the Spanish colony at Vera Cruz, Mexico. It was said that he, more than any other single pirate, was most feared by the English and Spanish during the 1680s and 1690s. It is not known whether or not he was ever captured or killed, but the Vera Cruz colony breathed a sigh of relief when his raids ended. Some black pirates were little more than a "flash in the pan." They did not remain in the profession very long.

Here are a few of the "flashes in the pan": Captain Bartholomew Roberts was a pirate who lived with a partially black crew in the waters off the coast of Virginia in the mid-1700s. Francisco Fernando had a brief, yet very successful pirating career. After taking 250,000 silver pieces-of-eight in his first act of piracy, he immediately retired, believing he had hit the jackpot. Abraham Sowell, a former slave from Martinique, retired from piracy to rule a kingdom in Madagascar after raiding just one ship.

With all of these early retirements, it is understandable why in 1742 a report declared that piracy on the southeast coast had been completely exterminated and vessels could sail without fear of being attacked and looted. With this news, insurance rates for cargo ships between New York and Jamaica dropped by 20 percent. (1)

❂
Loose Lips Sink Pirate Ships

Near the end of the 17th century, when Europe and the Virginia colony were thriving, scores of pirates made the Virginia Cape their hunting grounds. The pirates filled their treasure chests with slave-produced wealth and, in many instances, took the slaves themselves who shared in the profits.

One June day in 1688, the English frigate Dunbarton, captured a small boat coming up the James River. On board were three white men, one black man and a large amount of gold, silver, money and expensive cloth. After the three white men--Davis, Delawafer, and Hinson--were arrested and locked up in the James City Jail, the black man, Peter Cleiss, confessed that he and his companions were pirates who had stolen and possessed valuable items from numerous Spanish vessels.

Because now everyone knew they were pirates, the three white men, pleaded for leniency of the court and a return of their stolen loot, including Peter Cleiss, the Negro. Several months later, all four of the pirates, including the Negro, were released but the court kept the loot. Perhaps Peter Cleiss should have elected to stay in prison because when the three whites were re-arrested they listed among their effects "a Negro since dead."

With the only witness against them dead, the remaining three pirates won a permanent release and a pardon that restored all of their stolen property except 300 pounds, which was to be devoted to some charitable good. Early records of the College of William and Mary reveal the sum of 300 pounds paid to the college by Davis, Delawafer, and Hinson. (2)

✪
Slave Traders Committed Insurance Fraud

In 1781, the slave ship Zong, a British vessel, left Africa enroute to Jamaica with 400 slaves on board. Nine weeks later, 60 slaves and several whites died on board from an unknown disease.

Fearing that he would lose even more of his black cargo before reaching his final port, Captain Luke Collingwood, a man with a questionable reputation, decided to cover his losses by throwing 132 shackled blacks overboard. He believed that if he claimed accidental drownings he could trick the insurance company into covering his losses on both the drowned blacks and those who had died from the disease. When the ship reached port in Jamaica, the insurance company refused to accept Collingwood's accidental death claim.

When the slave trade investors all lost their money because the insurance company refused to honor the claim, they in turn sued Captain Collingwood. Whether or not they were successful in their suit is unknown, but the British Parliament responded by enacting laws regulating the terms under which insurance companies would be liable for the loss of slaves in transport.

The Zong incident was one of the most cruel cases recorded. It illustrates that slavery was a multi-level, cut-throat, heartless business, extending from slave procurers, to slave traders to slavery financiers. It demonstrated the low premium placed on black life when money, profit or some other "market advantage" was at stake. For nearly another century, potential slaveowners in America could purchase slaves at local open markets or special order them directly from Africa through others like Captain Collingwood. Using special catalogues, a person could special order blacks by size, height, weight, tribe or price range. After the Zong incident, financiers of slave traders purchased insurance coverage on the number and kind of slaves ordered. (3)

❂
The Ear That Started A War

By the third decade of the 18th century, the British held monopolies in slave trading African blacks as well as maritime shipping in the Atlantic Ocean. With such economic power, Britain was not reluctant to use its military weight against Spain and France to maintain dominance.

The British got their chance to go after Spain in 1739 when the Spanish, who were angry and tired of English pirates, decided to make a point and cut off the ear of an English smuggler named Edward Jenkins. Jenkins was little more than a common petty criminal, but when the British heard what the Spanish had done, they responded by declaring a war with the most interesting sounding name in history, the War of Jenkins' Ear. But, the Jenkins' Ear War was anything but. It was a nothing war with no point that lasted until 1742, but it did introduce two interesting pieces of American history.

First, it introduced Admiral Edward Vernon, whose nickname was Old Grog, because he issued a daily ration of rum and water that made his appreciative crew, groggy. Admiral Vernon's nickname and its effect on his sailors led to the drink being called grog. One of the Admiral's colonial officers, Lawrence Washington, a half brother of George, was so taken with Admiral Vernon that he named his Virginia slave plantation Mount Vernon in the Admiral's honor.

Second, it is worthwhile to note that during the non-interesting Jenkins' Ear War, the British began to refer to their colonial cousins as "Americans," rather than as provincials or colonials. The term, American, had been recorded as early as 1578, but in all previous instances, it applied only to native Indians. The Jenkins' Ear War called attention to a new American nation that was being founded upon stolen Indian land and expropriated black slave labor. (4)

✪

Just a Bunch of Good Ole Boys

The Ku Klux Klan, America's most infamous vigilante group, emerged in the South as an outlet for a bunch of "good ole boys" who were simply bored after all the fun and excitement of the Civil War. It began innocently in Pulaski, Tennessee, when six former Confederate soldiers decided they wanted some new excitement and adventure. So, in May, 1866, they formed a social club borrowing the Greek phrase "Kuklo Adelphon" from a college fraternity. The phrase means "circle of brothers," but was eventually modified into the Ku Klux Klan. Like college fraternities, it began with secret rituals. The pin head hoods and costumes were to add mystery and uniqueness to an otherwise "frivolous social club." But, it quickly lost its harmless image.

Having just lost the Civil War, the good ole southern boys could not accept the idea of their black ex-slaves voting, running for public office, attending school and seeking forty acres and a mule. They feared these social changes might encourage blacks to try to be equal to, or compete with whites. So, they took action "to keep blacks in their place" by preaching white superiority over blacks and any other vulnerable minorities. They had stumbled onto an ideology that instantly appealed to a large number of whites, especially in the South. The good ole boys were off and running, not as pranksters, but as America's newest terrorist group.(5)

A Black Joke of the Times

Typically, white slavemasters enjoyed impressing their black slaves. Without changing the status and authority relationship, many masters tried to be friendly by seeking a slave's opinions and advice. The slave would gladly give his opinion, but had to protect himself by "dumbing down." A real tricky slave would act dumb while making a "fool" out the master. The following conversation demonstrates the technique.

"Pompey, how do it look?" inquired the white master.

"O' Massa, mighty! You sho' look Mighty!"

"What do you mean! Mighty what Pompey?"

"Why sir, you looks just like a lion."

"Why, Pompey, where have you ever seen a lion."

"Well, I saw one down yonder field the other day, Massa!"

"Pompey, you foolish fellow, that was a jackass you saw!"

"Was it massa? Well suh, you still looked just like him." (6)

11
Politicians and Patriots
Am I not a man and a brother?

Mini Facts

• *In 1776, Bill Richmond, a young black slave, was the hangman at the execution of Nathan Hale, accused by the British of being an American spy. Richmond later became a heavyweight boxer in Europe.*

• *In 1814, after the British burned Washington, D.C., over 3,000 blacks, free and slave, built defenses to keep the British from burning the cities of Philadelphia and Baltimore.*

• *In 1901, after President Theodore Roosevelt invited Booker T. Washington to the White House, the South was incensed and reacted with violence against blacks across America.*

✪
The Burning of Jamestown

The landing of 20 Africans at Jamestown in 1619 from a Dutch ship, marked the "formal" beginning of the African-American experience in America.

For the next 20 years, African blacks struggled to avoid a developing caste system while poor whites struggled under British rule to avoid a developing white class system. White aristocrats and British officials feared that poor white frontiersmen and African blacks would band together to overthrow the British governor of Virginia. And, indeed, they did in 1676 in what history called Nat Bacon's Rebellion. It was the first popular rebellion in colonial America, and blacks, both free and enslaved, participated in it.

Nathaniel Bacon, a cousin to the scientist and philosopher, Sir Francis Bacon, led the troops in rebellion against the colonial governor of Jamestown, Virginia, which was established in 1607 as England's first permanent settlement in North America

Nat Bacon's Rebellion was the first of about 20 minor uprisings that demonstrated a new anti-authority attitude in America. For blacks, it was the beginning of a long-standing pattern. Blacks demonstrated their patriotism by burning down the capital of Jamestown. But, after the uprising was suppressed, Nathaniel Bacon was dead, and his black and white associates were either killed outright or hanged. Ironically, this black-white rebellion foreshadowed in nearly every respect and laid the ground work for the Revolutionary War which followed nearly a century later. (1)

❁

Jim Crowism Frames the 20th Century

Despite the fact that blacks had volunteered to fight in every war, even before this country was a nation, and were over-represented in the Korean and Vietnam conflicts, some members of white society continue to perceive them as less than patriotic. As far back as World War I, the United States government issued an edict demanding that "all men" work or fight; engage in productive labor, or join the Army. Enforcement of the directive, however, was directed most intensely at the black man.

As they had so often done, blacks heeded the military call and served with high distinctions. They were some of the most decorated and recognized soldiers in World War I. Black soldiers received so much positive publicity in Europe, it triggered a white backlash in the military as well as the civilian sector.

A secret memo went out on August 7, 1918 called, "Secret Information Concerning Black-American Troops." It was issued by General Black Jack Pershing himself. It informed the French people and Army that the Negro was really "an inferior human being." High-ranking administrative staff issued orders forbidding blacks to associate with French women. In response, General Ballosa of the French Army ordered blacks to stay away from places where they were not wanted. Although 1300 of the crosses in Flander's Field in France mark the graves of black American soldiers, those who survived were neither permitted to socialize with white women nor take part in the great Paris Victory Parade. (2)

Yankee Doodle May Have African Roots

Yankee Doodle, a popular national song of a century ago, may have an African origin. Yankee Doodle shows a strong similarity to a slave song from Surinam, which goes:

> Mama Nanni go to town
> Buy a little Pony.
> Stick a feather in a ring,
> Calling Masa Ranni. (3)

Woodrow Wilson Deceived Black Voters

Woodrow Wilson needed the black vote to win the presidential election in 1912. In a formal statement to blacks, Wilson said he, "Wished to see justice done to the colored people in every matter; and not mere grudging justice, but justice with liberality and cordial good feelings." Wilson further stated, "I want to assure them [the Negroes] that should I become President of the United States, they may count on me for absolute fair dealing, for everything by which I could assist in advancing the interest of their race in the United States."

With such a public pronouncement, black leadership abandoned the Republican party and rushed to support Wilson. W. E.B. Dubois was one of the first to champion Wilson's candidacy. He was followed by Booker T. Washington, the NAACP, The National Independent League and the Colored National Democratic League. Black America responded to their leadership and gave Wilson their votes. Their 100,000 votes put Wilson over the top and into the White House.

After Wilson won the election, Congress drafted and sent to the President for his approval, the greatest flood of new laws that discriminated against blacks that had ever been introduced by the United States Congress. The proposed laws advocated segregation on public carriers, in hotels and work places, and total exclusion of blacks from the military and federal jobs. President Wilson thumbed his nose at black people and approved all of the proposed laws that propelled black people backwards. Conditions became unbearable in the South and that triggered the great migration of blacks from the South to the large urban cities of the North between 1920s and 1930s.

Wilson encouraged the rigid maintenance of Jim Crow segregation in every department of the federal government. In offices that traditionally hired blacks, the jobs were given to "deserving white Democrats." Scores of blacks were summarily fired. Blacks were not allowed to compete economically. Throughout the South abuse escalated. Lynchings skyrocketed. Blacks, as well as their crops, were burned; their animal stock poisoned and kerosene doused on their cotton.

The little power or voice that blacks had was stripped from them. All sorts of schemes kept them from voting or having their cries of pain heard. While his black supporters were being killed and abused, President Wilson failed to issue a single-word in their defense. Like so many "great white leaders" before him, President Woodrow Wilson became just another Great Deceiver. (4)

✪
A Black Spy in Revolutionary War

In March, 1781, James Armistead was granted permission by his owner, William Armistead, to serve in the Continental Army and became one of the most important spies of the American Revolution. The information that James Armistead acquired aided his commander, Marquis de Lafayette, a Frenchman serving in the American army, to defeat the British at Yorktown, Virginia, on October 19, 1781. Lafayette became an immediate hero, Armistead returned to being a slave. Although Lafayette wrote a letter urging Armistead's freedom, it was not until 1786 that the Virginia General Assembly intervened and granted it. Armistead later showed his appreciation for being freed from slavery by adopting the name of the famous Frenchman, "Marquis de Lafayette." (5)

✪
A Black Hero at Bunker Hill

Although the black race was itself enslaved, free blacks fought and died to help America's white colonists win their freedom. Peter Salem, of Framingham,

Massachusetts, along with several other free black men, were among the Minutemen who launched the Revolutionary War at the Concord Bridge in April, 1775.

A couple of months later, in June, at Bunker Hill, Peter Salem fired the fatal shot that killed the British Commander, Major Pitcairn. Salem continued his efforts to free the nation from British rule, fighting in the battles of Saratoga and Stoney Point. Free blacks joined the revolutionary struggle to seek dual freedoms; first for the new nation, then for themselves and other members of the black race.

They hoped that helping the white colonists win their freedom from British economic bondage would translate into freedom for the black race. They helped to win America's independence, but black freedom did not come with the victory. (6)

✪
Blacks Betrayed in Revolutionary War

In November, 1775, Lord Dunsmore, the British royal governor of Virginia, proclaimed that all slaves "able and willing to bear arms" for the British would be liberated. The free blacks who followed Dunsmore were tricked. In fact, the British treated slaves as captured property, shipping a few of them to freedom in Canada, but most were reassigned into slavery in the British West Indies.

Some were returned to the British colony of Sierra Leone in West Africa. A few escaped from bondage in the confusion of war and migrated to either Canada or Florida as free people. About 5,000 blacks served in the British Army and Navy in non-combat status. In the end, a British promise of freedom for all, in fact, was freedom for a very few.(7)

✪
Black Politicians: A Rare Breed

The first black caucus came into existence in Congress during the Reconstruction Period of 1871 through 1876. They came with high visibility, but only in rare instances were black elected officials ever in charge of or in control of anything of importance within local, state or federal offices. Blacks were effectively shorn of real political power, and as a relegated labor class, they remained at the mercy of the ruling white power structure. But, their faith in the national political parties remained strong. From the 41st Congress through the 44th (1869-1877), a total of 14 blacks were at various times members of the U.S. House of Representatives. They were from South Carolina, Georgia, Mississippi, Florida, Alabama, North Carolina and Louisiana. There were two blacks in the U.S. Senate, a governor, and a commissioner of education. They were all members of the party of Lincoln, Republicans. Lacking an economic base, their election was more form than substance.

For all intents and purposes, their tenure ended with Reconstruction. During their short period in office, they were blamed for everything that was wrong in government even though whites held the reins of power, from Congress to the lowest local positions in county seats.

Long before the end of the 19th century, northern whites had abandoned blacks. Southern whites picked up the hint and began to use legal and extra-legal means to run blacks out of politics. With limited experience, resources and training, blacks on the whole actively fought for progressive legislation for their people. But, like the dinosaur, they disappeared.

In 1931, "Negroes" returned to the United States Congress after an absence of 30 years and for the first time since the end of Reconstruction. The Representatives were Oscar DePriest of Chicago, 1931-35; Arthur Mitchell of Chicago, 1935-43; and William L. Dawson of Chicago. There were two other Congressional Democrats, Adam Clayton Powell of New York and Charles Diggs of Detroit. They were flamboyant personalities, outspoken advocates for black people, who had little power to bring about significant changes, but boldly challenged the system.(8)

❂
Blacks: America's Most Patriotic

America's behavior has been oxymoronic when it comes to black slavery, Jim Crowism and structural racism. The dominant society systematically oppressed blacks at the same time it encouraged black people to be their loyal, patriotic protectors.

Since the founding colonies, blacks have defended this country from American Indians, various European, Asian, and Spanish nations. Some of the more notable conflicts were wars with the British, French, Germans, Italians, Japanese, Chinese, Russians, Koreans, Cambodians, Vietnamese, Canadians, Cubans, and Mexicans. Blacks willingly fought and died to get freedom for a never-ending influx of immigrants into America.

White society's need for blacks in its defense has evolved through a complete 360 degree cycle. As early as 1642, before they were officially enslaved, blacks were called upon to join the militia and defend white settlements against Indian attacks. At the same time, every colony and state enacted laws that prohibited blacks from arming and protecting themselves. Fear of black slave revolts, especially through joining forces with American Indians, prompted whites in the 1790s to impose a national immigration law that set a zero quota on blacks and a law that barred blacks from the army. Black Americans are the only racial and ethnic group that has fought in every major military conflict and whose mother country has never engaged in a military battle against this nation. No European, Asian, Hispanic nor Native Americans can make such a claim.

The British government was well aware of the hypocrisy that existed in America between the colonies' cry for freedom and their cry to maintain the enslavement of blacks. Some military commanders openly advocated a black slave revolt against the white colonies. The fact that blacks made up approximately 34 percent of the national population and as high as 65 percent of the population of Georgia and South Carolina, colonial whites feared enslaved blacks would revolt and join either the British army or the Indians.

When George Washington took command of the Continental Army, he insisted that slaves not be allowed to serve. He feared that arming the slaves would lead to conspiracies and insurrections. A national policy was established that prohibited blacks from routine military service until mid-1860 and the Civil War. After the war was over, blacks were again excluded from the nation's military forces by a national public policy that lasted until the mid-1940s.(9)

12
Runaways and Hideaways
You can run, but you can't hide.

Mini Facts

• *The first recorded slave revolt in North America occurred in 1526. Black Africans escaped from Spanish explorers on the coast of the Carolinas and sought refuge with Indians further inland.*

• *In 1788, the **Negro Union** in Newport, Rhode Island, called for free African Americans to emigrate to Africa, a position the Philadelphia Free African Society opposed.*

• *In 1825, Josiah Henson, the alleged model for Harriett Beecher Stowe's character "Uncle Tom," led a group of runaway slaves from Maryland to Kentucky, then to freedom in Canada.*

• *Following the Red Summer riots of 1919, in which hundreds of blacks were lynched or killed across the nation, more than a million blacks began migrating North to the Urban Promised Land.*

✪
The Grapevine: A Black Man's Telegraph

Black enslavement depended to a large degree upon white society's ability to keep blacks divided, uneducated and uninformed. To this end nearly every level of government enacted laws and policies to keep blacks in darkness and impede their ability to communicate.

Policies and laws that prevented blacks from communicating were rigidly enforced in the South where approximately 95 percent of all blacks in America lived until the beginning of the 20th century. Neither free nor enslaved blacks could work around or operate a printing press, beat on drums, use signal mirrors, read certain publications or newspapers, nor visit a library in southern states. To get around these impediments, blacks developed a grapevine or slave communication system. They broadcast important news by back-door whispers, through dances, in work song lyrics, and in religious sermons.

You can run, but you can't hide. Information often times moved so fast that the grapevine was likened to a telegraph system, especially when "the word" was about the underground railroad that carried blacks North to freedom. Bold and committed ex-slaves like Harriet Tubman and Sojourner Truth, who sneaked into the South on a regular basis and led slaves to freedom, depended upon the grapevine for reliable and current information. (1) Blacks published their first newspaper in the 1830s. But until the present time, they remain only weekly papers. Blacks remain dependent upon white forms of media in order to communicate with other blacks.

❂

The Destruction of Fort Negro

North Florida was just a few miles away from the slave plantations in Georgia and Alabama. Many black slaves ran away from southern plantations to sanctuary in Florida, which was Spanish territory. In Florida, blacks joined the Seminole Indians or created their own black communities. More than 300 slaves made a home in an abandoned British fort on the Apalachicola River in north Florida.

Under the leadership of an African black man named Garcia, the abandoned building became known as Fort Negro. Although the fort was a heavily armed and independent community in Spanish territory, it became a haven for runaway slaves and a threat to the slavery system in America. Slaveholders pressured the United States government to use its forces to destroy the fort.

The government made the destruction of Fort Negro a high priority in 1816 and sent the Navy and the Army up the Apalachicola River to attack the fort.

When called upon to surrender, Garcia refused even though the fort was primarily filled with women and children. The runaway slaves repelled the first attack on July 17, 1816. The Navy began the second attack with cannon bombardments.

One of the hot cannon balls rolled into the fort's magazine and set off an explosion that killed nearly 250 of the black inhabitants. Garcia escaped injury but was killed by a firing squad and the rest of the survivors were returned to slavery in the United States. (2)

❂

It Paid to Advertise

Throughout the slavery period, slaveowners and catchers routinely ran newspaper advertisement for black men, women and children who had run away. Under the various fugitive slave acts, all the advertisements or posters for runaways offered some kind of remuneration. Black runaways were money-making godsends for poor whites and Indians. Urban areas offered white slave catchers the opportunity to earn hundreds of dollars. In many instances, they would pick up free blacks, claim they were slaves and sell them for the full market value of a slave or simply collect the reward offered for a particular slave. Typically, Indians worked the wooded or uninhabitable areas. They were paid $20 for tracking or recapturing a black runaway unless their treaty with the federal government specifically stated a greater amount.

In addition to offering rewards for the capture, holding, or return of a slave, the ads described the slave's general features such as sex, age, height, weight, clothing, hair, speech, and skin color. Since most blacks were thought "to all look alike," it was equally as important to include distinctive features, unusual skills, habits or body mutilations and scars in poster descriptions.

The reward posters or advertisements themselves revealed a lot about the slaveowners, and often included details of how the slave had been treated. The ads alluded to missing body parts that slaveholders took credit for causing. Posters contained such statements as, "He has deep scars on his back that I inflicted with the lash," or an "R branded on the face from previous escapes."

One of the most bizarre and determined efforts to recapture a runaway slave occurred near Richmond, Virginia in the 1800s. The white slaveholder offered a reward for the return of this black slave who could easily be recognized by the fact that both legs had been previously amputated. (3)

❁

A Slave Takes a Chance

Like many slaves, Gilbert Adams expressed his hatred for enslavement by running away from his white master. Adams knew that unless he was able to become a passenger in the underground railroad, the odds against him safely reaching freedom in the North were remote, and the penalties inflicted on a captured runaway could be severe.

Slave codes authorized every white citizen, and non-citizens such as other blacks and Indians, to make a citizens' arrest and return runaway slaves to their masters. Like so many runaway slaves, Adams was caught and imprisoned.

Prison conditions quickly convinced Adams that maybe slavery was not so bad after all. One day, as his old master, French Tilgman, was passing by the local prison, he heard a familiar voice call out to him for help. It was the voice of his runaway slave, Gilbert Adams. "Marse French! Marse French! Over here!" Adams cried. "For God's sake, get me out of here!" Master Tilgman was very surprised to see Adams who he thought was some place up North or in Canada. He thought he would never see Adams again. Sure enough, he got Adams out of jail. Then it was Master Tilgman's turn to surprise Gilbert Adams. He immediately sold him once again to a slave plantation in the Deep South, as punishment for having lost favor with his white master. This black slave's experience with his master gave rise to an expression that is still in use, "being sold down the river." (4)

❁

They Mailed Themselves to Freedom

Two black slaves took the United States Postal Service at their word that nothing, "rain, sleet nor snow shall stop the mail" from going through, and mailed themselves to freedom.

Engraving of the Box in which HENRY BOX BROWN escaped from slavery in Richmond, Va.

Henry Brown's escape. (Library of Congress)

In 1856, Henry Brown mailed himself from Richmond, Virginia to freedom in Philadelphia, Pennsylvania. It seems physically impossible for Brown's plan to have worked. He built a box 3 ft. long by 2 ft. wide by 2 ft. and eight inches deep and packed a jug of water, a few biscuits, and a pry-bar to open the box from the inside. He had his friend, James A. Smith, another slave, to address the box to the home of an abolitionist, William H. Johnson, on Philadelphia's Arch Street. To lessen the hardship of being locked in the box, in a fetal position, Brown marked the outside of the box

"Handle With Care" and "This Side Up," so that he would travel with his head up.

The postal service did not follow outside instructions to keep the box right side up. After traveling upside down in the box for 25 hours, Brown arrived in Philadelphia at Johnson's home. Johnson took the box to the office of the Anti-Slavery Society. After members of the society pried the top of the box open, Brown jumped up and said, "How do you do, gentlemen!"

In 1859, William Peel Jones used Henry "Box" Brown as a model in planning his escape from slavery in a box aboard a steamship from Baltimore, Maryland, to Philadelphia, Pennsylvania. Jones had a special reason to attempt his escape. His white master had confided that he was liquidating his assets and intended to sell Jones and other slaves as soon as possible. Like Henry Brown, Jones acquired a box for his escape. But, in his haste, he picked a box that was too small for him, even in a fetal position. He was forced to keep his legs folded in a painful position throughout his voyage. In addition to the pain of leg cramps and bruises from the cramped space, Jones was ill-clothed for the cold sea air and moisture that penetrated the box.

Jones was finally rescued when the boat reached Philadelphia by the same friends who had mailed him and traveled by land to be in Philadelphia when the box containing Jones arrived. Jones' pain and his friends' teamwork paid off when they opened the box and Jones was alive and free. (5)

✪

Railroad Conductor Finds Lost Brother

In 1850, two separated brothers of slave parents found each other in the office of the Philadelphia Anti-Slavery Society, a major depot for the Underground Railroad.

William Still was working as a clerk and conductor in the Philadelphia office when Peter, a newly-freed slave, walked in and requested assistance in locating his lost parents. Peter explained to Still, the clerk, how he would still be a slave in the South had not a kind white man taken an interest in him and purchased his freedom from a wretched Alabama slaveholder. Now that he was a free man, Peter said he was committed to finding his parents, Levin and Cidney, who had escaped from slavery years earlier, but were forced to leave him behind. Peter expressed the love that he still felt for his parents.

As Peter described his parents, Still was impressed because the parents' descriptions were so much like his own parents. By the end of Peter's story, Still knew that Peter's parents were also his parents and Peter was a brother that he never knew existed. At the end of Peter's story, Still joyously announced that he knew where the lost parents were because they were lost brothers. The Underground Railroad had done its job. It had brought together lost brothers and lost parents into a happy family at last. (6)

❂
A Runaway Couple Passes to Freedom

One of the boldest escapes planned by black slaves was that of William and Ellen Craft, a slave couple from Macon, Georgia. William, a skilled cabinetmaker, took advantage of his white master's "rent a slave" policy that allowed him to hire himself out for odd jobs. But unlike most slaves who sought to earn money to buy their freedom, William saved his money for an escape plan he had devised for his wife, Ellen, and himself. The couple used the money to purchase common male clothing for Ellen, a light-skinned quadroon who was to assume the role of an ailing slaveowner going North for medical treatment.

Since Ellen could not read nor write, she pretended to be hard of hearing so no one would converse with her, and she wore her right arm in a sling so she would not be asked to sign a hotel or steamboat register. William, a dark-skinned black, played the role of a loyal and faithful servant traveling as an aid to his invalid white master. For five days, the couple traveled through the slave states, always in first-class style, as would be expected of a prosperous planter. Finally, as their train pulled out of Baltimore and crossed the Mason-Dixon Line, the couple openly danced and jumped for joy that their plan had worked. Their slavery days were over. (7)

❂
The Underground Railroad?

Black slaves began escaping from their masters as soon as slavery was formally established in America. Unassisted escaping slaves, commonly called runaways, maroons, or fugitives, did not have pre-established paths to freedom. They generally headed out in any direction they believed would lead them away from their master's land. Escape routes typically led West, South and North, or any combination of these directions determined mostly by the runaway's ability to obtain food, shelter, and security.

An estimated 30,000 to 60,000 slaves out of a population of four million deserted slavery via the Underground Railroad between 1830 and 1860. It is also true that the Underground Railroad's effectiveness has been exaggerated. A lot of slaves escaped and did not use the Underground Railroad. It is telling, however, that most slaves chose to remain in bondage for life.

Although the term "Underground Railroad" first appeared in print in the early 1840s as a mechanism for assisting slaves to escape to the North, the phrase was used as early as 1804. General Thomas Boude, an officer in the Revolutionary War, purchased a slave, Stephen Smith, and took him to Columbia, Pennsylvania. Smith's mother later escaped and followed her son to Pennsylvania.

The Boudes took Smith's mother in just before she was tracked down by her white mistress and they refused to turn the black female over to her white mistress. In the minds of some historians, this incident was the beginning of the Underground Railroad, which later developed into an organized network of way-stations that helped slaves escape from the South to free states and as far north as Canada. The way-stations were mainly homes whose residents and helpers were free blacks as well as whites.

As the Underground Railroad increased in popularity, other railroad-like terminology was added. The escaping slaves were called passengers, the homes were shelters or stations, and those who guided them were conductors. Most of the credit for the success of the Underground Railroad was given to whites who participated in the slave-runaway system. The truth, however, is that free blacks of the North and South, as well as the slaves on the plantations who had the courage to seek freedom at a risk to their own lives, deserve the bulk of the credit. (8)

✪
Easy Come, Easy Go

Although the value of slaves was tied into stock market prices, value also depended upon the whims and fortunes of a given slaveholder. Slaves were acquired in an endless number of ways. They were usually bought and sold at slave auctions, but they were also inherited, won in lotteries, card games, fights, and court suits. Slaves were also given as birthday, wedding, or Christmas gifts.

But, like most things in life that come too easily, there often is little respect or appreciation for it.

Senator John Hammond of South Carolina was an enthusiastic slaveholder who acquired black slaves by hook or crook. In 1844, he wrote of two of his slave workers who had just died, saying, "Neither slave was a serious loss. One valuable mule also died." (9)

❂
Gottaway Clean

An unidentified Virginia slave made out so well in escaping from slavery that he wondered why he had not done it earlier. Having spent most of his life enslaved, he never envisioned himself free. On the spur of the moment while driving a Confederate wagon between hostile lines, he decided to escape to the North. Confederate guards saw him escaping across the battle lines but could not stop him. The black slave was totally surprised by the success of his escape.

He was even more surprised and pleased when a Union army paid him several hundred dollars for the mules and the wagon he had stolen from the Southern Confederate army in his escape. (10)

13
Civil War and Reconstruction
Life has its own rewards and penalties.

Mini Facts

• *In 1859, nearly all whites and blacks in New England could read and write, while more than 20 percent of southern whites could not.*

• *In 1860, on the eve of the Civil War, a national report indicated that had Northerners voted to abolish slavery, probably no more than two percent would have done so.*

• *In 1861, the Secretary of the Navy stipulated blacks could enter the Navy, but they could achieve no higher rank than "boys," at a compensation of $10 per month and one day's ration.*

• *In 1860, black Americans owned and controlled approximately one-half of one percent of the nation's wealth. By 1990, blacks owned and control one and one-half percent of the nations wealth.*

❂
A Round Three With England?

Even though England and America had gone to war on two previous occasions, England was prepared to intervene in the American Civil War of the 1860s on the side of the Southern Confederacy. Like the American South, England profited economically and politically from black enslavement. International slavery, in general, and cash products from the American South had fueled England's industrial revolution in the 1790s. By the 1860s, the annual sales of slave-produced cotton generated more than $30 billion for England's cotton goods retail industry. An attack on slavery in America's South, therefore, was a threat to England's economic base, its textile industry.

Historians rarely, if ever, point out that up until the Civil War, the South functioned as a wholly independent nation in international trade. The firing on Fort Sumter had international economic repercussions. The Lincoln administration's greatest fear in foreign affairs was that European nations, but especially Britain, would extend diplomatic recognition to the Southern Confederacy. Britain's recognition of the South would have legitimized secession from the Union and undermined the U.S. Constitution. Intervention would have inevitably led to another British-American war. The prime minister, Lord Palmerston, who bore the ultimate responsibility for any decision to intervene into the American Civil War, insisted that Great Britain wait until a decisive Southern Confederacy victory over the Northern Union forces occurred, then they would jump in. The Prime Minister felt that on the heels of a defeat, the Northern Union could most easily be convinced to leave slavery and the Southern Confederacy alone. But, the key Confederate military victory that Britain was looking for never came. And neither did the third war between England and America. (1)

❂
Slavery Divided Families and the Nation

The Civil War is often referred to as the Great Dividing War. Although symbolically it was fought to preserve the Union, in reality it was fought to preserve slavery. Without slavery there would have been no resort to arms between the North and South. And the various racial, political, economic and familial divisions that split and threatened the viability of the nation and its families would not have occurred.

It was President Abraham Lincoln who said that a house divided against itself would not stand. He could have been speaking about his own household.

The Civil War reached inside the White House and touched Lincoln's family, the First Family of this nation, and divided it as it divided the nation itself, along lines of Union versus Confederacy.

The division within the Lincoln household became so great that the United States Senate Committee on the Conduct of the War felt it had to deal with it was a national issue. The committee met to consider charges of treason against the President's wife, Mary Lincoln. Lincoln came to her rescue and read a brief statement denying that any member of his family had collaborated with the enemy.

Four of Lincoln's brothers-in-law wore Confederate uniforms. One of them, Lieutenant David P. Todd, was charged with brutality against Union soldiers held as prisoners of war in Richmond, Virginia. Mary Lincoln's two sisters were married to Confederate officers, while her brother, Dr. George Todd, was a volunteer Confederate surgeon who called Lincoln an "unhung scoundrel." (2)

❂

Nation's Richest Were First Draft Dodgers

The first military draft by the federal government, called the Enrollment Act, began in 1863, one year after the Confederate draft. The act required all men between the ages of 18 and 45 to register with local militia units and be available for national service. There was an immediate negative reaction to the draft act. First, because the act exempted men in certain occupations, and those with physical disabilities or the ability to pay $300 for a substitute to stand-in for them. As with the most recent drafts, this exemption allowed wealthy persons to stay home and profit from the Civil War.

Those who protested the draft the loudest included J.P. Morgan, who soon became America's wealthiest man; Andrew Carnegie, not far behind Morgan; future President Grover Cleveland, then a young aspiring attorney; and the well-to-do fathers of Teddy and Franklin D. Roosevelt. These were but a few of the thousands who sat out the Civil War by paying others to go in their places. Since neither rich nor poor whites were willing to fight for freedom for black people, the cause of the war shifted from slavery to "preserving the Union."

The indifference to the plight and well-being of black people was a sad indictment of majority society. Even though blacks were the only racial or ethnic group who had fought in every major national conflict to gain and insure freedom for white Americans, and whose mother country had never been at war with this nation, the greater number of northern whites did not and would not fight a war for black freedom.

They bitterly resented the draft law and by the summer of 1863, angry protests and outbreaks of violence had occurred in every northern state. The headlines in one Pennsylvania paper read, "Willing to fight for Uncle Sam but Not for Uncle Sambo." Instead of fighting Confederate soldiers, Northerners turned on innocent and defenseless free blacks, killing hundreds of them. According to written reports, many blacks were literally butchered. White draft rioters looted businesses, killed and terrorized blacks for nearly a full week, before troops from West Point and Gettysberg battlefield arrived and restored calm. (3)

✪

The Truth About Grant?

Even though he was a modest and self-effacing man, General Ulysses Grant of the Union Army generated a lot of gossip. Rumors charged Grant with being an anti-semitic, drunkard and slaveholder who used the government for nepotism. Some of the charges were true, some were not. It is true that in 1862, he ordered all Jews expelled form the U.S. Department of the Treasury within twenty-four hours for "violating every regulation of trade and Department orders." It was true that he used government to bestow favors on his own family. He gave federal positions to 13 members of his family.

In racial matters, another accusation was true. Grant was a slaveholder who had voted for the southern Democratic ticket and had married into a pro-southern family.

In 1858 General Grant bought a mulatto slave, William Jones, 35 years of age, but gave him his freedom a year later even though he could have sold Jones and recaptured his investment. Further, in hopes of holding the Union together, Grant did vote for Buchanan, on the Southern Democratic ticket.

Grant is equally guilty of the last accusation. He, in fact, did marry Julia Dent of St. Louis, who owned at least three slaves; her family was pro-southern. Grant differed sharply with his father-in-law on slavery, and before the war, returned his wife's slaves to her family. Although guilty on all three counts,

General Grant did demonstrate concern for the humanity of black people and personally rejected their enslavement. (4)

⊛

A Lynching That Backfired

Whites demonstrated their life and death control over blacks through cruel and excessive punishment of slaves, especially the lynchings of black men. Up until the late 1930s, at least one black man was reportedly lynched every day in the year, most charged with "raping" a white woman. The word rape was broad and ambiguous. It included any and everything from sexual contact to "reckless eyeballing." Under the stringent social sanctions of black enslavement and Jim Crow segregation, there are few accounts in available records that show black men attacking or raping white women. With black men so vulnerable and suspect, it made little sense for a black man to approach a white woman for sex.

However, on at least one historical occasion, both the Union and Confederate armies used a charge of rape against a black male as a major wartime propaganda effort. On June 20, 1864, the Union Army hanged a black man, who had been charged with raping a white woman. He was hanged within plain view of the Confederate lines near Petersburg, Virginia. The Union purpose for lynching the black man in front of southern white males was to convince them that black males who touch white women would be severely and swiftly dealt with, even in the North if it won the war.

The plan backfired, and the Confederacy, which had been losing thousands of runaway black slave laborers, cleverly turned the incident to the advantage of the South.

The Confederacy marched hundreds of black slaves past the "lynching spot," pointing out just how inhumane northern white males were, how they were just as bad, if not worse than southern white males. Further, the Confederacy warned slaves that should they run off to the North, they would surely be lynched, just as white northerners had lynched the unfortunate black charged with rape.

Shortly thereafter, nighttime slave escapes and runaways all but ceased on that war front. (5)

❂
Free Blacks Wanted to Fight

Even though a 1792 law barred blacks from military service, the Union would not have won the war without the aid and involvement of blacks. White fears of arming blacks kept them out of uniform for the first year despite the eagerness of thousand of free blacks to enlist.

In April, 1861, the first blacks were appointed commissioned officers in the Civil War by the Confederacy in Louisiana. By war's end, 93,000 blacks served in the Confederate Army.

However, in August 1862, the Union's need for more manpower dictated a need for a new public policy on blacks in the military. Frederick Douglas and other prominent blacks petitioned the Union government to give blacks a chance to fight for their own freedom, even though that was not what the war was about. About 200,000 blacks fought in the Union Army and more than 65,000 were killed. There were 30,000 blacks in the Union Navy, about a quarter of the total number of sailors. Blacks in blue took part in 499 military engagements, 39 of which were major battles One of the first to act was Edwin M. Stanton, Secretary of War, who authorized the military government to enlist black ex-slaves in South Carolina. After the Emancipation Proclamation of 1863 authorized enlisting blacks, the governor of Massachusetts moved to organize a black regiment, the famous Massachusetts 54th. Swiftly thereafter, other states began to recruit black soldiers, and in May, 1863, the federal government established a Bureau of Colored Troops to supervise their enlistment. By the end of the war, one soldier in eight in the Union army was black. (6)

❂
A White Soldier's Poem About a Black Soldier

Private Miles O'Reilly, a white soldier, wrote this poem about black slaves joining the Civil War.

"Sambo As a Soldier"
Some tell us it's a burning shame

To make the naygiers fight;
 And that the trade of being kilt
Belongs but to the White;
But as for me, upon my scowl,
So liberal are we here,
I'll let Sambo be murdered in place of myself
On every day of the year.
So hear me all, boys, darlings
Don't think I'm tipping you chaff,
The right to be kilt, I'll divide wid him,
And give him the largest half. (7)

⊛
Why the North Won the War

The Union won the Civil War primarily because it had the industries, soldiers, technology and a centralized form of government. But, to their credit, the Southern Confederacy nearly won the war because the South had a greater concentration of wealth, trained military leaders and millions of unpaid slave workers whose labor provided food, military supplies, and supportive care for unattended white families and farms.

The presence of five million slaves in the South during the war was a knife that cut two ways. A small number of slaves refused to assist the South, choosing instead to organize and become a subversive force within the "belly" of the Confederacy. Thousands of black slaves crippled the South by serving as spies, saboteurs and guerrilla forces for the North.

Runaway slaves left fields and homes in the South unattended. What may have been more injurious was the fact that a large percentage of them joined and fought with the Union Army. They were not only soldiers but served as construction workers, cooks, personal servants, woodcutters, teamsters, and skilled craftsmen.

By the end of the Civil War, more than 200,000 black men had formally fought in the Union Army to defeat the Old Confederacy. (8)

✪
A Black's Post-Civil War Poem

We ain't what we oughta be;
We ain't what we wanna be;
We ain't what we gonna be;
But thank God,
We ain't what we use to be!
(Source: Unkown)

✪
Until Death Do Us Part

While President Lincoln was reluctantly and belatedly facing up to his oblig-ation to free America's black people from bondage, at least one Confederate leader freed the slaves that he personally owned.

On December 21, 1861, General Robert E. Lee, the commander-in-chief of the Confederate armed forces, instructed his wife in a letter to free any of his 63 slaves who wanted to be free upon his death. Lee's plantation was converted into the Arlington National Cemetery to both punish the South and to ensure the land could never again be used for slavery. The land of Lee's co-compatriot, Jefferson Davis, met a similar fate.

Following the South's loss of the Civil War, Jefferson Davis, who had been President of the Confederacy, was sent to a Union prison. Since the war had depleted his finances, Davis was forced to sell his plantation for $300,000 to Benjamin T. Montgomery, one of his former black slaves. Unfortunately, the old public policy of selling to blacks "on credit only," caught up with Montgomery. Southern whites began establishing Farmer Alliances in the late 1860s that excluded black farmers from banking development funds, product distribution systems, and marketing opportunities. After 15 years of payments, Montgomery, like thousands of other black farmers, lost his revenue base and ability to make mortgage payments. Davis' plantation then reverted into the hands of his family where it was converted into a museum. (9)

❂

Slavery Wealth Hidden On Wall Street

The Civil War allowed the origins of this nation's wealth to be transformed and hidden. It moved from South to North. From owning slaves to owning land. From investing in the institution of slavery to investing in Wall Street stocks and bonds. Prior to the Civil War, nearly all businesses were directly or indirectly selling products and goods produced by slavery. The nation's textile, tobacco, shipping, insurance, cotton, sugar, iron works, building, furniture, and agricultural industries thrived off slavery. Wall Street commodities were linked to and fluctuated with the rising and falling values of slaves. In the 1840s, there were only one or two millionaires. John Astor, with $16 million, one-fifth of the nation's wealth, was the richest man in America. He derived his $16 million wealth from businesses that profited from slavery.

The Civil War generated a rush of millionaires. Merchants who were able to sell slave-produced items, especially food, clothing, military supplies and weapons reaped fantastic profits from government contracts. Others made fortunes from the war over slavery by selling abroad. For instance, the "king and queen" of commodities, of course, remained cotton and tobacco. On the eve of the Civil War, England purchased approximately one billion pounds from the South. While the Civil War had depressed cotton prices in the South to a low of .03 cent per pound, cotton industries in England paid as much as .48 cents per pound for cotton. This sale produced approximately $500 for every white person in America. After the Union Navy began to blockade southern ports and harbors, the profit on 1,000 bales of cotton, with a "fast delivery" (that is, within two weeks), in one instance was about $250,000.

After the Civil War, the wealth was shifted into northern factories to profit from the pending industrial revolution. The U.S. government gave millions of acres of land to the newly-arriving European immigrants and the privately-owned railroads. The Baltimore and Ohio Railroad received free land that was the equivalent of the size of the state of Texas. Within a few decades, railroads and their stock exchanges had sold nearly all of it at an average price of $22 per acre. The Civil War produced new multimillionaires like the Vanderbilts and Carnegies. Their newly-acquired wealth was reinvested in railroads, shipping, oil, land, and Wall Street stocks. Slavery and cotton were no longer investment "kings."(10)

○

Lincoln Didn't Free Slaves

Historical facts suggest President Lincoln was everything but "the great emancipator of black slaves." During the earlier years of the Civil War, President Lincoln publicly claimed he would not and could not free black slaves. He even acknowledged that the Civil War was not about black people, but about national unity.

Lincoln was not passive in his support of slavery even when Union commanders issued orders freeing slaves in captured Confederate territory. Lincoln blocked such orders at least twice. Lincoln's position was strengthened by the U.S. Congress in 1861, when it passed and referred to the states in an amendment to the Constitution that guaranteed that Congress could never abolish black slavery in America. Few northern politicians had any interest in freeing black slaves. They were concerned about breaking the wealth and political power base of the South.

Most politicians knew that Lincoln's Emancipation Proclamation was a sham. Lincoln was President of the Union only. He could not and did not free black slaves. The Emancipation Proclamation spoke gloriously about freeing slaves in the deep South, over which the Union had no authority. Yet, it ignored blacks in the border states over which Lincoln did have authority. The attitude of Lincoln and his administration was succinctly put in Lincoln's letter of December 22, 1860, to Alexander Stephen, soon to become Vice-President of the Confederacy, "Do the people of the South really entertain fears that a Republican administration would, directly or indirectly, interfere with the slave, or with them, about the slaves? If they do, I wish to assure you, as once a friend, and still, I hope, not an enemy, that there is no more danger in this respect than it was in the days of Washington."

Even the British press regarded the Emancipation Proclamation as sheer hypocrisy. *The Times of London* sarcastically remarked that Lincoln considered himself "a sort of moral American Pope. Where he has no power, Mr. Lincoln will set the Negroes free; where he retains power he will consider them as slaves. Lincoln died holding the same views about blacks that he held firmly throughout his public life. (11)

❂

The Great Emancipator's Sick Joke

There is an old adage that whatever a man jokes about is what he truly feels in his heart. If there is any truth in this saying, it speaks poorly for President Abraham Lincoln. After Elijah Lovejoy, an anti-slavery editor had been killed by pro-slavery forces, Lincoln made a joke out of his death. In a speech in Worchester, Massachusetts, he said, "I have heard you have abolitionists here. We have a few in Illinois and we shot one the other day." The crowd roared with laughter. But, on the serious side, many of Lincoln's formal statements revealed he held no love for blacks, free or enslaved. (12)

❂

Douglas Attacked by Mob

During the Civil War, free blacks did not have the right to assemble and protest even in the North. On December 3, 1861 a pro-slavery white mob attacked a black rally in Boston organized by black activist, Frederick Douglas, in honor and memory of abolitionist John Brown. Brown had been executed by the federal government for his raid on Harpers Ferry, Virginia, attempting to seize weapons and free black slaves. Rather than protecting Douglas and his supporters from the white mob, the local police joined the attacking mob and broke up the rally. (13)

❂

Blacks Excluded From Civil War
Grand Military Review

On May 23, 1865, in Washington, D.C., the Union Army celebrated its Civil War victory over the South with the largest parade in the nation's history. It was called the Grand Review. Attending this historical occasion was President Andrew Johnson, Edwin Stanton, the Secretary of War, and all the top military officers including Generals Ulysses S. Grant, William T. Sherman, and Charles Wainwright.

Thousands of spectators gathered to watch a massive parade of all the Union troops in service at the end of the Civil War, with one exception. The more than 200,000 black soldiers and sailors were not recognized. The black Union regiments, some of which had fought substantially longer than the white units on parade, were intentionally excluded from the victory parade. *The Philadelphia Inquirer* explained their absence saying, "They [blacks] can afford to wait... Their time will come." The few blacks who did march in the parade were made to appear ridiculous. They paraded as the "pick and shovel" brigade to provide comic relief. For example, two large black soldiers dressed in colors rode small mules, so their feet dragged the ground. They drew laughter from President Johnson and the crowd.

In the Grand parade, neither the former black slaves nor free soldiers were to be depicted as heroes. Their exclusion signaled a clear message about the kind of Union the white veterans felt they had preserved. With the South back in the Union, white soldiers being honored and black ex-slaves providing the entertainment, the Grand Review was the visual embodiment of a reunited America. (14)

Ex-Slaves Entered Politics

Although a number of blacks became elected officials in high offices within five years of slavery, their political presence was deceiving in terms of their power, responsibilities, and the effect they had on the quality of life for blacks. They lacked a critical mass, influence and respect. Even though blacks were the dominant population in a number of southern states, none were ever elected governor. Fewer than a dozen served in Congress. Most were in state legislatures and held minor local offices such as constable, sheriff, and postal worker.

Black elected officials were unable to compete with white officials because they lacked education, were poor and politically unsophisticated. The social political climate also "kept them in their place." The majority of black elected officials came from the ranks of slaves who had been house servants or artisans, not field hands. Consequently, mulatto politicians were disproportionately numerous, and as a group, provided more conservative, non-threatening leadership for the race.

Regardless of their skin complexion, nearly all elected blacks surrendered the decision-making to whites in the belief that "whites could govern best because they were better equipped." Even though blacks had left the decision-making and control of resources in the hands of whites, after Reconstruction "failed," black elected officials were blamed and ridiculed by southern whites who took government back by the late 1890s. (15)

✪

Reparations for Slaveholders?

Abraham Lincoln was growing increasingly sensitive to and fearful of, the divisive and explosive issue of slavery. Early in the first term of his presidency, Lincoln offered reparations to southern slaveholders. Lincoln devised a scheme to free the slaves gradually over a period of some 30 years. He would offer reparations to the southern slaveholders and pay them for their "losses" out of the national treasury. To carry out his plan, he needed the approval of Congress to pay southern slaveholders nearly a half billion dollars, only a portion of their total $7 billion investment. This was an unimaginable amount of money for that period in history.

The federal government could not afford to compensate slaveholders to release their slaves. All the capital investments in the North, South, and the West together would not have been enough to cover the costs of reparations to southern slaveholders. Northern industrialists were another glitch. They were not interested in compensating southern slaveholders for their investments. They and northern politicians would not support reparations because they wanted to reduce the South's plutocratic control of the national government. The proposed reparations plan for slaveholders exceeded the total federal budget of $50 million and all the businesses in America combined. Of course it never happened. Congress denied the President's request.

14
Sports and Entertainment

Dominate in business wherever you dominate in population.

Mini Facts

• *In 1799, Gottlieb Graupner, a German immigrant who later founded the Boston Philharmonic Society, performed one of the early racist minstrel shows with blackface and southern dialect.*

• *On May 1, 1884, Moses Fleetwood Walker became the first black to join the all-white American Baseball Association. One year later, Frank Thompson, a black man, organized the first all-black baseball team, the Cuban Giants.*

• *In 1971, Leroy Robert "Satchel" Paige, the first black pitcher in the American League and to pitch in a World Series, became the first black to be elected to the Baseball Hall of Fame.*

• *On February 12, 1900, James Weldon Johnson and his brother wrote and introduced their Negro National Anthem, Lift Every Voice and Sing, at Lincoln's Birthday Celebration.*

• *In 1915, The Lincoln Motion Picture Company was founded in Los Angeles, California. Lincoln and Norman Productions in Jacksonville, Florida were the first black movie companies.*

✪

A World Dominated by Blackness

Like the rest of the world, from its inception, American society has been preoccupied with acting and reacting to the presence or absence of black people.

After centuries of wars and political movements, the world has gone "color-blind," pretending that blacks no longer exist. Yet, their notable visibility in our culture keeps us fixated. For examples: from 1850s -1930s, minstrel shows were the dominant form of popular entertainment; the longest running play ever was *Uncle Tom's Cabin*, about black slavery; the first American epic motion picture was *Birth of a Nation*, about a black rapist; the first talkie movie was *The Jazz Singer*, about a blackface singer; the biggest blockbuster movie was *Gone with the Wind*, about a fight for black freedom; the most popular radio show of all times was *Amos n' Andy*, with blackface comedians; the most popular television series ever was *Roots*, about black history; the basis of America's only true art-forms are black music, black dance and black slang; and black athletes have dominated many sports for more than a century. (1)

✪

Black Film Studios Tried to Compete

In 1914, on the eve of World War I, forward looking black business persons had entered the movie production industry. An independent black film company released its first movie, *Darktown Jubilee*, starring Bert Williams, an African-American comic. During the same period, whites were showing D.W. Griffin's, *A Birth of a Nation*, a movie that precipitated racial confrontations across the nation by portraying blacks in a negative manner and glorifying the Ku Klux Klan.

Birth of a Nation included an incendiary rape episode between a black man and white woman, and presented black people in such a derogatory light that it spawned a national anti-black backlash. The Ku Klux Klan, the Knights of the Camellia, the Black Horse Brigade and other white terrorist organizations arose. When the black movie *Darktown Jubilee*, which showed a black man in a positive and leading role, was shown in Brooklyn, New York, it was met with cat calls and boos from white audiences. The black producers had to take their film out of circulation for several years.

By 1918, blacks had established two national chains of movie theaters in black communities. The Lincoln and Lafayette theaters. Black film producers in Los Angeles, Chicago, New Jersey and Florida distributed their westerns, comedies, and religious movies through the black-owned theaters. These theaters showed black films, but were handicapped because white film distributors and producers withheld their movies from black theaters for as long as a year or more.

A billboard from a black film studio in Jacksonville, Florida. (Library of Congress)

There were not enough black-produced films to fill the black public's demand. Norman Film Productions, in Jacksonville, Florida, was a major film producer of black westerns, comedies, and mysteries. Oscar Micheaux, a pioneer filmmaker, produced and directed **Birthright** (in the 1920s), the first full-length black film. He became one of the most successful black filmmakers. His film company, Oscar Micheaux Corporation, located in Illinois, made more than 30 movies, including a film of his novel, the **Homesteader** and **Body and Soul**, in which Paul Robeson made his debut.

Micheaux made many low-budget films for the black movie circuit and sold stock shares in his company to blacks across the nation. He made his last film in 1948. (2)

⚙ Black Music Producers

Even though black music is the foundation of white music, more commonly called popular music, few blacks have ever established and maintained successful commercial businesses producing and marketing black music. Berry Gordy founded Motown Records in Detroit, Michigan, in the late 1950s and was the premier promoter of black music before he sold his interest in the 1970s.

Undoubtedly the most successful, Gordy was not the first African-American record producer of black music. As early as 1921, Harry Pace formed the Pace Phonographic Corporation, which issued records on the Black Swan label. His label featured blacks performing classical music, blues, spirituals, and instrumental solos, with such hits as *Down Home Blues* and *Oh, Daddy* sung by Ethel Waters. Even though society operated under a "separate but equal" public policy on race, white record producers sought to control both white and black record markets. White competition for manufacturing and selling black music to black listeners forced Pace to sell his business to Paramount Records, a white-owned company, in the 1920s. (3)

⚙ The Birth of Ragtime Music

Beginning at the turn of the century, ragtime music evolved and was spread throughout the country by black itinerant pianists. Ragtime music represented a blending of West African rhythms and European musical forms.

It appears to have originated in the Midwest around St. Louis. White musicians adjusted their styles and played the music for white audiences. Ragtime developed about the same time as jazz emerged in New Orleans. The styles were somewhat separate and did not merge for about 20 years. Scott Joplin, a black with classical training, was the greatest composer of ragtime. Attempts were made to incorporate ragtime into the

European tradition. However, the rhythms were too complex and culturally different for most white traditional musicians to play. The music, however, survived and thrived on street corners and bars in black neighborhoods throughout the mid-south. Protected by the walls of segregation, only white musicians who lived with or were good at feeling the pains of "being black" played ragtime and jazz with the right feeling. (4)

❁
Whites Enjoyed Blacks In Sports

The distance between the cotton fields and the sports fields was short for blacks because they were thought of as brawn and no brain, like beasts in the field. As the elite, educated society, whites felt that blacks were more suitable for hard back-breaking work and, therefore, had physical advantages over whites.

On Sunday and special days, like New Years, Christmas or Easter, slaveowners enjoyed watching demonstrations of blacks' physical prowess in special sporting events. Blacks participated in various kind of sports or other contests to entertain or for personal profit for their masters or themselves. Some of the more popular sporting contests were wrestling, chopping or picking cotton, shooting marbles, pitching horseshoes, coon hunting, or foot racing against dogs and horses.

One of the most unusual sports for black males was "head butting." Two black male slaves would grab each other by the shoulder and violently bang heads until one was rendered unconscious or gave in. In Virginia, Albert Woods and Colleen Hedging were two slaves who were widely known for their head butting ability and endurance. Head butting champions typically displayed their head scars for recognition and respect. These head butting contests were the rare instances when it paid for a black man to be "hard headed." (5)

❁
Black Baseball's Beginning to End

In 1920, Andrew "Rube" Foster brought the various black baseball teams together into an association similar to the white leagues. Rube Foster had been involved in every aspect of the game, beginning when he was a small boy. He had little formal education. When he was old enough, he quit elementary school and became a professional baseball player. Foster soon learned that he was a better organizer and businessman than he was a professional baseball player. His greatest achievement came when he organized black baseball leagues for all the aspiring young baseball players and fans.

Pre-intergration black baseball team. (Library of Congress)

He became known as "the father of black baseball," and his National Association of Professional Baseball Clans became known as the Negro National League. As the first president of the league, Foster provided black players a place to play and investors with financial opportunities. The Negro National League initially included such teams as the Kansas City Monarchs, the Indianapolis ABC's, the Chicago American Giants, The Detroit Stars, The St. Louis Stars, and the Western Cuban All-Stars.

Black baseball was so popular with blacks that two separate leagues evolved. Each league had eight to nine teams, with approximately 20 players. These black-owned teams had black coaches, managers, physicians, support staffs, equipment, facilities and fields. Black baseball heroes were covered by black news media. They had higher attendance around the country than did white baseball teams. The heavy attendance was too lucrative to be ignored. Professional black baseball was thriving outside of mainstream professional baseball. Things had to change.

On April 10, 1947, Jackie Robinson broke the color-barrier when he left the Kansas City Monarchs to join the Brooklyn Dodgers, an all-white National League team. Although Moses Fleetwood Walker, a black man, had been a catcher in the American Baseball League in 1884, Jackie Robinson was the first black baseball player in modern baseball. He was an outstanding player and the first black player in the white Baseball Hall of Fame. Other black baseball players and fans followed Jackie to the white baseball leagues. Within a few years, black base -ball leagues and teams disappeared. Black America had traded away its baseball leagues, teams, hundreds of players, equipment, support staffs, buildings, and hundreds of thousands of fans just to get one black onto a white team. (6)

❂
Where and What Is Dixie?

There are at least two theories about the origin of that emotionally-charged term, "Dixie."

Some people believe the word was derived from the Mason-Dixon line that divides Pennsylvania from Maryland. Others suggest that "Dixie" originated from the $10 bill issued by Louisiana banks. The bill had the word "Dix," a French word for "ten," in each corner. Eventually, people in the area sought these "Dixies" and called the deep South, "Dixieland."

As a descriptive term for the whole South, Dixie really didn't catch on until 1859, when a song titled *Dixie* debuted at a minstrel show. It instantly became a favorite in the South.

Dixie is an ironic microcosm of black people's history in America. It was first sung publicly in Mechanics Hall in New York by a white minstrel performer, Dan Emmett, who many believe was the song's composer. However, other reputable sources claim *Dixie* was written by a black family. Charles Christian, in his book, *Black Saga*, and in a 1993 Smithsonian Institution publication, claimed authorship of the song was credited to a family of black musicians, the Snowdens, who lived in Mount Vernon, Ohio. The story goes that Dan Emmett learned the song from them.

The authorship debate surfaced when cemetery markers of Dan and Lew Snowden were discovered, inscribed with the statement, "They taught Dixie to Dan Emmett." Records show that the Snowdens wrote many songs for minstrel shows and that, in 1843, they passed their work on to a blackface minstrel troupe that often returned to Mount Vernon to visit relatives who lived next door to the Snowdens.

President Abraham Lincoln, the "Great Emancipator," had feelings for the song *Dixie*, that added another ironic twist to its history. On April 8, 1865, just as Lincoln was returning by boat from a tour of his Union Army camps below the fallen Confederate capital of Richmond, he asked a young French Count who was sitting beside him if the nobleman had ever heard the song. When the Count shook his head "no," Lincoln requested that the boat's band play the tune. Then he said to the Count, " The tune is now federal property, and it's good to show the southern rebels that with us in power, they will be free to hear it again. It has been a favorite of mine, and since we have captured it, we have a perfect right to enjoy it."

Whether it was a geographical location or a song, *Dixie* in every respect, played a divisive role in the lives of blacks and whites. For whites, the word "Dixie" personifies the good old magnolia days, when free or cheap black labor made life and "living so easy." For blacks, the word "Dixie," both the place and song, is a reminder of centuries of suffering, death, debasement and exploitation of their race at the hands of an oppressive majority group. *Dixie* is played to this present day at social, sporting, and political events throughout the South.(7)

❂
America's Only Real Art Form

Along with the fruits of their labor, black people gave America their greatest gifts and only true artform, black music and dance. Rooted in history, in the enslavement of people of Africa, the seeds of black music and dance crossed the Atlantic with the slave ships. Dancing and singing were not only the favorite pastime of slaves, but were also the most accessible vehicles of self-expression. Black musical expressions were a blend of "Africanisms," Protestant hymns, revival songs and emotional responses to an oppressive world of whiteness. Blacks developed a repertory of songs for all occasions and constantly improvised new ones. They made up spirituals for their religious expressions; work and folk songs to break the monotony of endless work; story songs to communicate with other blacks; blues to convey their sadness; rhythm for their joy, and jazz for their desolation and peace.

From the very beginning, whites were fascinated with the creative, rhythmic, uninhibited, sensuousness of blackness. Some pious whites condemned black music and dance as sinful. They called blues "race music." Jazz became a shortened label for "jack ass music." Ragtime was called "coon music." The gutsy cries and grunts in Rhythm and Blues was referred to as "soul music." What whites saw they liked. What they liked, they sought to imitate, manipulate and control for commercial markets. For centuries, black music, dance, slang and even comedy assimilated into mainstream "popular culture." Paradoxically, Rock and Roll, another name for black music, is a 100 billion dollar industry, from which black people derive less than one percent. Whites, not blacks, have franchised jazz and blues clubs across America. (8)

✪
The Origin of Tap Dance

Like music, blacks have demonstrated a genius for creating dances that the dominant society has learned and enjoyed for centuries. While most dances rise and fall with their popularity, tap is one dance that has remained popular through the years. William Henry "Juba" Love, considered the father of tap dancing, began performing in urban saloons as a teenager in the early 1840s. He combined European and African "jigs" with hand jive to produce tap, a dance form that was new to the minstrel stage. His hand jive was similar to an African stick dance in which the dancers performed intricate foot-stomping and hand clapping rhythms, and slapped sticks against their bodies. Love was praised for the dance innovations and the manner in which he beat time with his feet. At the height of his career in the late 1840s, he competed in a series of challenge dances with John Diamond, the greatest white minstrel dancer of the time. Love consistently won each contest. Love died in 1852 at the age of 27. (9)

15
Medicine and Education
The wasteful person is condemned.

Mini-Facts

• *Simon, a black man, was able to "bleed and draw teeth." This was the first written account of a black practicing dentistry which appeared in a Pennsylvania newspaper in 1740.*

• *In 1900, under its "separate but equal" policy, South Carolina's Department of Education was allocating $9 for a black child's education and $54 for a white child.*

• *On April 10, 1941, Dr. George Washington Carver, a black scientist at Tuskegee University gave the John Andrew Clinical Society a new drug to treat the gum disease, pyorrhea.*

• *In 1971, it was revealed that for more than 40 years, black men were used as guinea pigs in a federal government sponsored syphilis experiment at Tuskegee University.*

✪
On Being Black In America

Numerous sources, including the federal government's Centers for Disease Control reported in the 1980s that being black in America is hazardous to one's health. Being black in America means higher mortality rates, lower levels of education, lower levels of occupational status, lower income, lower levels of wealth, lower levels of health, poorer housing, fewer two-parent households, higher unemployment, greater contact with the criminal justice system and higher levels of marital disruption than the white population.

The report suggested that socioeconomic conditions among blacks, to a large degree, stemmed directly from the structural economic and social inequalities produced by centuries of slavery, Jim Crowism, and benign neglect. Since the black man is the primary target of racism, it is the report explains, in large measure, why black men are disproportionately burdened with health problems and the shortest life expectancy of any race or gender. (1)

❂

Myth Exposes Blacks to Yellow Fever

In 1793, an epidemic of yellow fever broke out in Philadelphia, Pennsylvania. The disease mystified most physicians who struggled to find a cure and stop the number of deaths growing in the white community.

Benjamin Rush, an eminent physician of that day, believed that blacks were immune to the disease. That myth would eventually kill many blacks. Dr. Rush had the city's mayor ask the Free African Society to supply black nurses and black men for burial duty. The Free African Society also believed the myth, and responded to the city's request for humanitarian aid. Hundreds of blacks volunteered. But, contrary to Dr. Rush's medical supposition, and the Free African Society's belief, hundreds of blacks who volunteered contracted yellow fever.

Unlike the white community, they did not have doctors, access to medical services, and most of them could not afford medical attention even if they had access, so most of the infected blacks died. After the epidemic passed, the City of Brotherly Love's interest in blacks also passed. Not only did the city fail to express its appreciation to the many blacks who responded to the crisis and sacrificed their own lives, one white newspaper writer even managed to turn the community against blacks with unfounded allegations that black volunteers had looted the possessions of the whites who had died.

Free blacks had answered white society's call for humanitarian assistance, but they received no brownie points for their behavior. The city's black population remained excluded and deprived. (2)

A Slave Prescribes Cure for VD

In the late 1700s, an unknown Virginia slave was credited with devising a cure for syphilis, a venereal disease unknown in Africa, but widespread in Europe.

Early in the 18th century, William Gooch, Governor of the Virginia Colony, wrote to the Bishop of London that he was shipping to England a box of "roots and barks" which, in equal quantity, being made into a concoction that was, in the colonies at least, "curing most venereal disease, especially syphilis."

Gooch wrote in his letter, "Here only mankind will be the better for what has been a secret in the hands of a black for many years in this country where he practiced with success, until I thought it worth my endeavor to get this concoction from him."

Typically, blacks who formulated medical cures for diseases, or what were thought to be cures, were eligible for meritorious manumission from slavery by either their masters or a grateful government. Records do not tell the ending of this story. (3)

Blacks Used as Guinea Pigs

The United States Public Health Service conducted a study of 412 black men in rural Macon County, Alabama, in the late 1930s which was called the "Tuskegee Syphilis Study." Some of the blacks were infected with syphilis when they entered the study, others were not. The government researchers wanted to study the effects of untreated syphilis.

For more than 30 years, public health officials pretended to treat the infected black men. Tons of reports, films and experiments were conducted, not to aid the blacks, but to record how the disease progressed and would ravish and destroy the human body. The black patients received neither new drug therapy nor those already in use in medical circles to treat the disease. Nearly 70 years later, no one has been punished for the crime against these black men and their families, nor has the federal government compensated the victims and their families.

The practice of using blacks as guinea pigs for medical research continued into the latter part of the 20th century. The federal government admitted that it used prisoners to test new drugs. In some instances, the prisoners were offered candy, money, and special privileges for voluntarily participating. Most of the prisoners were black and were simply "drafted" into the medical testing program.

In the 1950s, the United States Department of Energy and other federal agencies sprayed cities with large black populations, like Detroit, Michigan, to determine the impact of "certain chemicals" through airborne spraying. Neither the nature of the chemicals, purpose of the studies, nor the impact on blacks were ever fully disclosed to the public. In 1994, the U.S. Department of Energy at a Congressional hearing promised to make the studies public. They have yet to do so.

Many recent live black volunteers have come from the ranks of the homeless. On December 20, 1996, *The Washington Post* carried a story that described how Wishard Memorial Hospital at Indiana University was using homeless people in medical tests. Since the majority of the homeless population is black, it is reasonable to assume that blacks were the primary guinea pigs at Indiana University. Ironically, when informed of the circumstances, the federal government's National Institutes of Health (NIH) seemed more concerned that Indiana University did not have government approval to conduct human medical experiments for Eli Lilly and Company rather than the fact that the experiments were conducted at all. Apparently it was OK to do medical experiments on blacks so long as it was sanctioned by some level of government. (4)

❂

The First Inoculation Using Smallpox

An African was the first to introduce the practice of inoculations for smallpox. In 1721 a Boston slave named Onesimus instructed Cotton Mather, a noted clergyman of that period, about an inoculation technique that was used commonly in Africa. Mather tried the technique. In his journal he described how he injected infected fluid from a smallpox victim into the blood of an uninfected person and found that the second person became immune to the disease.

In order to overcome opposition from the medical profession, Mather wrote a pamphlet on the technique to show its African origin and effectiveness. He called his report, *An Account of the Medho and Success of Inoculating the Smallpox.* (5)

○

Tuskegee Study Revisited in Africa?

Even while suspicions and rumors continue to reverberate through black America that AIDS was intentionally introduced into the black race by World Health Organization experiments in Kenya, Africa, in the early 1980s, yet another medical study on blacks surfaced in 1997. According to an article in the *Wall Street Journal*, the NIH and the Center for Disease Control (CDC) are sponsoring research in Africa in which pregnant black women infected with HIV, the virus that causes AIDS, are treated with placebos, instead of actual medicine.

Researchers claim it is too expensive to give pregnant African mothers "real medicine," and have not used some of the drugs proven effective against the disease. Although such an experimental medical study would now be unethical in the United States, the researchers felt it was justified in Africa because: 1) African women gave their informal consent; 2) the research information may prove beneficial; 3) since the women would not be able to afford medical intervention anyway, they are no worse off receiving the "pretend" medicine; and 4) such studies are necessary to find affordable treatments for use in poor Third World countries. Government officials professed not to see the similarities between this study and the "infamous Tuskegee Syphilis Study." (6)

○

First Freedman Hospital

The first freedman hospital was built in the nation's slave capital, Washington, D.C. In 1868, O. O. Howard ordered the Freedmen's Hospital to be established at 5th and W Streets, N.W., in Washington. The purpose of the hospital was to serve the thousands of blacks who had migrated to the nation's capital during and after the Civil War. A black man, Dr. Charles Purvis, was appointed to head this 300-bed facility, and became the first black man to head a civilian hospital.

The hospital had an awesome obligation since so many blacks, both enslaved and free, had no previous access to appropriate health care. In 1866 some 23,000 of the city's 31,500 blacks were said to be suffering some type of untreated illness or disease. The hospital staff accepted its responsibility, and their superhuman efforts did reduce some of the suffering of the ex-slaves. The hospital stands today as Howard University Hospital. (7)

❖
Howard University, a School for Mulattos

In 1867, General O.O. Howard also established Howard University, the paragon of black education, in Washington, D.C. The initial and unannounced role of Howard was to educate the mulatto offspring of white Congressmen. Howard remained a school primarily for the so-called "elite" blacks, until the black Civil Rights Movement of the late 1950s.

But, like all black schools, Howard grew out of the ashes of the Civil War. General O.O. Howard, a well-known hero of the Civil War, was the founder, first president, and namesake of the school. Because of its mulatto students and special relationship to Congress, it was the only black school that received large federal funding. It was authorized to teach a full complement of standardized academics with professional courses, including medicine and law, and prepared black children to compete with white children, breaking an old taboo.

Chartered by the U.S. Congress, Howard assumed the name and rank of a college from the beginning, unlike other black colleges throughout the South that started out as elementary schools, and had to work their way up to become a college. Situated in the nation's capital, Howard was the "capstone school" for blacks. (8)

❖
The Brilliant Mind of Negro Tom

Thomas Fuller, more popularly known as "Negro Tom," born in Africa, brought to America as a slave at the age of 14, became a self-taught mathematician.

Denied a formal education, he could neither read nor write, but he could calculate complex mathematical problems in his head within a matter of minutes. He was especially adept at figuring time, distance and space.

Zorah Colburn, a noted mathematician of the 19th century once challenged Fuller to calculate in his head the number of seconds a man had lived who was 70 years, 12 days, and 12 hours old. Within a matter of minutes, "the African Calculator" had his answer. Colburn, figuring on paper, obtained a different answer, but Fuller reminded the mathematician that he had neglected to count leap years. On figuring once more, Colburn was forced to admit that he was wrong and Fuller was right.

Regardless of how remarkable Fuller's ability was, he never received his freedom from slavery, so his mathematical brilliance was wasted. He could not use it to help himself, his family or his race. Sadly, like most blacks, he spent his life in cotton and tobacco fields rather than classrooms. An educational organization, The Columbia Centennial, called him a prodigy, a mathematical genius who, without a doubt, would have been equal to Sir Isaac Newton had he had an appropriate formal education. (9)

✪

For Blacks: Compulsory Ignorance

Throughout the slavery period, blacks were subjected to compulsory ignorance. Laws and societal customs forbade teaching slaves how to read or write, so learning became incidental to whatever tasks they were performing in and around the plantations. The 1860 Census reported national literacy rates of 55 percent for whites and approximately 1 percent for all blacks.

National public schools were mandated by law after the Civil War, but they were profoundly different in both quality and quantity between whites and blacks. The country needed new schools to educate and acculturate the large number of European immigrants and their children who were pouring into the country. As the national economy expanded, it generated white collar and semi-skilled jobs for these "new citizens."

The opposite was true for black Americans who were still subordinate and outside of the social system. Worse, following emancipation, no measures were taken to identify and correct the psychological, social, economic and educational damage that 260 years of slavery and abuse had inflicted on the black race. The dominant society pretended that slavery had never happened. While a peonage system was being prepared for blacks, the new public policies introduced them into separate and inferior public schools. But, even under these poorest of educational conditions, blacks were able to reduce their illiteracy from 98 percent in the mid-1860s to 40 percent by 1900, and to just 20 percent by 1920.

By overcoming centuries of planned ignorance and inferior schools, black educational achievement far exceeded that of the newly-arriving European immigrants who received first-class citizenship with better schools. The 10 million European immigrants who arrived in this country in the decade following the Civil War had an illiteracy rate of approximately 95 percent. By 1900, black ex-slaves had reduced their illiteracy rate twice as fast as European immigrants who had access to much better educational resources. (10)

⊙
Where Are All the Black Ph.D's ?

The complaint is frequently heard that America has produced too many people with doctorate degrees. This charge could not possibly apply to blacks. In a seven-year period between 1965 and 1972, as the black quest for more education and advance degrees peaked, America's universities awarded more than 120,000 Ph.Ds, but, less than 200 to blacks. To find 2,000 blacks with doctorates, one would have to count all the way back to 1920. For example, in the 1993-94 school year, of more than 1300 Ph.Ds awarded in business, only 38 went to black Americans. The chart below depicts the number of degrees that universities awarded nationally in business and management for the indicated years. Like most things that are positive or beneficial, black Americans remain fixed around two percent or less.

African Americans Awarded Ph.Ds in Business and Management

School Year	Total Awarded	Number of Blacks	Percentage
1988-89	1,149	19	1.5%
1989-90	1,142	18	1.5%
1990-91	1,243	25	2%
1991-92	1,242	27	2%
1992-93	1,346	29	2%
1993-94	1,364	38	2%

Source: The National Center for Education Statistics, Washington, D.C., 1996. (11)

⚙
There's a Will, There's a Way

For black people, the struggle for education was essential to the struggle for freedom from slavery. They were aware that the national public policy opposed their learning. The policy was summarized in the words of a member of the Virginia House of Delegates who spoke of educating black slaves in 1832 saying, "We have, as far as possible, closed every avenue by which light might enter their minds. If we could extinguish the capacity to see the light, our work would be completed; they would then be on a level with the beasts of the field, and we would be safe... to use them to build wealth, power and personal comfort."

Colonel Auld, Frederick Douglas' master, upheld the policy when he stopped his wife from teaching Douglas. In his letters to her, Colonel Auld argued that, " If you teach that Niggar to read, there would be no keeping him. It would forever unfit him to be a slave."

Frederick Douglas and many other blacks proved Colonel Auld right. The laws and policies could not quench black people's desire to be literate, even though becoming literate could result in death or their children being sold. Many blacks would not be denied. They sought out white friends, abolitionists and anyone else willing to teach them. They were creative and resourceful. Some black slaves manufactured their own pens and ink, using chicken feathers and berry juice, then practiced in secret.

Gus Fester, a white sympathizer, recalled how one black slave creatively taught himself. He said that on Saturdays and Sundays, the slave would slip off from white folks. He would cut out blocks for counting from the bark on pine trees. He would use the sticks from oak trees for an ink pen, and drop oak balls in water, which would turn to ink if left over night. The slave persevered and eventually learned how to write his name, read, and do some figuring in math. (12)

⚙
Black Student Makes a Perfect Score

Ms. Skylar Byrd, a black female senior student in the Washington, D.C. school system, in May, 1996, achieved a notable first for a student. She entered the record books as the first student to ever achieve a perfect score on the Scholastic Achievement Test (SAT), a national test used for college admission. Paradoxically, Ms. Byrd's father, a professor of special education at Bowie State University, a historical black college, specializes in training teachers to recognize and educate talented and gifted children.

In support of Professor Byrd's educational philosophy, the Bethune-Dubois Foundation, a national organization that promotes youth achievement and leadership, publicly recognized Ms. Byrd for her unprecedented and outstanding achievement in June, 1996. (13)

❂
Notable Note

Around the turn of the 20th century, some teachers in white public schools kept a "nigger stool" in their classrooms. To embarrass and punish white students for being "dumb, " the teachers made them sit in the corner on the "nigger stool." (14)

❂
Immigrants Blocked Mobility Paths

European, Asian and Hispanic immigrants have historically entered this country in advantaged positions over blacks. Their presence places a downward pressure on blacks, even though 99% of the blacks in America were here before 99% of all the European, Asian and Hispanic ethnics ever arrived.

The pattern of white immigrants taking jobs from native-born blacks first appeared during the great Irish and German migrations of the early 19th century. An 1838 article in the *Colored American Newspaper* complained, "The impoverished and destitute beings transported from transatlantic shores are crowding themselves into every place of business and of labor, and driving the poor colored Americans out. Along the wharves, and in other situations, [Negroes] are being substituted by foreigners or European whites."

In 1853, Frederick Douglas wrote, "White men are becoming house-servants, cooks, and stewards on ships and in hotels; they are becoming porters, stevedores, wood-sawyers, brick-makers, white-washers and barbers, so that the (free) blacks can scarcely find the means to subsistence."

Following the Civil War, entering ethnics displaced blacks from the skilled trades, and the artisan class of businesses that blacks had monopolized for centuries. Nearly 10 million new immigrants were brought to America between 1868 and 1880. According to 1865 Census data, blacks made up more than 100,000 of the 120,000 tradesmen in the South. Yet, less skilled immigrants formed unions, locked blacks out, and took over the skilled trades based upon skin color. Blacks were bumped out of the northern factories, shipyards, mines, lumberyards, and other trade craft areas.

In 1865, nearly 60% of the southern farmers were blacks. Just as white immigrants were shutting blacks out of jobs and unions in the North, whites across the South created Farmer's Alliances that locked blacks out of the agribusiness, market places and banks. After 150 years, blacks have yet to successfully break whites' unions, Farmer Alliances, and "red lining" banks. Other minorities, while they may encounter some discrimination, have not experienced this protracted exclusion from the mainstream society. Asian and Hispanic immigrants sued and gained access to the agri-markets in the early 1900s.(15)

❂
America's Fastest Typist

In 1944, Cortez W. Peters, a black man, was a world typewriting champion who typed 130 words per minute while at the same time carrying on a conversation with other persons on an entirely different subject. Mr. Peters was a celebrity and inspiration in black communities across the nation. He established his own typing training school and regularly visited and demonstrated his "superman skills" in black schools. Even using the bulky and mechanically slow World War II typewriters, Mr. Peters' typing speed was still twice as fast as any other known speed typist in the nation. (16)

16
Blacks, Indians and Women

Minorities, minorities everywhere, but only one was enslaved and Jim Crowed.

Mini Facts

• *As a result of the Revolutionary War, less than 4% of the nation's real and personal wealth changed hands, and the nation had less than 1% unemployment.*

• *In 1830, Andrew Jackson forced various southeastern Indian tribes to relocate to Oklahoma, a Choctaw word meaning "land for the red people." The U.S. Army reported, however, that nearly one-third of the relocated Indians were of mixed African descent.*

• *In 1920, white women received the right to vote, but black women were not included. They received voting rights with all blacks when voting laws were enacted half of a century later.*

• *In 1996, the federal affirmative action set-aside policy at the U.S. Small Business Administration was modified to exclude blacks and replace them with preferences for women and Indians.*

❂

Black Man Pretended to be an Indian

While many blacks found comfort in proclaiming how much Indian blood they had in their veins, in one instance, a black even passed himself off as a full-blooded Indian.

Tony Simpson, a humble Louisiana Negro, posing as Prince Antonio Apache of Arizona, became the social darling of the elite of New York and Philadelphia in 1903. Among those who feted him in their drawing rooms or at the Metropolitan Opera were Mrs. John Jacob Astor, Mrs. Howard Gould and Mrs. John R. Drexel. Even President Theodore Roosevelt was taken in by Simpson. The President consulted "Prince Apache" several times on Indian affairs at the White House.

The "Prince" was tall and imposing, dressed like a Beau Brummel, and had high society manners. He wore a wig attached to a tuft of his own woolly hair. The willingness of the highest echelons of government and society to accept a person they thought was an Indian may explain why so many people claim some Indian ancestry. But, there is a greater question. If Indians were always so much worse off than blacks, why would Tony Simpson or any black person claim to have "Indian blood?" If blacks are better off than Indians and other groups in America, why aren't Indians, Asians, Hispanics and whites eagerly proclaiming their "black blood"? (1)

✪
Indians' Unpaid Debts to Blacks

In the early development of colonial America, Europeans included incentives to dissuade alliances between blacks and Indians in nearly every Indian treaty. Culturally, politically and economically, Indians were classified above blacks.

Many Indians adopted the racial attitudes that blacks were inferior, their skin color the outward sign of their predestined status as slaves. There were major differences in the way Indians and blacks were treated. The dominant white society felt a sense of indebtedness to Indians and taught them they were superior to blacks. Whites respected Indian heritage, culture and religion. Therefore, it was acceptable for Indians to assimilate with the white race, to become educated and farm the land. On the other hand, government treaties required Indians to aid in the capture of runaway slaves and to turn them over to local white authority or owners.

Like whites, Indians found slave trading to be extremely profitable. By the close of the 1700s, all five of the so-called civilized Indian societies were slave traders and owners, and fought alongside the Southern Confederacy in the Civil War to maintain slavery.

The degree of slave trading and ownership among Indians varied from tribe to tribe. The Cherokee, Choctaw and Chickasaw had the most anti-black reputations. These figures tell a part of the story. In 1824, there were 1,277 black slaves being held among 15,560 Cherokees.

On the eve of the Civil War in 1861, the situation between blacks and Indians had worsened. In that year, 25,000 Choctaw and Chickasaw Indians owned more than 5,000 black slaves. The Chickasaw tribe offered the following explanation for supporting slavery and the Southern Confederacy during the Civil War, "Our geographical position, our social and domestic institutions, our feelings and sympathies, all attach us to our southern friends. As a southern people, we consider their cause our own."

After the Southern Confederacy and the Indians lost the Civil War, neither southern whites nor Indians wanted blacks to have their "forty acres and a mule". Consequently, a committee of Colored People of the Choctaw and Chickasaw Indian nations filed a letter of protest with the U.S. Senate and House of Representatives of the United States Congress in January, 1870. They argued that as ex-slaves of Indians they were still being deprived of their rightful economic inheritance.

In a treaty at Fort Smith, Arkansas, in September, 1865, the Choctaws and Chickasaws were paid $300,000 by the U.S. government for a district of lands west of the 98 degree longitude. The treaty provided that the United States government pay the Choctaw and Chickasaw Legislatures $300,000 plus 5% interest for the land contingent upon the Indians drafting laws and rules to free all their black slaves, and give "each black slave and their descendants, 40 acres of land from each nation."

In addition to the 80 acres to have been given to each slave, each tribe was to give each slave "$1.00 per capita." The treaty further stipulated that should the Indian legislatures not craft these laws for black slaves within a two-year time period from the ratification of the treaty, the $300,000 shall cease to be held in trust for the Indians and given instead to the black ex-slaves. A contingency of ex-slaves traveled to Washington, D.C in the early 1870s and complained to Congress that they never received the 80 acres of land nor the monies. More than a century later, blacks are still waiting to collect from their Indian slavemasters. (2)

✪

Only Custer's Black Courier Was Not Scalped

Crazy Horse and his band of Indians got their revenge on General George Armstrong Custer at the Little Big Horn by taking the scalps of "General Yellow Hair" and his company of white soldiers. Isaiah Dorman was the only black member of the company headed by General George Armstrong Custer. Dorman was one of the 264 American soldiers who died that day. Curiously, the Sioux did not scalp and mutilate Dorman as they did the white soldiers. No explanation was ever given. Dorman had served as a courier for the War Department in the Dakota Territory. Since he knew the territory, the language, and may have been part Sioux, he was requested by Custer to serve as an interpreter and courier. Dorman was at the wrong place at the wrong time. But, unlike his white companions, he did not ride into glory nor the history books. (3)

✪

Congressman Shifted Civil Rights to Women

Throughout the 1960s, southern Congressmen were relentless in their efforts to stop black Americans' efforts to achieve freedom and equality of opportunity. President Lyndon Johnson pushed hard to enact civil rights legislation for blacks against much conservative opposition. Congressman Howard K. Smith, a Virginia Republican, was a long-time combatant against civil rights legislation. While the 1965 civil rights bill was still in the hands of the House Rules Committee, Smith managed to switch the focus from race to gender. Decades before, Smith led the attack against FDR's New Deal social policies.

At a critical moment during the combat over the 1957 civil rights bill, Smith managed a delay, saying he had a personal emergency and needed to return home to inspect a barn that had burned. Democratic Speaker Rayburn quipped that although he knew Howard Smith would do anything to block a civil rights bill, "I never knew he would resort to arson and burning down his own barn."

Finally, during opening proceedings before the Rules Committee in January, 1964, Smith proved again that he had an inexhaustible bag of parliamentary tricks when day after day he scheduled hearings on what he called this "nefarious bill." At last, voted out of the Rules Committee, the measure had then to run the House gauntlet of days of debate on complex provisions and amendments.

Smith threw members of the House into confusion by moving to add the word "sex" to the list of forbidden discriminations-- race, creed, color, and national origin. Designed more to kill the bill than to promote equal rights for women, his amendment prevailed after vigorous lobbying by the National Women's Party. (4)

Frederick Douglas Explained Feminism

For more than a century and half, radical feminists have piggybacked upon gains made by blacks.

When Congress enacted constitutional amendments that mandated the right to vote for former slaves before white women, and omitted the word "sex" from the phrase that outlawed discriminations based on "... race, color, or previous condition of servitude," northern white women were enraged.

To his credit, Frederick Douglas, the most visible and prominent black freedman, understood the difference between sexism and racism, and how to keep the issues in their proper perspective. Writing from Rochester, New York, on September 27, 1868, Douglas explained to a former abolitionist and white liberal, Mrs. Josephine White Griffin of Washington, D.C., why he felt the question of Negro suffrage to be of greater urgency at the time than that of women's suffrage. He said:

> My dear friend: I am impelled by no lack of generosity in refusing to come to Washington, D.C. to speak on behalf of women'ssuffrage. The right of women to vote is so sacred in my judgment as that of a man, and I am quite willing at any time to hold up both hands in favor of this right. It does not, however, follow that I come to D.C. or go elsewhere to deliver lectures upon this special subject. I am devoting myself to a cause, if not more sacred, certainly more urgent, because it is a life and death to the long enslaved people of this country, and

that is: Black Suffrage. While the Negro is mobbed, beaten, shot, stabb-
ed, hanged, burned and is the target of all that is malignant in the North
and all that is murderous in the South, his claim may be preferred by
me without exposing myself to the imputation of narrowness or mean-
ness towards the cause of women. As you very well know, women
have a thousand ways to attach herself to the governing of power of the
land and already exerts an honorable influence on our legislation. She
is the victim of abuses, to be sure, but it cannot be pretended, I think
that her cause is as urgent as that of ours. I never suspected you of
sympathizing with Miss Anthony and Mrs. Stanton in their cause. Their
principle is that no Negro shall be franchised while a woman is not.
Now, considering that white men have been franchised always and
colored have not, the conduct of these white women, whose husbands,
fathers, and brothers are votes, does not seem generous.

It appears that on the modern day discussions of the issues of sexism and racism,
Frederick Douglas said it all nearly 135 years ago. (5)

✪
Women's Movement Kidnapped Affirmative Action

Even before the ink was dry on this nation's affirmative action policy in the late
1960s, women in general, and white women in particular, had usurped blacks.

The women's issue is a class issue and should never have been equated to
that of blacks. Women are not minorities in any sense of the word. Nor have they
ever been segregated, enslaved, castrated or required to be uneducated. They
have always had access to this nation's socioeconomic resources through the
white male. It is disingenuous to give white males a choice between assisting
women or blacks. The historical role of the white male is protector of white
womanhood. Everything in his culture drives him to share with women because
as a majority, their paths will surely intertwine. White women will be his daughter, wife, mother, sister or another female within his race.

Women came out of the homes and onto the employment rolls to increase
their family income just as blacks were coming out of centuries of "no-pay"

White woman slaveholder. (Library of Congress)

enslavement and "low-pay" Jim Crowism. Women were much more preferable to blacks. So, where the term "minority" was used and women were included, women always out-paced blacks in terms of getting benefits.

The growth in women-owned businesses and the parallel decline in black-owned businesses reflect policy changes instituted by conservative forces in Congress and the executive branch of government. In 1996, the Small Business Administration (SBA) revised its policies and removed blacks from its list of targeted groups. Today, only small businesses, American Indians, and women receive preferences in these set-aside programs. Women are the primary beneficiaries of preference policies throughout the nation. The SBA policy simply formalized what is already happening in government procurement programs across the country.

For example, of all of the contracts for services and goods that were set aside for minorities in the state of Texas in 1994, white women received 78%, Hispanics received more than 21% and blacks received 9/10 of 1%. By 1996, business ownership by white women had surged nationally. The number of women-owned businesses grew faster than growth of businesses overall. In 1992, women-owned businesses accounted for 34 percent of all the firms in the country. In the Washington area, women owned 122,007 businesses in 1992, generating $10.7 billion in revenue. Those firms accounted for 39 percent of all the businesses in the region.

Contrarily, black businesses remained marginal. Even though the number of black businesses doubled during the past three decades, on a per 1,000 basis, blacks had more businesses in the 1920s than they have in the 1990s. Worse, even though the number of black businesses doubled over the last 30 years, the gross revenue from sales remained the same. Rather than business growth, twice as many black businesses are chasing the same dollar. (6)

❂

Tubman Stiffed by U.S. Government

Harriet Tubman, an escaped slave, abolitionist, friend of John Brown, fighter for women's rights, nurse, scout, civil war spy and fighter for black freedom until her death in 1913, was truly a towering figure in American history. During the Civil War, Tubman performed spy services for the Union army. But, she was never fairly compensated either as a black person or as a spy. She never received the promised 40 acres and a mule, and in 1898, she petitioned the United States government for back pay for her spy services in the Civil War.

She was poverty-stricken in her old age and had no tangible means of support. Based upon military disability regulations, she was eligible for military aid. She submitted documentation of her war time service to the Secretary of War and various army officers, but no action was taken for 30 years. Finally in 1897, a Senate Committee recommended that Harriet Tubman be given $25 a month for the rest of her life. But, before the bill for her compensation was approved in 1898, a southern Congressman reduced the amount by $5. (7)

17
Civil Rights and Religion

If I laugh loud enough, maybe no one will hear me cry.

Mini-Facts

• *The famous "separate but equal" doctrine, accepted by the U.S. Supreme Court in 1896, originated in a Massachusetts court in 1847.*

• *In 1896 there were 130,000 registered black voters in Louisiana. Four years later, after the Plessy vs. Ferguson "separate but equal" ruling, there were only 5,320 registered black voters.*

• *In 1965 Rev. Martin Luther King, Jr. was surprised to find black sharecroppers on plantations in Alabama who had never in their lives seen real U.S. currency.*

• *The first civil rights bill was enacted by Congress in 1875. The U.S. Supreme Court ruled the act unconstitutional eight years after it was enacted.*

✪
Dred Scott Decision Still Lives

One hundred and fifty years later, the U.S Supreme Court's Dred Scott decision of 1857 is still alive and well. This infamous court decision drug the U.S. Constitution to an all time low and set the stage for the Civil War. To this day, it has not been reversed by the court.

Dred Scott was a slave, owned by a military surgeon. In 1833, Scott's master took him from the slave state of Missouri to the free state of Illinois. In 1836, they moved to Fort Smelling in the federal territory near what would become the city of St. Paul, Minnesota. Congress had banned slavery in the northern portion of this federally-owned property in 1846.

Having entered non-slaveholding federal property, Scott and his wife sued for their freedom. It took 11 years for the case to reach the U.S. Supreme Court. The court ruled 7-2, that no black person, free or slave, was or could ever be a citizen. Chief Justice Roger Taney, writing the majority opinion, commented that, "Blacks were so far inferior to whites that they had no rights which the white man was bound to respect; and...might justly and lawfully be reduced to slavery for their benefit."

The decision was often cited as a major contributor to the Civil War. The Scotts were freed by their white master soon after the decision in spite of the Supreme Court ruling. After being granted their freedom, the Scotts remained in St. Louis where Dred Scott worked as a hotel porter and his wife worked as a laundress.

The Dred Scott decision provided a powerful legal precedent to abridge the rights of all blacks, whether they are enslaved, free, Jim Crowed, or benignly neglected. For more than 150 years, the Dred Scott decision has been denounced and repudiated, but the Supreme Court has never reversed it. (1)

⚙

No 40 Acres and a Mule for Blacks

In 1862, Union Brigadier General Rufus B. Saxton, a West Point Cavalry soldier and late-blooming abolitionist, was appointed military governor for blacks on southern plantations. Saxton pressed vigorously for the sale of land exclusively to blacks who would be allowed to buy their homesteads from the government at nominal prices and make payments in modest installments.

But a faction within the government, led by the U.S. Treasury Department's tax commissioner, was strongly opposed to Saxton's plan. Behind the tax commissioner was an array of northern land speculators who conspired to control and personally profit from abandoned or tax-available land in the South. Out of nearly 200 plantations in South Carolina, more than half of them went to northern white land speculators not to landless ex-slaves. (2)

✦
The Black Power Movement

The Black Power Movement of the 1960s in the United States was seen by its advocates as the latest in a series of efforts to correct the injustices that existed in almost every dimension of life between black and white Americans. The term "Black Power" stood for a range of concepts and meanings that galvanized blacks and frightened whites.

Some people saw the Black Power Movement as a "quasi-violent" effort on behalf of black people to destroy the political and economic institutions of the United States. Others saw it as an effort to counter one of the negative effects of the Civil Rights Movement that injured black Americans; confusing the racial issue and diffusing any resources due blacks. Others saw it as an effective pressure group with tactics to counterbalance the Ku Klux Klan and other racist white organizations.

Lastly, some saw the Black Power Movement as an attempt to instill dignity and pride in black people, with respect for their culture and communities, and to redistribute some control and wealth into the hands of black people.

Regardless of the view, the Black Power Movement helped highlight the importance of skin color in a socioeconomic context. Great black bridge builders like Harriet Tubman, Frederick Douglas, W.E.B. Dubois, de-emphasized the importance of race and skin color. However well intended, their attitudes ignored the fact that in a democracy, ethnic and group identifications are imperatives for competing. (3)

✦
The Southern Manifesto

In response to the 1954 Supreme Court desegregation decision, most southern whites remained adamant about keeping blacks subordinated, excluded, powerless and poor, regardless of what blacks and the rest of the nation believed. Determined to maintain the historical public policy on the treatment of blacks, in 1956, 96 southern Congressmen crafted what was called the *Southern Manifesto*.

According to *Webster's Standard Dictionary*, a manifesto is a public and formal declaration of principles or intentions, usually issued by a political group.

In defiance of the Supreme Court's 1954 desegregation decision, the document denounced the ruling and called for "all lawful" means to be used to bring about a reversal which they felt was contrary to the U.S. Constitution.

The Southern Manifesto had a pronounced effect on desegregation in the South. The pace of integration slowed to a trickle. While 200 new southern school districts integrated in the first two years following the court decision, only 38 did so in the third year. Contrary to the Supreme Court directive that southern schools must "desegregate with all deliberate speed," the *Southern Manifesto* encouraged schools to show little speed and much deliberation. The Manifesto inspired foot dragging on desegregation, caused social disruptions, loss of life and property, as well as a loss of black people's faith in the nation's commitment to democratic principles. (4)

⬡
The Black Manifesto

In April 1969, civil rights activist, James Foreman, led a conference in Detroit to discuss the state of black America. The conference produced a *Black Manifesto* that demanded that white Christian churches, Jewish synagogues and other white religious institutions pay $500 million in reparations to black people for the sacrifices of African-Americans under slavery. Any reparation funds were to be used for economic rehabilitation of the urban ghettos.

Although the reparations were never paid, some churches and synagogues increased their out-reach and funding to help the so-called "urban poor." Thirty years after the *Black Manifesto* was written and publicized, blacks are beginning to voice concern that reparations should again become a national issue. (5)

⬡
Was J. Edgar Hoover A Gay Racist?

Jack Mingo wrote a revealing biography of J. Edgar Hoover. He described a Hoover who was America's top law enforcement agent for five decades, and also this nation's chief blackmailer, homosexual, tyrant and hater of blacks. Throughout his reign as the head of the FBI, he used his office to enrich himself, reward his friends and to punish any person or racial group that he disliked. He did not wait until he was an adult to display his true self. He came out of the closet at a very early age.

Hoover was born on January 1, 1895, barely a year before this nation's Plessey v. Furguson, "separate but [un]equal" public policy went into effect. By his 13th birthday, Hoover demonstrated skill and interest in collecting bits of information about everyone around him. After college he landed a government job and used it to avoid being drafted into military duty during World War I. As a conservative right-wing Republican, he used his talent to identify and punish suspected communists and people he did not like. His skills found a good outlet when he was appointed to head the Federal Bureau of Investigation.

According to Mingo, Hoover engaged in numerous homosexual affairs with FBI proteges and young teenage boys. He occasionally enjoyed dressing in women's clothing. Even though he was a homosexual known in many circles, one of his favorite political tricks was to label an enemy as homosexual. Mingo also reports that Hoover kept records on other well-known personalities, including Congressmen, crime figures, and nearly every President from Roosevelt to Lyndon Johnson and John F. Kennedy. Not only did he keep records, he used them for blackmail as needed. Few could compete with the power that Hoover had at his fingertips.

Hoover used the power of government to satisfy his own bigotry towards blacks and gays. His abuse of power went unchallenged for more than half a century. He used the agency to screen blacks out of nearly every level of government employment. Even as late as the 1960s, after the Civil Rights Movement, Hoover still refused to hire black FBI agents. Instead he gave "promotions" to black servants and janitors, but deceptively called them "agents" on the Bureau's employment rolls. In the late 1960s, the FBI had only 20 black investigative agents out of 16,000 staff members.

Even after it became politically incorrect, Hoover tried to smear Martin Luther King, Jr., by labeling him both a communist and a homosexual. Hoover ordered illegal wire taps of Martin Luther King's hotel room and sent copies of the tapes to his wife, alleging that King had been caught in the act of committing adultery. When King was killed three years later by a sniper, Atlanta agents cheered and one shouted, "We finally got the son of a bitch." The FBI dragged their feet on investigating the assassination of King. Hoover's hatred for blacks did not stop there. He later opposed making Martin Luther King's birthday a national holiday. In addition, he allegedly orchestrated a plan to criminalize and kill off the Black Panther Party and other civil rights organizations.

He spent his life labeling and attacking groups of people. In 1972, he died in the nation's capital, alone and virtually reclusive. (6)

✪
Million Man March Sets Record

On October 16, 1995, Minister Louis Farrakhan, the leader of the Nation of Islam, called for and got the largest gathering of people, black or white, in the history of the nation's capital. Minister Farrakhan called a million black men to march on Washington, D.C. for a "day of atonement and redemption." Black men came from all over this nation, not so much to atone, but in search of new black leadership, a greater sense of black unity and community, a national economic and political self-empowerment plan, an opportunity to rebuff the establishment, and a chance to be a part of history in the making. The National Park Service reported that less than a half million black men participated in the March. Numerous other sources, however, tallied the number in excess of a million. Either way, the Million Man March was an historic event. (7)

✪
The Rosewood Massacre

Something terrible happened in the little black Florida town of Rosewood in 1923. A mass murder of blacks took place. No one wanted to talk about it until 1995, when it was brought up for public discussion by a contingency of black Florida legislators. The massacre started with a lynching and ended with the entire town burned to the ground, its middle-class black residents killed or chased into the swamps.

Rosewood was dead, but the memory of that town burned through the years in the hearts of those who had lived there. Seventy years later, amid great anguish and political resistance, the State of Florida acknowledged the terrible wrong that had been done and voted to pay the survivors a small reparation award.

Although the few black survivors of the Rosewood massacre had avoided discussing the incident, Arnett Doctor, the son of a survivor, learned about what really happened in Rosewood when he began to interview senior citizens about the town's history. Nearly a century ago, Rosewood was a town of about 200 black people. The massacre of blacks started when a white woman in a nearby town claimed to have been raped by a black man. A mob of armed white men headed straight for Rosewood.

They knew that because of gun control laws, most black communities were unarmed and defenseless. For a week the white men ravaged and burned the black town of Rosewood. Newspaper reports from the time listed eight dead, six blacks and two whites. But reports of mass graves filled with black bodies persisted through the years.

Some sources charged that more than 100 blacks were slain. No one will ever know the true number of the dead. But the property records could not be clearer. Land that had been owned by black men and women was confiscated and sold for taxes to white buyers. The black families of Rosewood lost all they had spent their lifetime earning.

Not all whites actively participated. But most did nothing to stop the slaughter of blacks. A few did rescue some blacks who were hiding in the woods and swamps. The larger white community collectively chose to put the event behind them, even after the white woman who claimed she was raped by a black man confessed to having lied. There had been no justice for the black people of Rosewood for more than 70 years. And pressure was applied to stop the Rosewood Massacre from becoming a public issue.

In 1994, with the nation's newspapers and television stations looking on, Florida's nearly all white legislature took an historic giant step and voted to pay $2 million in compensation to the black Rosewood survivors. Although no amount of money could redeem the losses blacks suffered in the Rosewood incident, reparations from the state of Florida at least acknowledged and apologized for some of the suffering and lack of justice for blacks. (8)

⊛
Majority Should Protect the Minority

The *Federalist Papers* were foundation documents for the U.S. Constitution. These writings were used to explain and promote the ratification of the U.S. Constitution. One of the most important principles the papers stressed was that in a social democracy that operated on the principle of majority rule, it is the majority population's responsibility to protect the rights of the "minority population." The drafters of the Constitution understood that when the rights of the minority are constantly abridged, the nation is at risk of a revolt.

Thomas Jefferson was absent from the Constitutional Convention in Philadelphia, at which time the *Federalist Papers* were drafted, but he backed a legislative system based on the "majority will rule." While Jefferson talked grandly about a majority rule, he also stressed the right of the minority to revolt when their rights are ignored and abused. Jefferson, Madison, and other founding fathers believed that not only must the majority respect the rights of the minority, but they must "... never impede the minority from becoming the majority the same way the existing majority formed." Should the majority abuse the minority or cause the minority to be a "permanent" minority, then the "abused minority" has no obligation to respect any laws or authority established by the ruling majority. A permanent minority then, is abused and suffering tyranny. Fresh from under British tyranny, Jefferson and the founding fathers were confident that a majority of free Americans would never trample on the liberties of fellow Americans as guaranteed in the Bill of Rights. They were blind to the fact that they had nearly a million blacks enslaved. (9)

Notable Quote
" Someone will at last arise who will champion our cause
and compel the world to see that we deserve justice."
A lonely black slave's prayer

✪

Blacks Were Double Victims of the Holocaust

Even though they are never mentioned in public discussions, black people were double victims in the Jewish Holocaust in the late 1930s and early 1940s. First, they were victims of Nazi war crimes just like Jews were. Yet, blacks as Holocaust victims remain one of the world's best kept secrets of recent history. They are conspicuously absent from the vast majority of Holocaust movies, museums, commemorations and financial reparation policies. As quiet as it is kept, black people lived in Germany before and during the Jewish Holocaust. As far back as World War I, many blacks had been recruited into the Geman army from its African colonies. Others had later migrated to Germany. Blacks in North Africa and the German colonies were also killed and forced into labor camps to produce war materials and supplies.

Nazi Germans hated and perceived blacks to be an inferior race of people. Blacks were arrested, persecuted, placed in German concentration camps and executed prior to and during World War II. When the Jewish Holocaust began, black Germans were also targets, but unlike Jews, they fought hard against the mounting Nazism. For example, a black German, named Lari Giles, was murdered by the Nazi SS Police for the role that he played in leading a resistance group in his hometown of Dusseldorf.

More than three million blacks were registered in the United States military during World War II. Blacks served and died as front line combat soldiers, pilots and support personnel but justice and recognition continue to elude them. The Holocaust accounts have focused on religious, not racial persecutions. Blacks died with and for Jews. Yet, as victims or soldiers, they remain an after-thought. Blacks have received none of the more than $52 billion paid to Holocaust victims since the end of World War II.

18
Odds and Ends

You can fool some of the people all of the time.

Mini Facts

• *In the 1866, Memphis, Tennessee riot, whites burned down every black church in the city. In 1995-96, more than 70 black churches were burned throughout the Southeast.*

• *In the late 1800s, Henry Ossian, a West Point graduate and one of the leaders of the Buffalo Soldiers, was set-up by jealous white officers and court martialed for embezzlement.*

• *In 1990, TLC Beatrice Inc. was the largest black-owned company in the United States, with total revenues of $8.81 billion.*

❂
Media Routinely Degraded Blacks

Throughout the Reconstruction period, major social and economic forces used the print media to maintain the status quo on black people, using negative stories, cartoons, and product advertisements.

From the social section to the news, papers and magazines used labels, names, and language that were outright racist. These terms included nigger, nig-gah, darkey, coon, pickaninny, mammy, buck, uncle, aunt, high yaller, yaller hussy, and light-complexion yaller man. They affixed names to blacks that poked fun at them, such as Colonel, Senator, Sheriff, Apollo, George Washington, and Napoleon Bonaparte.

Many of these images were further exaggerated and promoted commercially on post cards, calendars, outdoor billboards and consumer products, like pancake flour, rice, soap, tobacco, and dolls. Lacking competitive print media, political power and their own independent economic structure, black Americans were totally vulnerable and incapable of countering the negative media images.

That pattern continues today. Integration killed off black-owned, community-based newspapers. Blacks acquired their first radio station in the late 1940s. It took 50 years for them to own less than 2%, or just 176 of more than 10,000 radio stations in the nation. The 1996 Telecommunications Act, passed by Congress and signed into law by President Clinton, stripped blacks of their meager gains. The Act lifted radio ownership caps, created a frenzy of consolidation and mergers, and blacks lost more than 30% of their stations in just one year. At the current rate that black stations are being bought up and forced out of business, blacks will again be inconsequential in the media business. With capital so firmly fixed in the white community, it is no wonder that whites own more than 97% of all the country's radio stations. It seems that if you were not there when the goodies were passed out, you will always be relegated to the crumbs. (1)

❂
Familiarity Shows Contempt

The familiar names slaveowners gave black men and women signaled status and reflected the power relationships. Black men within the inner domestic circle of a white family were called boys until they became senior citizens, then they were called "Pappy" or "Uncle." Black females were called girls, until they were up in age, then they were called "Auntie." If the black female was young and attractive she was called a "Jezebel," to indicate she was loose sexually and disruptive to white men and women's relationships.

"Mammy" was a popular familiar name for a black woman that emerged in the mid-1800s. It was the name for older women who took care of and raised white children. As subtle as it might be, the term "Mammy" stripped a black woman of her dignity, normal sexuality, her own family responsibilities and made her a nurturing, caring female authority dedicated to white society.

Mammies usually had a degree of authority in the white household. They ranked next in line to the white wife or mistress.

A black Auntie ranked lower than a black Mammy based upon who she worked for and the skin-color of the children that she was raising. Mammies raised white children. Aunties raised black children. Auntie, like her male counterparts, Uncle and Pappy, carried practically no authority in white households. While a black person's first name could be added to the titles of Pappy, Uncle, Auntie or Mammy, it was strictly taboo to give a black person a formal, nonfamiliar title such as Mr., Mrs., or Miss. (2)

❂
They Never Get the Word

Blacks have seldom taken steps to preserve, mark and close their communities and culture as European, Asian and Hispanic ethnics do. Some groups mark and close their communities with posted signs such as "Little Italy" or "Frenchtown." Others use fences or another kind of barrier. Sometimes it is more subtle, with archways, language or distinctive street signs. Whatever the technique of marking and closing, ethnic groups establish and maintain the sanctity, unity, and control of property value by marking and closing off their communities.

Hispanics in south Florida are an example of marking and controlling territory. When Hispanics took control of the Dade County Commission and Miami City Council, they declared Spanish to be an official language equal to English. This action significantly reduced the necessity of Hispanics to learn English. Instead, non-Hispanics are obliged to learn Spanish to do business within Hispanic communities. Spanish language radio and television programs dominate the commercial airways in those cities. All public signs and instructions must be in both English and Spanish. Many street signs are now in Spanish.

Business owners and government offices want employees who are bilingual and fluent in the Spanish language. Non-Spanish speaking whites and blacks are effectively shut out of the social, political and economic systems. Are the non-Spanish speaking residents victims of language discrimination? Are they being denied the right to earn a living?

Dirty Little Secrets

216

Marking and closing communities appears to be a new concept only to blacks. Ethnics have used their culture and language to mark and close their community streets for nearly a century. In 1933 in Chicago, Illinois, Italian immigrants pressured the city government to change 7th Street in their community to Balboa Avenue. The name change reflected an Italian presence and gave honor to a "great Italian navigator." A few years earlier, the black community had the same opportunity to make a statement about their group, but failed to see the importance of the control of symbols within their communities. In an attempt to promote black culture and heroes in Chicago, a few blacks moved to have Washington Park Court renamed Du Sable Court in honor of the black man who settled and founded the City.   Almost immediately, the larger black community objected and demanded reinstatement of the name to Washington Park Court, after the first President of the United States. (3)

✪

The Glass Ceiling in Organized Crime

Organized crime, like politics and businesses, was a microcosm of American society and provided a path to mainstream society for most groups.

Crime was organized with and through legitimate businesses, beginning in the early 1930s. Black crime was disorganized and outside of mainstream society. It lacked a business structure and was therefore relegated to blue-collar or the lowest level of crimes against person and property. In the 1930s, however, a few blacks started their own form of gambling called "playing the numbers."

This form of illegal gambling was accepted in black communities as an alternative economic system. Black gangs did reasonably well until Italian mobsters found out how well they were doing, then the Italian mobsters moved blacks out. Now, playing the numbers has gone legit or mainstream. Today, it is called the lottery, and blacks spend heavily to purchase lottery tickets. Now, instead of the mob operating an alternative income system in black communities, it is state governments that siphon those dollars from black citizens into state coffers.

Although blacks are heavy lottery players, they do not control the game's employment or the revenue flow. Blacks' lack of political and economic cohesiveness and muscle has always left them vulnerable to 'take-over' by others.

Ethnic control of criminal activities produced more than mere economic impact. It gave them greater control over their culture, employment opportunities, political clout, as well as social mobility and acceptance. There was an aura of acceptance for the Irish, Jews, and Italians when they participated in organized crime. The gang communities created economic and political opportunities. The communities accepted them and their gifts. (4)

❁

The Most Recognized Black Woman

No racial image or food trademark has ever equaled Aunt Jemima in national recognition, popularity or longevity. Her clean, ready-to-serve with a crisp smile image, along with her intuitive knowledge and distinctively Southern manners, was a successful advertising creation that epitomized black servility. In addition, it was an example of racial exploitation.

According to the white version, the Aunt Jemima story began in St. Joseph, Missouri in 1888 when Chris Ruff, an editorial writer for the *St. Joseph Gazette* and Charles Underwood, a friend in the milling business, purchased an existing mill along the Black Snake Creek and formed the Pearl Milling Company.

The two partners developed a self-rising pancake flour. The name "Aunt Jemima" came from a cakewalk tune heard by Rutt at a minstrel show. The character who was performing was costumed in an apron and bandanna in the tradition of southern cooks. And so Aunt Jemima began. Rutt and Underwood organized their company and registered the Aunt Jemima trademark. However, their business did not do well.

By 1890, without merchandising success and no capital, the company faltered. Within a few months, the partners reorganized into the Aunt Jemima Manufacturing Company with Underwood's brother Bert as fancier and promoter. The business failed under Bert, too. Rutt returned to the *Gazette* and Charles Underwood found employment with R.T. Davis Milling Company, the largest miller in St. Joseph. Shortly thereafter, Davis purchased the recipe and set out to improve and promote the product. With the addition of rice flour and corn sugar to improve the flavor and the addition of powdered milk for simplicity, the mix was ready for promotion.

Davis envisioned a living Aunt Jemima to demonstrate the self-rising pancake flour and to bring the trademark to life. Bring it to life they did with friendly, 59-year old Nancy Green, born a slave on a plantation in Montgomery County, Kentucky. She became the first Aunt Jemima in the flesh. For more than 30 years, she presided at promotional events for Davis across the country, including the 1893 Chicago World's Fair. Purd Wright, advertising manager for Aunt Jemima accompanied Davis and Green to various fairs.

Over the course of the next generation, the company's ownership went through several changes, but caught another wind when Quaker Oats took it over. Nancy Green, the original Aunt Jemima died on September 24, 1923, after being struck by a car in Chicago. Green was replaced by a succession of large black females who exhibited the appropriate personal qualities. The pictures on the cartons also changed through the years. The bandanna was replaced by a headband, then the headband was replaced by soft, curly, gray-streaked hair, pearl earrings and a new lace collar. Today, Aunt Jemima's face and famous pancakes are as much of an American institution as apple pie. (5)

❂
Race and Class in the Bathroom

Until the mid-1800s, there were few so-called bathrooms or indoor personal hygiene amenities. The bathroom first appeared in America around 1791 and was clearly a wonder that only the rich and primarily white enjoyed. Woods and outhouses served private needs in rural areas, while city dwellers found comfort in alleys, dark streets, and chamber pots. Porcelain or metal "chamber pots" or "slop jars" were commonly found in the bedrooms under the beds. Louis Philippe, who became the King of France, reported with dismay that while on a trip through the United States in 1797, he asked for a chamber pot and his host told him there were none available, but invited him "to make free use of the window," an offer he politely turned down. It was not until the 1820s, that toilets began a slow move indoors.

Like everything else, bathrooms trickled down to blacks last. Blacks, especially those living in the deep South, were the last to find bathroom comforts.

Prior to the 1950s and the Civil Rights Movement, the majority of southern blacks still used private outhouses and segregated public facilities that reflected racial inequalities. Although toilet paper first appeared around 1880, well into the early 1950s, black outhouses typically contained old newspapers, store catalogs, and corn cobs as alternatives to toilet paper. For most blacks in the South, toilet paper was relatively new and rare until after World War II.

Throughout history, levels of hygiene and social sophistication were a direct reflection of racial inequalities and classism. (6)

⚙

Black Humor

A dialogue exchanged between a black and white in 1868:

White cotton field overseer asked, "Sam, what makes your nose so flat?" Sam, the black tenant farmer, answered, "Don't know, boss, but I figure it's to keep me from sticking it into other people's business."

⚙

Gagged for Gossiping

During slavery, plantation slaves in household service were skilled at listening, reporting, pilfering, signifying and gossiping. The "grapevine" from the masters house to the slave cabins and from plantation to plantation were critical message channels for sharing needed items as well as information. The information the household slaves circulated often assisted other blacks to run away or plan slave uprisings. All slaveholders were concerned about slaves who spied and passed on information, especially through gossiping.

For slaves, gossiping was a form of communication, entertainment and fun. Some masters tried to stop gossiping by associating it with pain and suffering. To keep slaves from gossiping and talking about "white folks' business," a special gagging device was invented and sold to slaveowners who had habitual gossipers or a female servant with a loose tongue.

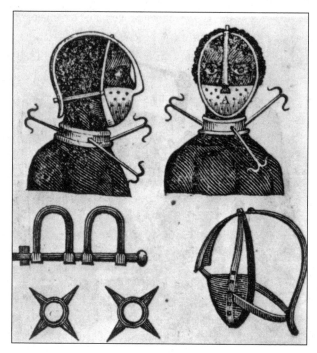

Control devices of slavery. (Library of Congress)

The gagging device was a circular iron band which protruded into the mouth and around the lower part of the slave's head. A thick piece of metal was attached that covered the tongue and prevented the slave from talking. Modern day soap operas and talk shows on radio and television, thrive on gossip. During slavery, gossiping could be dangerous to a slave's health. (7)

✪

Founders and Builders of Cities

Brick by brick, black hands built nearly every one of the nation's great cities. In many cases, blacks were the brains as well as the brawn. Many served crucial but seldom recognized roles as chief architects and designers of major cities.

Free blacks helped found and build New York, Los Angeles, Chicago and Washington, D.C., the nation's capital. Surely most people are unaware that Jean-

Baptiste Point DuSable, a black man, established the first settlement at the present-day site of Chicago and operated its first trading post. Similarly, few people know that Benjamin Banneker, a black surveyor, designed the District of Columbia after being appointed by President George Washington to a three-member commission to map out the city. When Pierre Charles L'Enfant, the head of the commission grew tired of criticisms and resigned, President Thomas Jefferson appointed Benjamin Banneker to head up and finish the mapping of the nation's capital. Today, Washington, D.C. is still considered an outstanding example of urban design.

Not many people know that of the 44 original founders and developers of Los Angeles in the early 1850s, 26 were black. During the following century, nearly all of the lands were either sold or taken from the original black owners. The children and grandchildren of the remaining founding blacks inherited large blocks of land in Los Angeles. Maria Rita Valdez, the granddaughter of a black founder owned Rancho Rodeo de Las Aguas, now known as Beverly Hills. Another black, Francisco Reyes, initially owned the entire San Fernando Valley.

In New York City in 1644, 11 blacks received a large court-ordered grant of swamp land on the edge of New Amsterdam. The area was essentially a black settlement for more than 200 years. Today this property is known as Greenwich Village and Washington Square. It is difficult to determine exactly when blacks lost ownership of the Greenwich Village land because of the circular migration patterns of blacks and whites. (8)

❂

Artifacts of Hate Are Hot Sellers

Three decades after the end of the Civil Rights Movement, the marquee of an old theater in Laurens, South Carolina, read, "The World's Only Klan Museum: The Redneck Shop." The owner, John Howard, sold Klan souvenirs to raise money for a first-of-its kind Klan museum he wanted to open in the theater. Photographs of cross-burnings, men in hoods and white robes, including one of a Ku Klux Klan kiddies rally, were for sale in the store. Stacks of segregation-era signs such as "Colored People Must Sit In Balcony," "No Dogs, Negroes, Mexicans" sold for $1 a copy. Making a play on a modern day black expression, Howard sold tee-shirts with a picture of a Klan hood with the lettering, "The original boys in the hood."

Inside the store, Howard displayed a black mannequin inside a coffin, with a rope around its neck. White customers openly supported the store. One white female customer who purchased the memorabilia said, " I am not ashamed. I am a Klan supporter because I believe in the southern ways. " The store owner was the Grand Dragon of the South Carolina Ku Klux Klan and he sold photos of himself in his Klan robe, yet, he asserted he was not a racist. He was "just concerned about the future of the white race."

The popularity of hate artifacts was supported by a Halloween incident in Saybrook, Illinois, in October, 1997. According to a *Washington Post* article, the local Lions Club awarded first prize in a Halloween costume contest to a 14-year old girl dressed in a Ku Klux Klan robe. On the robe were swastikas and the phrases, "Kill them all" and "White Power" Both the girl and the Lion's Club representative indicated no offense was intended. (9)

❂

Sambo Ads Used to Promote Pizza

In 1996, *The Michigan Chronicle* brought to the public's attention a "Sambo" pizza advertisement used by Domino's Pizza in Guatemala to sell pizza. Domino's Pizza is a domestic and international business that is based in Ann Arbor, Michigan. The advertisement featured cartoon-like drawings of dark-skinned people wearing bones in their curly dark hair. These pictures were accompanied by a written message in Spanish which when translated read, "We realize that you work like blacks... and naturally, you will eat like cannibals..." The ad proceeds to offer a special on its pizzas with a Coca-Cola.

The Michigan Chronicle pointed out that in some Spanish-speaking countries, the word "Negroes" can be translated as either "blacks" or "slaves," depending on the context. In the ad it was possible to insert either meaning. According to the article, a Domino's representative claimed the company did not create the ad. "Our franchisee ran the ad. Domino's is a franchised business and franchisees produce their own marketing. We found that the ad was discriminatory and extremely offensive...When Domino found out about the ad, the local franchisee was ordered to stop running it."

Even on the eve of the 21st century, many still feel at liberty to use degrading images of black people in advertisements. (10)

❁

Memorabilia Regains Popularity

White racism, by its very nature, forced black people to be pathetic, ignorant, comical figures and the butt of jokes. Stripped of their African heritage, history, language, humanity and a broad sense of peoplehood, they were given ill-fitting names, clothing and titles, then required to respond inappropriately or in a child-like fashion in adult situations. They were denied an education to keep them ignorant; the fruits of their own labor to keep them poverty-stricken; open immigration to keep them a permanent minority; and access to political tools to keep them powerless and under control. Without status and dignity, it was predictable that businesses would develop around the creation and selling of artifacts that disparaged blacks and portrayed them as ugly, ignorant, uncivilized Sambos, clowns, jesters and buffoons.

In the 1700s, black images appeared on a limited number of manufactured items, such as dolls and fine porcelain figurines that were produced by Japan, Germany, France, England, Austria and the United States. By the 1800s, negative black images could be found on souvenir items such as salt and pepper sets, tablecloths and towels, lawn jockeys and other household items.

Two American companies located in New York and Ohio dominated the negative artifact market by the early 1900s, but had to compete with general businesses that used negative black images to promote and advertise their products. On the eve of the 21st century, negative images still appear in toothpaste and pizza commercials in Latin America and Japan.

At the turn of the 20th century, negative blackness continued to sell commercial products up to the black Civil Rights Movement of the 1960s. Negative images of blacks adorned every conceivable product. The most popular images were those of the black Mammy, Old Uncle, and pickaninnies. Black faces appeared on Quaker Oats products, Old Virginia Bread Pans, Mammy Shanty Restaurant, Aunt Jemima Waffle Mix, Mammy's Orange Soda, Luzianne Coffee, Duncan Admiration Coffee, Mammy's Charcoal Aide, Ole Virginny Cashews, Mammy's Favorite Coffee.

Images and caricatures of black men appeared on the label of Cream of Wheat, Uncle Ben's Rice, Colgate Toiletries, Warrenton Rum Cakes, Bixby's Satinola Shoe Polish, Dr. LeGear's Lice Powder, Negro Head Brand Oysters, Old Black Joe Beans, and Uncle Remus Syrup.

Images and caricatures of young children were used as ads for Pickaninny Coffee Shop, Sambos Pancakes and Restaurants, Sambo Chocolate Drink, Coon Chicken Inn, Cotton Patch Restaurant, Darkie Toothpaste and Peppermints, Gold Dust Twins Soap Products, Sharpoint Cobbler's Nails, Boyce Typewriters, Soriba and Fatou Matches, Just-Rite Barbecue, Dixie Kid Cut Plug Tobacco, Cantelope Smoking Tobacco, Mascot Baking Powder, Mason's Shoe Polish, Sunny South Peanuts, Niggar Hair Tobacco, Fun-To-Wash Washing Powder, Honey Child Sweet Shop, Whitman's Pickaninny Peppermint, Alexander's Tomatoes, and Nigger-Toes Nuts used primitive characterizations of blacks.

Comedic postcards with degrading depictions of blacks were also very pop-

Advertisment for soap products. (Roger Lewis Collection)

Commercial advertisment (Roger Lewis Collection)

ular and profitable. By the 1930s, American companies increased their profits by contracting the manufacture of those products to Japanese, Chinese and other Asian companies that had a low-wage labor market and ready inclination to produce negative black artifacts for American consumers. Asian countries continued to be major producers until the 1950s Civil Rights Movement made degrading blacks unacceptable. By the 1980s, with a rising tide of national conservatism, black memorabilia was a growing industry with collectors paying a thousand percent markups on the original cost of negative black artifacts, figurines, advertisements, lawn jockeys and post cards. Clearly, there are endless ways to make money by making fun of black people. (11)

Sources

1
Notable Firsts and Lasts

1. Bontemps, Arna. *Story of the Negro.* (New York: Alfred A. Knopf), 1953.

2. Boyd, Herb. *The Glory Road.* (New York: Avon Books), 1995.

3. Loewen, James W. *Lies My Teacher Told Me.* (New York: A Touchstone Book), 1995, p. 93.

4. Rogers, J.A. *100 Amazing Facts About the Negro.* (Florida: Helga M. Rogers), 1965, p. 37.

5 Katz, William Loren *African American Eyewitness: A Living Documentary of the Contribution to American History.* (New York: A Touchstone Book), 1995, p. 37.

6. Bushman, Richard L. *The Refinement of America.* (New York: Knopf), 1992, p. 434.

7 Quarles, Benjamin *The Negro in the Making of America.* (A Touchstone Book: New York), 1987, p. 87.

8. Christian, Charles M. *Black Saga: An African American Experience.* (New York: Houghton Mifflin Company), 1995, p. 136.

9. Boskin, Joseph. *Sambo: The Rise and Demise of American Jester.* (New York: Oxford University Press), 1986, p. 24.

10. Printed in *"365 Days of Black History"*, 1997 Engagement Calendar, California: Pomergranate Calendars and Books.

11. Katz, William, *Eyewitness: A Living Documentary of the African American Contribution to American History.* (New York: A Touchstone Book), 1995, p. 219-300.

12. Potter, Joan and Constance Claytor. *African-American Firsts: Famous, Little -known and Unsung Triumphs of Blacks in America* (New York: Pinto Press), 1994, p. 259.

13. See August page of *"365 Days of Black History, 1997 Engagement Calendar,* California: Pomergrante Calendar and Books.

14. Christian, Charles M. *Black Saga: The African American Experience..* (New York: Houghton Mifflin Company), 1996.

15. Ibid. , 185 & 211.

16. Shenkman, Richard And Kurt Reiger. *One-Night Stands with American History*. (New York: Quill), 1992, p. 89.

17. Senna, Carl. *The Black Press and the Struggle for Civil Rights*. (New York: The African American Empower), 1993, p. 18-19.

18. Bergman, Peter M. and Mort N. Bergman. *The Chronological History of the Negro in America*, (New York: A Mentor Book), 1968, p. 132.

19. Berlin, Ira *Slaves Without Masters*. (New York: The New Press), 1974, p. 76-78.

20. Christian, Charles M. *Black Saga: An African American Experience*. (New York: Doubleday), 1966, p 185.

21. Bergman, Peter M. and Mort N. Bergman. *The Chronological History of the Negro in America*. (New York: A Mentor Book), 1968, p. 218.

22. *Michigan Citizen*, December 7, 1997, page 3.

2
Heroes and Heroines

1. Bennett, Lerone. *Pioneers in Protest*. (Chicago: Johnson Publishing Company), 1968, p. 62.

2. Katz, William Loren. *Black Indians*. (New York: Atheneum Publishers), 1986, p. 63.

3. Arno and New York Times. *The American Negro, His History and Literature*. (New York: Arno Press), 1969, p. 53.

4. Tuleja, Tad. *American History in 100 Nutshells*. (New York: Fawcett Columbine), 1992.

5. Lee, George L *Interesting People: Black American History Makers*. (New York: Ballantine), 1989, p. 8.

6. Ibid. , 10.

7. Combs, Norman. *The Black Experience in America*. (New York: Hippocrene Books), 1972, p. 81 & 82.

8. Logan, Rayford W. *The Betrayal of the Negro*. (New York: Collier Books), 1967, p. 140-142.

9. Boyd. Herb. *Down the Glory Road*. (New York: Avon Books), 1995, p. 28.

10. Mullane, Deirdre. *Crossing the Danger Water*. (New York: Doubleday), 1993,p. 74.

Sources

11. Ibid.

12. Jordan, Ervin L. *Black Confederates and Afro-Yankees in Civil War Virginia.* (New York: University of Virginia), 1995.

13. Jones, Jacqueline. *Dispossessed: America's Underclass from the Civil War to the Present.* (New York: Basic Books), 1992, p. 20.

14. Katz, William Loren. *African American Eyewitness: A Living Documentary of Contribution to American History.* (New York: A Touchstone Book), 1995, p. 40.

15. Anderson, Claud. *Black Labor, White Wealth.* (Maryland: Duncan & Duncan, Inc.), 1994.

16. Christian, Charles M. *Black Saga: The African American Experience.* (New York: Houghton Mifflin Co.), 1996, p. 41.

17. Unknown black slave.

18. Quarles, Benjamin. The Negro in the Making of America. (New York: A Touchstone Book), 1964, p. 176.

19. Garraty, John A. *The American Nation.* (HarperCollings Publishers), 1991, p. 240.

20. Davis, Kenneth. *Don't Know Much About History.* (New York: Avon Books), 1990, p. 126.

21. Ibid. , 126.

3
Freedmen and Free Labor

1. Scott, John Anthony. *Hard Trials On My Way.* (New York: Alfred A. Knopf), 1974, p. 268.

2. Loewen, James W. *Lies My Teacher Told Me.* (New York: A Touchstone Book), 1995, p. 138.

3. Anderson, Claud. *Black Labor; White Wealth.* (Maryland: Duncan & Duncan, Inc.) 1994.

4. Ibid.

5. Christian, Charles M. *Black Saga: The African American Experience.* (New York: Houghton Mifflin Co.), 1996, p. 144

6. Bryson, Bill. *Made In America.* (New York: William Morrow and Company), 1994, p. 151

7. Notes from Author: Unknown source. Willie Lynch and his infamous speech are well known in black America. It is routinely reprinted in distributed literature and was even referenced by Minster Louis Farahkan in his historical Million Man March on Washington, D.C. on October 17, 1995.

8. Bryson, Bill. *Made In America*. (New York: William Morrow and Co.), 1994, p. 28.

9. Christian, Charles. *Black Saga: The African American Experience*. (New York: Mifflin Co.), 1996, p. 32.

10. Nat Hentoff. *"Blind Eye to Slavery"*, *The Washington Post*, June 16, 1996.

11. Reprinted from an old posted advertisement for slave labor. Original source unknown.

4
Sex and Sensibility

1. Arno and the New York Times, *The American Negro: His History and Literature.* (New York: Hastings House), 1940, p. 13.

2. Jordan, Winthrop D. *White Over Black: American Attitudes Toward the Negro, 1550-1812..* (New York: W.W. Norton and Company), 1968.

3. Shenkman, Richard & Reiger, Kurt. *One Night Stand with American History.* (New York: Quill), p. 49.

4. Ibid. , 28.

5. Shenkman, Richard and Kurt Reiger. *One-Night Stands with American History.* (New York: Quill), p. 26.

6. Bryson, Bill. *Made In America.* (New York: William Morrow and Co.), 1994, p. 305.

7. Zacks, Richard. *History Laid Bare.* (New York: HarperPerennial), 1994, p. 350; and Burke, Davis. *The Civil War: Strange and Fascinating Facts.* (New York: Wings Books), 1994, p. 158.

8. Jordan, Winthrop D. *White Over Black: American Attitudes Toward the Negro: 1550-1812.* (New York: W.W. Norton and Co.), 1968.

9. Sowell, Thomas. *The Economics and Politics of Race.* (New York: Quill), 1983;Stevenson, Brenda. *Life in Black and White.* (New York: Oxford University Press), 1996, p. 4.

5
Adventurers and Artists

1. Wright, Kathleen. *The Other Americans*. (New York: Fawcett), 1971, p. 15.

2. Bontemps, Arna. *Story of the Negro*. (New York: Alfred A. Knopf), 195 , p. 43.

3. "*The Negro in World History: Antar the Lion*". Tuesday Magazine, p. 16, A Supplement to The Times-Union, (March, 1970),

4. Quarles, Benjamin. *The Negro in the Making of America*. (New York: Touchstone Books), 1996.

5. Loewen, James W. *Lies My Teacher Told Me*. (New York: A Touchstone Book),1996, p. 53.

6. Zinn, Howard *A People's History of the United States*. (New York: Harper Perennial), 1990, p. 1-5.

7. Stewart, Jeffery C. *10001 Things Everyone Should Know About African American History*. (New York: Doubleday), 1996. p. 3.

8. Bennett, Lerone. *The Shaping of Black America*. (Chicago: Johnson Publishing Company), 1974.

9. Richard Shenkman and Kurt Reiger. *One-Night Stands with American History*, (New York: Quill), 1995 p. 29.

10. Source: Mark Twain, *Huckleberry Finn.*

6
Colonizing and Colorizing

1. Arno Press and the New York Times. *The Negro in Virginia*. (New York: Arno Press), 1969, p. 4.

2. Christian, Charles M. *Black Saga: The African American Experience*. (New York: Houghton Mifflin Co.), 1995, p. 76.

3. Anderson, Claud. *Black Labor, White Wealth*. (Maryland: Duncan & Duncan Inc.), 1994.

4. Anderson, Claud, Ibid.

5. Anderson, Claud, Ibid.

6. Boorstein, Daniel. *The Americans: The National Experience*. (New York, N.Y.: Random House), 1965, pp. 381-82.

7. Christian, Charles. *Black Saga: The African American Experience*. (New York: Houghton Mifflin Co.), 1996, p. 537.

8. Stamp, Kenneth. *The Peculiar Institution*. (New York: Vintage Books),
    1956; and John Ashworth. *Slavery, Capitalism and Politics in the
    Antebellum Republic*. (Mass.: Cambridge UP), 1995.

9. Bergman, Peter M. and Mort N. Bergman. *The Chronological History
    of the Negro In America*. (New York: Mentor Books), 1969, p. 67.

10. Garraty, John A. and McCaughey, Robert A. *The American Nation*. (New
    York: HarperCollins Publishers), 1991.

11. Blockson, Charles L. *Black Genealogy*. (New Jersey: Prentice-Hall, Inc.),
    1977, p. 60.

12. Mullane, Deidre. *Crossing the Danger Water*. (New York: DoubleDay),
    1993, p. 173

13. Black, Eric. *Our Constitution: The Myth that Binds Us*. (Colorado:
    Westview Press), 1988, p. 76.

14. Bryson, Bill. *Made In America*. (New York: William Morrow and Co.),
    1994, p. 52.

15. Cose, Ellis. *A Nation of Strangers*. New York: HarperCollins, 1990; and
    The World Book Encyclopedia. (Chicago: Field Enterprises Education
    Corporation), 1976.

7
Conservatives and Sambos

1. Arno Press and the New York Times. *The Negro in Virginia*. (New York:
    Arno Press), 1969, p. 8.

2. Berlin, Ira. *Slaves Without Masters*. (New York: The New Press) p. 273.

3. Ervin L. Jordan, Jr. *Black Confederates and Afro-Yankees in Civil War
    Virginia*. Charlottesville: University of Virginia), 1995; p. 15.

4. Stewart, Jeffery C. *1001 Things Everyone Should Know About African
    American History*. (New York: Doubleday Publishers), 1996, p. 121.

5. Berlin, Ira. *Free At Last*. New York: The New Press, 1992, p. 274.

6. Berlin, Ira. Ibid., 275.

7   Bergman, Peter and Mort N. Bergman. *The Chronological History of the
    Negro In America*. (New York: Mentor Books), 1969, p. 67.

8. Watkins, Mel. *On the Real Side*. New York: Simon and Schuster), 1994.

9. Editor of the North Carolina newspaper, Gunnar Mrydal, *Man's Most*

Dangerous Myth, 1964.

10. Rogers, J. A. *100 Amazing Facts About the Negro*. (Florida: Helga M. Rogers), 1957, p. 6.

11. Anderson, Claud. *Black Labor; White Wealth*. (Maryland: Duncan and Duncan Co.), 1994.

12. Christian, Charles. *Black Saga: The African American Experience*. (New York: Houghton Mifflin Co.), 1996, p. 83.

13. Christian, Charles. Ibid., 86.

14. The Hayward Shepherd Monument was erected by the United Daughters of the Confederacy and the Sons of Confederate Veterans, at Harpers Ferry, Virginia to honor Hayward Shepherd for sacrificing his life to maintain slavery.

15. Anderson, Claud. *Black Labor; White Wealth*. (Maryland: Duncan & Duncan), 1994.

16. Ayers, Edward L. *The Promise of the New South: Life After Reconstruction*. (New York Oxford University Press), 1992, p. 324-326.

17. Anderson, Claud. *Black Labor, White Wealth*. (Maryland: Duncan and Duncan), 1994, p. 17.

18. Mullane, Deirdre *Crossing the Danger Water*. (New York: Doubleday) p. 743.

19. Gerhart, Groer. "The Reliable Source", *The Washington Post*, Wednesday, October 30, 1996, D3.

20. Johnson, Haynes. *Sleepwalking Through History*. (New York: W.W. Norton & Co.), 1991, p. 74.

8
Businesses and Inventors

1. Herbert Gutman, et al. *Who Built America?* (New York: Pantheon Books), 1989, p. 210-11.

2. A number of the inventors were taken form a Table of Inventions by Negroes in the *Encyclopedia of Black Folklore*, by Henry D. Spalding. p. 418 and Aptheker, Herbert. *A Documentary History of the Negro People in the United States*. (New Jersey: The Citadel Press), 1972, p. 873.

3. Potter, Joan and Claytor, Constance. *African-American Firsts: Famous, Little-Known and unsung Triumphs of Blacks in America*. (New York: Pinto Press), 1994, p. 234.

4. News Wire, The Democrat , West Alabama Community Newspaper, Wednesday, Oct., 16, 1996, Vol. 106, No. 41. p. 1.

5. "Journey of the African", *The Detroit Free Press* Section 6C, February 26, 1996.

6. "*The American Negro, His History and Literature,*" Arno and the New York Times. (New York: Arno Press), 1969, p. 54.

7. Bergman, Peter M. *The Chronological History of the Negro in America.* (New York: A Mentor Book), 1968, p. 158.

8. Arno and The New York Times, *The American Negro: His History and Literature.* (New York: Arno Press), 1969, p. 54.

9. Arno and The New York Times, *The American Negro: His History and Literature.* (New York: Arno Press), 1969, p. 56.

10. Bennett, Lerone. *The Shaping of Black America.* (New York: Penguin Press), 1975.

11. Notes from Author: Information on inventors can be found in *Created Equal: Black American Inventors* by James M. Brodie. (New York: William Morrow), p. 72. Spalding, Henry. *Enclyclopedia of Black Folklore and Humor.* (New York: Jonathan David Publishers), 1990.

12. Note from Author: See memoribilia: *Collectibles of Aunt Jemima by Jean William Turner.* (Penn.: A Schiffer Publication), 1994; and *More Black Memoribilia* by Jan Lindenberger. (Penn.: A Schiffer Publication), 1995.

13. Steward, Jeffery C. *1001 Things Everyone Should Know about African American History.* (New York:Doubleday Publishers), 1996. p. 133.

14. Notes from Author: See the book, *The New Negro*, p. 363.

9
Blood Lines and Blood Phobias

1. The Holy Bible, (Genesis 2:7 and 2:8); "The African Experience," by Roland Oliver, Harper Collins, New York, 1991. and Science Notebook, "Genetics: DNA Points to African Origins," *The Washington Post*, March 1, 1996, p. 2.

2. Historical information extracted from *The World Book Encyclopedia* and Ross D. Brown, *Afro-American World Almanac*. (Chicago: Truth Seekers Temple), 1943, p. 68.

3. "The Negro in World History: The Queen of Sheba," *The Times-Union*, Tuesday Magazine, December, 1968, p. 18

4. Bontemps, Arna. *Story of the Negro*. (New York:Alfred A. Knopf), 1953, p. 45.

5. Rogers, J.A. *The Five Negro Presidents*. (Florida: Helga M. Rogers),1957, p. 6.

6. Rogers, J.A. Ibid.

7. Rogers, J.A. Ibid. , 10.

8. Rogers, J.A. Ibid. , 12-13.

9. Brown, Ross D. *Afro-American World Almanac*. (Chicago), 1943; Rogers, J.A. *100 Amazing Facts About the Negro*. (St. Petersburg, Florida: Helga M. Rogers),1957, p. 9.

10. Brown, Ross D. Ibid , 76.

10
Scoundrels and Other Outcasts

1. Kenkor, Kenneth. "From the Seas: Black Men Under the Flag." *American Vision Magazine*, April/ May, 1995, p. 28-29)

2. Arno and the New York Times. *The American Negro, His History and Literature*. (New York: Arno Press), 1969, p. 17.

3. Mullane, Deirdre. *Crossing the Danger Water*. (New York: DoubleDay), 1993; and Stewart, Jeffrey. *1001 Things Everyone Should Know about Black History*. (New York: Doubleday Publishers), 1996.

4. Bryson, Bill. *Made In America*. (New York: William Morrow and Co.), 1994, p. 28.

5. Notes from Author: Quotes are from Peter Randolph's 1855 narrative, From Slave Cabin to Pulpit as printed in *On The Real Side*, by Mel Watkins.

6. Watkins, Mel. Ibid.,p. 67.

11
Politicians and Patriots

1. Davis, Kenneth C. *Don't Know Much About History*. (New York: Avon Books), 1990, p. 36.

2. Aptheker, Herbert. *Afro-American History: The Modern Era*. (New Jersey: The Citadel Press), 1971, p. 168.

3. Bryson, Bill. *Made In America*. (New York: William Morrow and Co.), 1994, p. 154.

4. Bergman, Peter L. and Mort N. Bergman. *The Chronological History of the Negro in America*. (New York: A Mentor Book), 1969, p. 368

5. Source: Christian, Charles. *Black Saga: The African American Experience*. (New York: Houghton Mifflin Co.), 1996.

6. Mullane, Deirdre. *Crossing the Danger Water*. (New York: Doubleday), 1993.

7. Garraty, John A. *The American Nation: A History of the United States to 1817*. (New York: Harper/Collins Publishers), 1991, p. 126.

8. Meier, August and Elliott Rudwick. *From Plantation to Ghetto*. (New York: Hill & Wang), 1970.

9. Anderson, Claud. *Black Labor; White Wealth*. (Maryland: Duncan & Duncan), 1994.

12
Runaways and Hideaways

1. Notes from Author: See Carl Senna. *The Black Press and the Struggle for Civil Rights*. (New York: The African American Empower), 1993, p. 18-19.

2. Stewart, Jeffery C. *1001 Things Everyone Should Know About African American History*. (New York: Doubleday Publishers), 1996, p. 28.

3 Scott, John Anthony. *Hard Trails on My Way*. (New York: Alfred A. Knopf), 1974, p. 87-90.

4. Jordan, Ervin L. *Black Confederate and Afro-Yankees in Civil War Virginia*. (Charlottesville: University Press of Virginia), 1995, p. 82.

5. Stewart, Jeffery C. *1001 Things Everyone should Know About African American History*. (New York: Doubleday), 1996, p. 37-38.

6. Stewart, Jeffery C. Ibid. , 42.

7. Quarles, Benjamin. *The Negro in the Making of America*. (New York: A Touch Stone Book), 1996, p. 94.

8. Spalding, Henry D. *Encyclopedia of Black Folklore and Humor*. (New York: Jonathan David Publisher), 1972.

9. Katz, William Loren. *Breaking the Chains: African-American Slave Resistance*. (New York: Athheneum Books), 1990, p. 22.

10. Jordan, Ervin L. *Black Confederates and Afro-Yankees in CivilWar Virginia*. (Charlottesville: University Press of Virginia), 1995, p. 120.

13
Civil War and Reconstruction

1. Jones, Howard. *Union In Peril*. (Chapel Hill: University of North Carolina Press),1992.

2. Davis, Burke. *The Civil War: Strange and Fascinating Facts*. (New York: Wings Books), 1994, p. 24; Quarles, Benjamin. *The Negro in the Making of America*. (New York: A Touchstone Book), 1996.

3. Davis, Kenneth C. *Don't Know Much About the Civil War*. (New York: William Morrow Co.), 1996, p. 315.

4. Davis, Burke. *The Civil War: Strange and Fascinating Facts*. (New York: WingBooks), 1994, p. 177; and Shenken, Richard and Reiger, Kurt. *One-Night Stands with American History*, (New York: Quill), 1982, p. 89.

5. Davis, Burke. Ibid. , 159-160.

6. Mullen, Robert. *Blacks in America's Wars*. (New York: Monad Press), 1973, p. 22-23, 31.

7. Logan, Rayford W. *The Betrayal of the Negro*. (New York: Collier Books), 1967, p. 293.

8. Jones, Jacqueline. *Dispossessed: America's Underclass from the Civil War to the Present*. (New York: Basic Books), 1992, p. 20.

9. Lebergott, Stanley. *The Americans: An Economic Record*. (New York: W.W. Norton & Co.), 1993, p. 235.

10. Davis, Burke; *The Civil War: Strange and Fascinating Facts*. (New York: Wings Books), 1994 p. 40-41.

11. Notes from Author: See Jones, Howard. *Union In Peril*. (Chapel Hill: The University of North Carolina), 1992; and Bergman, Peter M. and Bergman Mort N. *The Chronological History of the Negro in America*. New York:Mentor Books, 1969, p. 226.

12. Taken from public material. Source unknown.

13. Christian, Charles M. *Black Saga: The African American Experience* (New York: Houghton Mifflin Co.), 1995, p. 183.

14. McConnell, Stuart. *Glorious Contentment: The Grand Army of the Republic*, 1865-1900. (Chapel Hill, N.C.: The University of North Carolina Press), 1992, p. 8.

15. Anderson, Claud. *Black Labor; White Wealth*. (Maryland: Duncan & Duncan), 1994.

16. 7.

14
Sports and Entertainment

1. Anderson, Claud. *Black Labor; White Wealth*. (Maryland: Duncan & Duncan), 1994.

2. Potter, Joan and Claytor, Constance. *African-American Firsts: Famous, Little-Known and Unsung Triumphs of Blacks in America*. (Elizabeth Town: Pinto Press), 1994, p. 57.

3. Potter, Joan and Claytor, Constance. *African-American Firsts: Famous, Little-Known and Unsung Triumphs of Blacks in America*. (Elizabeth Town: Pinto Press), 1994, p. 5.

4. Bergman, Peter M. and Mort N. Bergman. *The Chronological History of the Negro in America*. (New York: A Mentor Book), 1969, p. 319.

5. Jordan, Ervin L *Black Confederates and Afro-Yankees in the Civil War Virginia*. (Charlottesville:University Press of Virginia), 1995.

6. Potter, Joan and Constance Claytor. *African-American Firsts: Famous, Little-Known and Unsung Triumphs of Blacks in America*. (Elizabeth town, N.Y: Pinto Press), 1994, p. 267.

7. Davis, Burke. *The Civil War: Strange and Fascinating Facts*. (New York: Wings Books), 1994, p. 184-185.

8. Anderson, Claud. *Black Labor; White Wealth*. (Maryland: Duncan &Duncan), 1994.

9. Watkins, Mel. *On the Real Side*. (New York: Simon and Schuster), 1994.

15
Medicine and Education

1. Christian, Charles M. *Black Saga: An African Experience*. (New York: Houghton Mifflin), 1995, p. 481.

2. Christian, Charles M. Ibid. , 71.

3. Jordan, Ervin L. *Black Confederates and Afro-Yankees in Civil War Virginia*. (Charlottteville: University of Virginia Press), 1992, p. 75.

4. Notes from Author: See Christian, Charles M. *Black Saga: An African American Experience*. (New York: Houghton Mifflin Co.), 1995, p. 458. and *The Washington Post*, "NIH Queries University on Use of Homeless in Tests", December 20, 1996.

5. Stewart, Jeffery C. *1001 Things Everyone Should Know about African American History*. (New York: Doubleday Co.), 1996, p. 341.

6. "Tuskegee Revisited", by Marcia Angell. *The Wall Street Journal*, October, 28, 1997, p. A22.

7. Stewart, Jeffery C. *1001 Things Everyone Should Know About African American History*. (New York: Doubleday), 1996, p. 343.

8. Notes from Author: See August Meier and Elliott Rudwick, *From Plantation to Ghetto*; and Peter L. Bergman and Mort. N. Bergman. *The Chronological History of the Negro in America*.

9. Weyl, Nathaniel, and Weyl, Marina, William. *Slavery and the Negro*. (New York: Arlington House), 1971.

10. Hill, Herbert. *Black Labor and the American Legal System*. (Wisconsin: University of Wisconsin Press), 1985.

11. Printed in The National Center for Education Statistics, Washington, D.C., 1996.

12. Scott, John Anthony. *Hard Trails on My Way*. (New York: Alfred A. Knopf), 1974, p. 69.

13. Notes from Author: During the month of June, 1996, this young student was recognized and awarded for having achieved a perfect score on the SAT by Bethune-Dubois Fund atit's national annual dinner in Washington, D.C.

14. Boskin, Joseph. *Sambo: The Rise and Demise of An American Jester*. (New York: Oxford University Press), 1986.

15. Michael Lind. *The Next American Nation*, (New York: The Free Press), 1995, P. 71.

16. Rogers, J.A. *100 Amazing Facts About the Negro*. (Florida: Helga M. Rogers), 1957.

16
Blacks, Indians, and Women

1. Rogers, J.A. *100 Amazing Facts About the Negro*. (Florida: Helga M. Rogers), 1957, p. 15.

2. Oaks, James. *The Ruling Race: A History of American Slaveholders*. (New York: Alfred A. Knopf Co.,) 1982, p. 45-47.

3. Christian, Charles M. *Black Saga: The African American Experience*. (New York: Houghton Mifflin Co.), 1996, p. 250.

4. Burns, James MacGregor. *The Crosswinds of Freedom*. (New York: Alfred A. Knopf Co.), 1989, p. 375-376.

5. Aptheker, Herbert. *A Documentary History of the Negro People in the United States*. (New Jersey: The Citadel Press), 1972, p. 627-628.

6. "Women-Owned Firms' Surge Mirrored Here", D'Vera Cohn and Kirstin Downey Grimsley, *The Washington Post*, Business Section, Wednesday, March 6,1996, p. D1.

7. Aptheker, Herbert. *Afro-American History: The Modern Era*. (New Jersey: The Citadel Press), 1971, p. 789.

17
Civil Rights and Religion

1. Black, Eric. *Our Constitution: The Myth that Binds Us*. (Boulder, Colorado: Westview Press), 1992, p. 45.

2. Anderson, Claud. *Black Labor; White Wealth*. (Maryland: Duncan &Duncan), 1994.

3. McCartney, John T. *Black Power Ideologies*. (Penn.: Temple University Press), 1992, p. 188.

4. Christian, Charles M. *Black Saga: The African American Experience*. (New York: Houghton Mifflin Co.), 1995, p. 393.

5. Stewart, Jeffery C. *1001 Things Everyone Should Know about African American History*. (New York: Doubleday Publishers), 1996, p. 173.

6. Mingo, Jack. *The Juicy Parts*. (New York: A Perigee Book), 1996, p. 220- 221.

7. Anderson, Claud. *Black Labor; White Wealth*. (Maryland: Duncan and Duncan), 1994.

8. The Way We Live Section, *Detroit Free Press*, Wednesday, February, 28, 1996, p. 2C.

9. Burns, James MacGregor. *The Crosswinds of Freedom*. (New York:Alfred A. Knopf), 1989, p.88.

18
Odds and Ends

1. Christian, Charles. M. *Black Saga: The African American Experience*, (New York: Houghton Mifflin), 1995, p. 258.

2. Garraty, John A. *The American Nation: A History of the United States to 1817, 7th ed*. (New York: Harper/Collins Publishers), 1991 p. 367.

Sources

3. See Ross Brown's *Afro-American World Almanac*, 1943, p. 61.

4. Lind, Michael. *The Next American Generation*. (New York: The Free Press), 1995, p. 78.

5. Turner, Jean Williams. *Collectible Aunt Jemima: Handbook and Value Guide*. (Penn: Schiffer Publishing Ltd.), 1994, p. 4.

6. Bryson, Bill. *Made In America*. (New York: William Morrows and Co.), 1994, p. 220.

7. Anderson, Claud. *Black Labor; White Wealth*. (Maryland: Duncan & Duncan), 1994.

8. Bennett, Lerone. *The Shaping of Black America*. (New York: Penguin Books), 1975, p. 286-287.

9. "Bygone Signs of Hate Now Carry a Price Tag", by Ricki Morell, *The Washington Post*, Monday, March 18, 1996, p. A6; and "Around the Nation," *The Washington Post*, Wednesday, November 5, 1997.

10. Notes from Author: See Front Page of *The Michigan Chronicle*, September 29-Oct. 5, 1996, Vol. XVIII, No. 45.

11. Notes from Author: See *Collectibles Aunt Jemima and More Black Memoribilia*, published by A Schiffer Books.

Index

A

Abolitionists, 30, 31, 59
Abraham Africanus the First, 127-128
Adams, Abigail, 86
Adams, Henry, 28
Adams, Gilbert, 152
Advertisement for slaves, 50, 51-52, 87, 111, 151
Aesop, 124, 125-26
Affirmative action, 195, 200-202
Africa, 123
African culture, 123, 124, 125, 143
Africa Town, 18
Afro-American Almanac, 124
Aladdin and his Lamp, 67
Alamo, Battle of the, 80-81
Allen, Richard, 29
Ali Baba and the Forty Thieves, 67
Althesa, 87
AME Church, 30
American Indians, 23, 72, 77, 133, 195-198
Anderson, Jo, 115
Antar, the Black Lion, 67
Anti-boycotting law, 122
Anti-smoking campaign (the first), 84
Arabs, 42, 49-51, 123
Arizona, 10
Asiento de Negroes, 1
Atlanta Compromise Speech, 106
Aunt Jemima, 120-121

B

Beard, A.J., 112
Bestiality, 59
Berlin Conference, 41
Berry, Harrison, 93
Bible, 6, 123-24, 125
Biddle, Nicholas, 13

Bill, Cherokee, 11
Bill of Rights, 88
Biological sciences, 183
Black barbers, 117
Black(s)
  actors, 65, 67, 174-75, 98
  artifacts and memorabilia, 65-66, 223-225
  athletes, 12, 21, 173, 177-78, 177-179
  businesses, 111-121, 213
  education, 1, 183
  entertainers, 173, 174, 176, 180, 181
  explorers, 71, 72
  governor, 10
  Holocaust, 41
  imitating Whites, 5, 84, 195
  ministers, 6-7
  minstrel, 15, 16, 173
  nationalism, 30
  newspaper, 14
  patriotism, 141, 142, 144, 145, 146, 147
  poets and poetry, 5, 35, 46, 73
  policeman, 14
  politicians, 145-146
  presidents, 126, 127-129
  recording artists, 1, 173, 176, 181
  religion, 6, 7, 49
  revenge, 31
  slaveholder, 4, 91, 92-93
  taxes, 2, 84
Black codes, 94
Black gold, 79-80
Black grapevine, 149-150
Black Labor; White Wealth, i
Black Mary, 25
Black films, 173, 174-175
Black landowners, 220-221
Black music, 1, 176
Black power movement, 205, 206
Black railroads, 112
Black Sal, 55-57
Blackbeard (the pirate), 134-135
Blackburn, A.B., 112
Bonoparte, Napoleon, 39